Women and poverty in Britain
the 1990s

edited by

Caroline Glendinning
Senior Research Fellow
University of Manchester

and

Jane Millar
Reader in Social Policy
University of Bath

HARVESTER
WHEATSHEAF

New York   London   Toronto   Sydney   Tokyo   Singapore

First published in Great Britain in 1992 by
Harvester Wheatsheaf
Campus 400, Maylands Avenue
Hemel Hempstead
Hertfordshire, HP2 7EZ
A division of Simon & Schuster International Group

Typeset in 10/12 pt Ehrhardt
by Columns Design & Production Services Ltd, Reading
Printed and bound in Great Britain
by Hartnolls Ltd, Bodmin, Cornwall

British Library Cataloguing in Publication Data

A catalogue record for this book is available
from the British Library

ISBN 0 7450 10393 (hbk)
ISBN 0 7450 10407 (pbk)

3   4   5   96   95   94

Contents

List of contributors

Carol Buswell teaches Sociology at Newcastle Polytechnic. Prior to her research on youth training she researched and published widely on secondary schooling and is currently directing a project on equal opportunities and employment. She is the author of *Women in Contemporary Society* (Macmillan, 1989).

Claire Callender has been a Research Fellow at the Institute of Manpower Studies, located at Sussex University, since 1989, undertaking research on employment and training for the public and private sector. Prior to that she taught Social Policy at the Universities of Cardiff, Leeds and Bradford. Her main interest is in women and the labour market and especially government and employers' policies.

Juliet Cook is Project Director for the Diploma in Youth and Community Work in the Department of Community Education at the Open University. She has been involved in a wide range of teaching and research posts in Britain and abroad, including the University of the West Indies, the University of Oxford and Coventry Polytechnic. Her current teaching and research interests are in the fields of 'race', gender and social policy. She has two children and two stepchildren.

Caroline Glendinning is a Senior Research Fellow, Department of Social Policy and Social Work, University of Manchester and previously worked for fifteen years in the Social Policy Research Unit, University of York. She manages to combine research and writing in the areas of community and 'informal' care, disability and social work services with bringing up her two children.

Hilary Graham is Professor of Applied Social Studies at the University of Warwick. She has worked previously at the Universities of Bradford and York, at the Open University and at Coventry Polytechnic. Her research has centred on women's experiences of caring in poverty, looking in particular at how women cope with caring for young children.

Dulcie Groves is pursuing an academically active early retirement as Honorary Lecturer in Social Policy/Women's Studies at Lancaster University, where she taught to 1989. She has published extensively on income maintenance and community care, especially women's access to pensions and the financial circumstances of carers.

Heather Joshi is concerned with work and the family as observer and participant. She was born in 1946, her children in 1982 and 1985. Mainly employed at the Centre for Population Studies, London School of Hygiene, she is also in the team at City University studying the 1958 birth cohort, and is a Fellow of the Centre for Economic Policy Research.

Hilary Land is Professor of Social Policy, Royal Holloway and Bedford New College, University of London. She teaches and researches in the area of the family and social policy, past and present, and has written various articles on social security, community care and women's work, both paid and unpaid.

Jane Lewis is Professor of Social Policy at the London School of Economics. Her main research interest is in women and social policy, past and present. She is the author of *Women and Social Action in Victorian and Edwardian England* (Edward Elgar, 1991); (with David Clark and David Morgan) *Whom God Hath Joined: The work of marriage guidance, 1920–1990* (Routledge, 1991); and (with Barbara Meredith) *Daughters Who Care* (Routledge, 1988).

Susan Lonsdale is a Senior Lecturer in Social Policy at South Bank Polytechnic in London. She is the author of *Work and Inequality* (Longman, 1985), and *Women and Disability* (Macmillan, 1990), and has co-authored *A Survey of Incomes In and Out of Work* (HMSO, 1991). She is currently on secondment to the Department of Social Security, working on an analysis of female unemployment and a study of invalidity benefit.

Jane Millar is a Reader in Social Policy at the University of Bath, having previously worked at the Universities of Ulster and York, and as a researcher for the Department of Social Security. Her research interests are mainly in the area of social security policy and in the relationship between policy and changing family and employment patterns. Recent publications include *Lone Parent Families in the UK* (with Jonathan Bradshaw) (HMSO, 1991).

Gillian Parker is a Senior Research Fellow and Assistant Director of the Social Policy Research Unit at the University of York. She is the author of *Getting and Spending: Credit and debt in Britain* (Avebury, 1990) and of a number of articles on consumer credit and debt, and the editor (with Robert Walker) of *Money Matters: Income, wealth, and financial welfare* (Sage, 1988).

David Piachaud is Professor of Social Administration at the London School of Economics and Political Science. He previously worked at DHSS (1968–70) and in the Prime Minister's Policy Unit (1974–9). He is the author of books and articles on the causes of poverty, the costs of children, the redistribution of incomes, international comparisons of social security, and work and welfare.

Alan Walker is Professor of Social Policy and Chairperson of the Department of Sociological Studies, University of Sheffield. He has written widely on the subjects of poverty and old age. His books include *Community Care* (ed., Basil Blackwell/Martin Robertson, 1982), *Social Planning* (Basil Blackwell/Martin Robertson, 1984), *Ageing and Social Policy* (ed. with Chris Phillipson, Gower, 1986) and *The Caring Relationship* (with Hazel Qureshi, Macmillan, 1989). He is currently conducting research on the social care of older people, the employment experiences of older workers and the impact of social and economic policies on older people in EC countries.

Shantu Watt is currently a Lecturer at the University of Warwick in the Applied Social Studies Department. She has previously worked in a variety of generic roles in social work before becoming a Staff Development Officer and Senior Lecturer in social work. She also acts as a consultant to a range of organisations.

Gill Whitting is Associate Research Director, ECOTEC Research and Consulting Limited in Birmingham and is currently responsible for the European System of Documentation on Employment. Previously Research Fellow at the Universities of Bath and Bristol, she has completed many research and evaluation studies on European poverty, urban deprivation and policy, equal opportunities, employment and training. She has particular experience in the development and application of evaluation methods.

Acknowledgements

We would like to thank Jean Ashton for her patience and meticulous word-processing expertise; Marie-Anne Doggett for preparing the bibliography and index; and Hilary Strickland for preparing the diagrams. And, of course, grateful thanks must go to our contributors for their patience and goodwill in coping with the demands we made on them.

PART 1

The social divisions of women's poverty

1 'It all really starts in the family'[1]: gender divisions and poverty

Jane Millar and Caroline Glendinning

In Britain in the early 1990s about one person in five lives either in poverty or in circumstances so constrained and restricted that poverty is just a step away. This means that there are almost 12 million people – men, women and children – whose family incomes cannot stretch to meet their needs. Ten years ago there were about 5 million people in this situation so the 1980s have been a decade in which poverty has increased and, as state support has been reduced, the lives of poor people have become more difficult and more circumscribed (Oppenheim, 1990; Millar, 1991c).

Poverty is not, however, simply a random misfortune. The risk of poverty, and the chances of escaping poverty, are very variable: some people will never experience poverty, others will find it impossible to avoid. The major social divisions of class, race and gender are clearly associated with different poverty risks. In Britain working-class people are more likely to be poor than middle-class people; Black people than white people; women more than men. This book focuses upon the last of these social divisions – on women's experiences of poverty and thus on how gender divisions mean that 'her' poverty and 'his' poverty are not the same, either in cause or effect.

There are two main aims to this book. The first is to document the *extent* of poverty among women. Until very recently women's poverty has been largely invisible, hidden within mainstream analyses which, in general, have defined poverty in relation to the financial circumstances of families or households and taken little or no account of what goes on within these units. Instead, the contributors to this book describe the experiences of women in a variety of contexts (training schemes, employment, redundancy, retirement); and in a variety of different roles (as paid workers, lone parents, wives, mothers, carers). These accounts of women's poverty and economic disadvantage in three main spheres – the labour market, the welfare state and the family – provide the main structure for the book.

Simply documenting the extent of poverty among women would not be adequate without also examining how government policy in recent years has affected women and their risk of poverty. The first edition of this book was published in 1987 (Glendinning and Millar, 1987) and the material in it related mainly to the mid-1980s. We have now reached the end of a decade in which social and economic policies have been driven by powerful ideological forces. Government policies in the 1980s have exacerbated women's vulnerability to poverty. Deregulation of the labour market, the shifting boundaries between public and private provision and the emphasis on family obligations and responsibilities have all resulted in substantially greater disadvantages for women. For example, labour market policies have done little to improve the low earnings of millions of women employees but have instead led to a worsening of job security and employment conditions. Reductions in social welfare services have generally resulted in more work – largely unpaid – for women in the private domain, as the care of children, sick and frail elderly people increasingly falls to them.

This second edition therefore contains more than just a series of statistical updates. It also incorporates discussions of the impact of recent policies. Thus, for example, Susan Lonsdale looks at recent changes to employment protection in the context of her discussion of women's particular employment patterns and earnings; Dulcie Groves considers the government-supported growth of private pension schemes and their impact on women; Jane Millar discusses the 1991 Child Support Act as it is likely to affect lone mothers; and so on.

In addition, three new chapters have been added to highlight specific policies. Hilary Land argues that women have lost significantly as a result of the decline of the 'social wage' – the services such as housing and child care which are so important in determining women's living standards. Gill Whitting looks at the impact of European Community policy on women's poverty in Britain, especially in relation to labour market issues. Caroline Glendinning presents new evidence about the impact of caring for elderly or disabled people on women's current and future economic situation, in the light of 'community care' policies.

The first aim of this book, then, is to document the extent of women's poverty and to analyse the role of policy, especially in recent years, in relation to this. The second aim is to explore the *causes* of poverty for women. As Jane Lewis and David Piachaud demonstrate in their chapter, both the extensiveness and the causes of women's poverty have altered little over the past century. Broadly speaking, poverty is a consequence of an inability to generate sufficient resources to meet needs. As the quotation from Margaret Thatcher at the beginning of this chapter indicates, for women this is a consequence of the gender division of labour, which assigns their primary role to the home and the primary role of men to the labour market. This division has profound consequences for the situation of women in the labour market, for their treatment within social welfare systems and for their status and power within the family.

In relation to the labour market, we have argued elsewhere (Millar and Glendinning, 1989) that women are defined as secondary workers in two senses. First, the paid work which women do is considered to be secondary to their domestic role. Jobs must therefore be fitted in around the demands of the domestic role – of husbands, children, other family commitments – so women tend to have periods out of the labour market and/or periods of part-time employment while fulfilling these obligations. Secondly, women's employment is considered to be secondary to that of their husbands, with the man providing the main or primary family income which is supplemented by the women's earnings. To these can be added a third sense in which women are secondary workers; they form a very substantial proportion of what has come to be known as the 'secondary' or 'peripheral' labour market, characterised by part-time, short-term, casual and low-skilled employment, often in service sector industries (Barron and Norris, 1976; Rodgers and Rodgers, 1989).

In all three senses, this secondary role carries costs for women and these are described here in the three chapters by Carol Buswell, Susan Lonsdale and Heather Joshi. Carol Buswell looks at how training schemes channel young women into traditionally female jobs, training them in the process to expect and accept low pay as part of their experience of employment. Two-fifths of employed women have part-time jobs and Susan Lonsdale shows how such part-time work is often insecure and low-paid, with few of the other material rewards (such as membership of occupational pension schemes) that full-time employment can bring. Other forms of women's employment, such as homeworking and working in family businesses, often mean even worse pay and conditions. Heather Joshi adds up the 'cost of being female' and the 'cost of caring' in terms of the wages that women lose through breaks in employment for child-rearing, with the subsequent part-time employment and loss of seniority. Women have steadily increased their share of employment – by the turn of the century almost half of the workforce in the UK will be women – but have done so on terms that are far from equal with men.

Women are also disadvantaged in access to social security benefits, public and private. Such benefits rarely meet the particular needs of women. For example, only six in ten women workers qualify for maternity leave and subsequent reinstatement (McRae and Daniel, 1991). Thus the contingency that affects the employment of many women, but no men – pregnancy – is far from adequately covered either by employment protection legislation or income replacement provision. Caroline Glendinning, in her chapter, gives another example of the way in which the 'risks' experienced by women are not given adequate social security protection. Many women provide often quite substantial levels of care for others (and thereby, of course, save the state considerable sums of money). For those whose earnings are restricted by having to provide such care, the income replacement available is hard to get and very low. Jane Millar, in her chapter, looks at the situation of lone mothers who rarely have access to the types of services, especially affordable child care provision, which might enable them better to support themselves and their children.

But while women's particular risks are not adequately protected against, at the same time they are usually not so well protected as men against the more general risks of unemployment, sickness and retirement. Although social security benefits are now generally available to women on the same conditions as men, the nature of these conditions – and in particular the way in which they are often tied to full-time work – means that many women fail to qualify.[2] Thus, as Claire Callender shows in her chapter, many women who lose their jobs are excluded from redundancy payments and unemployment benefit, so that their unemployment often goes unregistered and uncounted. Alan Walker and Dulcie Groves look respectively at state and private provision for retirement and show how women are often excluded or given lower benefits than men. This contributes directly to the very high rates of poverty found among elderly women.

The gender division of labour also structures relationships between men and women in the family. The type of work which women do outside the home (often for low pay) mirrors the type of work which women do in the home (for no pay): women are service sector workers both in and out of the family. This gendered division of paid and unpaid work has a number of consequences for women's poverty. First, the unpaid servicing work done by women within the home frees men to pursue their employment and hence to maintain, or even enhance, their earning power largely unencumbered by family or domestic responsibilities. Women give men time for paid work by looking after their homes and families – and women working part-time are especially likely to also be carrying out the bulk of the domestic and child-caring work (Henwood *et al.*, 1987). Secondly, women's earnings from paid work contribute to family income and prevent many families from falling into poverty. As Juliet Cook and Shantu Watt point out in their chapter, the low wages of very many Black men make this poverty prevention role especially important for Black women workers.

Thirdly, women play an important role in managing scarce household resources and protecting other family members from the worst impact of poverty. It is this aspect – women's role as household managers – which Hilary Graham and Gillian Parker examine in the last two chapters of the book. Hilary Graham looks at how women are responsible for meeting the health needs of their families, and their strategies for doing this on a limited income. One such strategy involves cutting back on their own consumption, with both short- and long-term consequences for their own health and welfare (see also Payne, 1991). Gillian Parker looks at another managing strategy for poor women – borrowing money – and describes the anxieties, problems and difficulties this can give rise to. Both chapters show how inequalities in power relationships within the family are reflected in differential access to family resources. Thus men command more of the family resources (of money, of food, of space and so on) and this is legitimated by their status as breadwinners. So the circle turns: women are prevented from equal participation in employment by their family responsibilities but because they are not 'providing' for the family they have less claim on the family's resources.

Underpinning and legitimating these gender divisions is the assumption that women are, or should be, financially dependent upon men. This dependency has traditionally been assumed to protect women from poverty – women do not need an income of their own because the men with whom they live will financially provide for them. Low pay and lack of access to social security benefits are, according to this assumption, entirely justified by the notion that women do not really 'need' an adequate income of their own. However, not only are there many women (single women, lone mothers, widowed women) who do not live with a man and so have no access to male earnings; but even those women who do live with men are not necessarily protected from current or future poverty. Inequalities in the distribution of income within the family can mean women living in poverty when other family members do not, or living in deeper poverty than other family members. In addition, if the family breaks down (as is increasingly likely) then women are very often plunged immediately into poverty as lone parents. Thus the financial dependency of women on men exacerbates, rather than reduces, the risk of poverty for women. Indeed, as Lister (1990) points out, this gendered notion of dependency reduces women's rights:

> Even dependency on means-tested income support, with all its inade-
> quacies and inequalities, can for some women be preferable to dependence
> on an individual man . . . at least [it] . . . provides some enforceable rights
> and some sense of control over money, once received. (Lister, 1990,
> pp. 452–3)

The causes of poverty among women are thus a result of complex but mutually reinforcing threads, which have their origins in the limitations placed upon women by the current gendered division of labour and by the assumptions of female financial dependency upon men. However, gender is not the only social division which structures women's lives and which affects their life chances. There are also divisions of class, race, age and disability, which interact with gender in ways that are still not clearly delineated. In particular, there has been little theoretical or empirical work focusing specifically on race and poverty. As Juliet Cook and Shantu Watt and Hilary Graham point out in their chapters, there is increasing evidence that Black people have a high risk of poverty (being more likely than the white population to be low-paid or unemployed) but only a few studies of poor people have even included Black people, let alone focused on their experience of poverty. This has two main consequences: first, it means there is a large gap in our understanding of poverty and how poor people live, since a large section of poor people have been excluded from detailed study. Secondly, just as a focus on gender challenges traditional ideas about the nature and causes of poverty, so too a focus on race is likely to raise issues that are currently largely ignored (Williams, 1989). For example, analyses of the relationship between the family and the labour market have drawn almost entirely on the experiences of white women. But for Black women the relationships between family, home and work can be very different (Westwood and Bhachu, 1988b). Analysing these differences – and the similarities – would add to our understanding of the processes that lead to economic disadvantage and poverty.

One of the main themes in our introduction to the first edition of this book was the traditional *invisibility* of women's poverty (and we have also elaborated this argument elsewhere: Millar and Glendinning, 1989; Glendinning and Millar, 1989; Glendinning and Millar, 1991). This invisibility operates in a number of ways: providing no separate information on women and men in data on poverty; presenting results which show women to be more at risk of poverty than men but ignoring or trivialising this; or conceptualising poverty in ways such that women's poverty is obscured. This latter, we have argued, is inherent in conventional approaches to defining poverty which employ household or family-based measures and which thus ignore the distribution of income *within* households.

Measures of poverty, or of material well-being, which are based on aggregate units rest on the assumption that within those units resources and living standards are shared more or less equally. In the first edition of this book we pointed to the emerging evidence that this was not so, and that differences in power within households enable men to command more of the family's resources than women. The evidence then was mainly small-scale, based on detailed in-depth interviews with relatively small numbers of couples, usually with children; another line of evidence came from studies of lone mothers, looking back on their marriages. However, Vogler (1989) has now examined within-household income distribution in a sample of about 1,200 households. Her analysis is based on the accounts of both partners and the results are a clear confirmation of the earlier small-scale evidence. She concludes that only 20 per cent – one in five households – used an egalitarian 'pooling' system and that women generally command less of the 'family' income than men:

> Financial equality depends on a wife's full-time employment, since part-time work simply operates to reduce calls on the husband's wage, without increasing wives' influence over finances . . . where the constraints of the labour market are greatest, wives are more likely to shoulder the burden of managing an inadequate income single-handedly and, at the same time, more likely to experience higher levels of financial dependence and to have less access to personal spending money than husbands. (Vogler, 1989, pp. 24–6)

Vogler's study thus further confirms that within families there is often substantial inequality between women's and men's access to resources. Such research calls into question the whole approach to measuring poverty which is based on aggregate units. Treating the family as a single unit clearly does not reflect the reality of the way resources are actually distributed within families. Nor does it reflect the fact that individuals cannot always rely upon the family or household units to secure their personal financial well-being. This evidence therefore

> leads us towards a concept of *independent* capabilities, and a measurement approach within which a woman's capabilities cannot be satisfied simply by sharing a household with, that is being *dependent* on, a man . . . Even if one is confident that within-household arrangements at some given point in time are satisfactory, individual capacities for economic independence are of significance because marriages break up and partners die. (Jenkins, 1991, pp. 464–5, his emphasis)

We would therefore argue that any valid definition of poverty must focus on the capacity of individual people to support themselves without relying upon others. People who are financially dependent upon others must be considered vulnerable to poverty.

Such data as are available suggest that many women are indeed very vulnerable in this way. For example, Evason (1991) has estimated the number of women in Northern Ireland who do not have an independent income above the level of income support. She identified three main groups of women in this situation – non-employed women, low-paid women and women on income support – and estimated that as many as three-quarters of adult women in Northern Ireland fall into one of these categories. Similarly, Esam and Berthoud (1991) have estimated the proportion of men and women in Britain with independent incomes of less than £25 per week. In 1990/1 this added up to about 4.6 million women, compared with just 0.4 million men. Thus when income is measured on an individual basis, women are ten times more likely than men to have very low incomes: 20 per cent of adult women compared with only 2 per cent of adult men were below the £25 level.

Income is, of course, only part of the picture: time is needed first to earn income and then to convert it into living standards. In both respects women's time is valued less than men's: women, being in general paid less than men, work longer hours to reach the same level of income; and the time needed to convert income into living standards is expended mainly by women in the course of their unpaid domestic work. Finding ways to measure poverty on an individual basis and taking into account not only income, but wider measures of access to resources, are likely to be very complex (Jenkins, 1991) but are nevertheless essential if we are ever to get an accurate picture of the extent of poverty, experienced not just by women but also by men.[3]

Women's lives have changed very substantially in recent decades and the 'double burden' of paid and unpaid work is now the experience of the majority of women. Thus measures to reduce women's vulnerability to poverty must address both the public and the private spheres. Improving women's access to an independent income (through employment or through the benefit system) is one side: relieving women of some of the unpaid work they do in the home is the other. The first without the second will simply double women's workload and their responsibilities (Bransbury, 1991). Therefore one essential condition for any reduction in women's poverty is that the men must change – women will always remain at greater risk of poverty than men, as long as the current gendered division of labour continues.

Notes

1. Speech by Margaret Thatcher to WRVS national conference, 19 January 1981.
2. The High Court has recently ruled that while it may be indirectly discriminatory not to give part-timers the same employment rights as full-timers (because most of the former are women and most of the latter are men), this discrimination can be justified on economic grounds. These grounds are that the extension of employment rights to part-timers would reduce the supply of part-time employment and so increase unemployment among women (*The Guardian*, 16.10.1991). Thus discrimination against part-time workers will continue, in effect on the grounds that women must be satisfied with either being cheap labour or with having no jobs at all.
3. In the 1980s poverty research has become simultaneously very technical and very controversial. The government's replacement of the 'low-income families' series with the 'households below average income' series raised both technical and political objections (see, for example, Johnson and Webb, 1990; Oppenheim, 1990; Johnson and Webb, 1991; Townsend, 1991a and 1991b). From the point of view of analysing women's poverty, both series are of limited value: neither provides a breakdown by sex; both focus only on income; and both measure poverty in aggregate units (although in this respect the household measure probably obscures women's poverty more than the family measure, since among those who share households are young low-paid or unemployed women and elderly widows). Our official statistics on poverty are very much in need of revision.

2 Racism, women and poverty

Juliet Cook and Shantu Watt

In this chapter, we are concerned that clear links are made between the multiple effects of racism on Black women, together with the impact of poverty that is captured in the 'feminisation of poverty' debates. We want to draw particular attention to the differences of meanings, definitions and experiences attached by the dominant values towards households headed by Black women.[1] There is also a lack of data about Black women's position within British economic structures. It is hoped that the 1991 Census will provide relevant information for future strategies and policies around Black families' economic marginalisation.

Evidence of Black families' experiences of service delivery, both as workers and as recipients (Ahmed *et al.*, 1986; Watt and Cook, 1989; Ballard, 1989; Patel, 1990), from major welfare organisations points to the perpetuation of institutional racism within British society. We aim to show how the racial position of Black people in British society has a crucial effect on their experience of poverty, and on the strength and determination of Black women in particular to survive and resist these processes. In most literature there has not been any detailed analysis of older Black women's experiences or Black lesbian women's experiences in relation to poverty. In the absence of any integrated policy strategies, much of the documentary evidence available implies that Black people have been passive recipients of an unjust welfare system. However, Black women activists throughout history and presently have systematically resisted and created positive platforms of reforms for Black communities. While the wider social debate continues about where responsibility lies for creating changes to institutional operations, Black women have continued to 'chip away' at the apparatuses of society that sustain racial and sexual ideologies, at the same time explicitly maintaining and managing everyday acts of resistance within the existing political and economic structures.

But the rhetoric cannot remain within theoretical discussions. The ideologies of race and gender are central to the evaluations of poverty for women. The implicit and explicit stereotypes around Black families must be challenged and exposed in day-to-day practice. Images of women, and Black women in particular, have too often focused on women as 'victims' and not as strong, responsible, self-directed people in whatever circumstances they find themselves. Black women are part of a worldwide herstory where exploitation, abuse, violence and poverty are often features of their lives. However, without romanticising their struggles, they are also part of a herstory of fighting back, of organising and challenging oppressive structures and processes, of caring and creativity as well. The position of Black women in Britain today illustrates these themes clearly, in that class, race and gender inequalities combine in complex ways to produce poverty and other inequalities for many Black women. Equally, it illustrates the ways in which Black women have resisted these processes, both as individuals and as members of groups. A good example is the very effective Organisation of Women of African and Asian Descent (1978–83) which organised Black women on a national basis and encouraged the growth of a multiplicity of local groups which still exist today (Bryan *et al.*, 1985).

Poverty has been defined in many ways, but most definitions include not only the lack of financial and other economic resources, but also related qualitative dimensions such as the lack of family and other social relationships, the lack of opportunities for fulfilment, and feelings of insecurity (Townsend, 1979). We want to capture not only the quantitative aspects of poverty for Black women and their families, but also the qualitative aspects – for example, being at the receiving end of stress from racism and living in poverty and the impact of immigration controls on family life – as well as the resourcefulness of women in maintaining families and communities in the face of such pressures. In modern capitalist societies such as Britain, there is a clear relationship between class (however defined) and poverty. Racism and sexism also play a vital role in making poverty an everyday reality for many Black women.

In recent years, there have been considerable developments in understanding and explaining sexism as both a past and contemporary phenomenon. However, many Black women have rightly pointed out that many of these theories are predicated on assumptions which apply only to white women and do not address the ways in which racism is always an overriding force in the lives of Black women. Racism is therefore likely to magnify and/or focus the effects of class and gender in producing poverty for Black women. Parmar (1982, p. 237) has stressed the need to understand 'racially constructed gender roles'. The centrality of racism in producing a differential experience of domestic violence for Black British women (an issue of fundamental importance for any form of feminism) has recently been documented by Mama (1989). Ramazanoglu (1989) also makes the case for stressing an autonomous role for racism in any analysis of women's oppression. Such theoretical arguments reflect the reality of Black women themselves: 'If you're a Black woman, you've got to start with racism. It's not a choice. It's a necessity' (cited in Bryan *et al.*, 1985, p. 174).

Black and white women may seem to share some common experiences of the various social oppressions, but racism divides them. For example, Westwood's (1984) study shows how Black and white women fought together at work for pay rises and improved conditions, but at the same time the Black women also experienced racism from their fellow workers. Racism also divided their social lives outside the factory.

Racism, and sexism, complicate Black women's relationship to class and to poverty. First, women are class members because of their role in production as paid workers. They are usually poor as paid workers because of low pay. Secondly, women have a further relationship to class because marriage or cohabitation may bring them more resources through access to men's wages. For Black women, however, racism means that these wages are less because Black men are paid less than white men. Thirdly, women can be seen as having an indirect relationship to class via their unpaid domestic labour which, it is argued, helps to service the economy by supporting male workers (Kaluzynska, 1980). Historically, however, this relationship is different for Black women because a high proportion of their paid labour under capitalism has been domestic labour (Parmar, 1982). Finally, the disproportionate effects of unemployment on Black workers, including women, and the low levels of state benefits combine to produce poverty for Black women.

To take the analysis still further and to keep racism at the top of the agenda, there are two additional assumptions that need to be challenged if a real understanding of Black women's poverty is to be developed: first, the notion that Black women are the economic dependants of men; and secondly, that the Black family is oppressive for Black women. It is a mistake to assume that Black women were or are the economic dependants of men. Both historical and contemporary evidence shows that Black women have always made significant contributions to the economic well-being of their families in a variety of ways (Carby, 1982; Davis, 1982; Parmar, 1982; Morokvasic, 1983). The active involvement in the labour market of women migrants from the Caribbean is well recorded from the 1950s onwards in, for example, the history of the National Health Service. Less well known, perhaps, is the increasing participation of women of Asian origin in the British labour market (Westwood and Bhachu, 1988b). In many areas of social policy, however, including the key arena of immigration and nationality law, Black women are treated as the dependants of men. Thus, in 1982, the Home Office (unsuccessfully) defended its 1980 Immigration Rules against the accusation of sex discrimination on the grounds that 'society still expects the man to go out to work and the woman to stay at home' (WING, 1985, p. 147). In situations of marriage breakdown, widowhood or other forms of family disruption, including domestic violence, Black women can become even more financially vulnerable because of the effects of such assumptions within immigration law (Gordon and Newnham, 1985; Mama, 1989).

The Black family in popular thinking and in some feminist literature is seen as oppressive to Black women. The stereotypes run deep and apply in slightly different, but equally negative, ways to Asian and Afro-Caribbean families (see Westwood and Bhachu, 1988b; Phoenix, 1988b). The fact that racism constantly has the effect of seeking to divide and, *in extremis*, to decimate Black families is overlooked in such discussions. Writers such as Carby (1982) and Parmar (1982) stress the contradictory nature of the family for Black women in a racist society such as Britain. The family does not always operate in an oppressive way for Black women because it serves as a major 'site of political and cultural resistance to racism' (Carby, 1982, p. 214). In other respects, the family in Asian communities acts as a positive support for women and a focus for activities such as networking that can give women considerable influence in informal family and community spheres (see, for example, Werbner, 1988). The obsessive media concern with the evils of arranged marriages for young Asian women is belied by the careful concern for their daughters manifested by the overwhelming majority of Asian parents, both mothers and fathers (Ahmed, 1978; Jamdagni, 1980; Edmonds, 1981).

Single parenthood is frequently seen as the dominant form of the Afro-Caribbean family, a form that is defined as deviating from the 'norm' of the two-parent (white) nuclear family. A second unacceptable characteristic is, therefore, that Afro-Caribbean mothers leave their children in an irresponsible way in order to take paid work. Phoenix (1988b) challenges these assumptions both empirically and in terms of their negative connotations. The value of the family to women of Afro-Caribbean origin and their vital role in its maintenance is overlooked.

Collins' (1990) recent work has highlighted the central role of the family and the church in the Black community in the USA. Equally, she has emphasised the support that these institutions give to Black women in the development of an Afro-centric feminist epistemology. Hooks (1991) also emphasises the overriding value of the 'homeplace', particularly to African-American women. A recent series on the Black church in Britain (*Black Faith*, 1990) highlighted some parallel issues in the British context.

Black women, as we would expect, play a vital role in their family systems and also frequently gain support and status from them. There are both practical and social benefits to be derived from these systems. In both Asian and Afro-Caribbean communities, family networks play an important role in offering financial support in times of need. The Asian practice of pooling resources to buy a house is perhaps better known than the 'pardner' system in Afro-Caribbean communities (Rex and Moore, 1967; Bryan *et al.*, 1985). More recent studies show that women have an important role in these systems (Westwood and Bhachu, 1988b).

British social policy (in particular, immigration policy) has not facilitated the economic strengths of Black women nor the unity of Black families. Indeed, British immigration law has been criticised by the European Commission for Human Rights for its racial bias and for dividing families (*The Guardian*, 4 December 1979). An historical analysis shows that racism and sexism, through the key concepts of nation and family, have had a decisive influence on the content and direction of social policy in Britain over the last century (Williams, 1989). As a result, Black women have been unable to rely on state support to any extent in their fight against poverty.

Black women and the labour market – employment, unemployment and low pay

There has been little change over time in the racism faced by Black workers in the labour market in Britain. Black men are located in rather different sectors of work from white men and are more likely to work in jobs with low pay and poor conditions. Brown's (1984) study (which remains the most comprehensive national survey on a wide range of 'race' issues, although the research was conducted in 1982) shows that 82 per cent of West Indian men and 73 per cent of Asian men are manual workers compared with 58 per cent of white men. Black men are also more likely to have to do shift work than white men. As far as job levels are concerned, Black men are less likely than white men to hold supervisory positions. The effects of these differences on median weekly earnings are striking. The 1982 figures showed that median earnings for white men were £20 per week higher than for West Indian men and £18 per week higher than for Asian men (Brown, 1984).

Black women of varying backgrounds have relatively high levels of involvement in paid work. Women of Afro-Caribbean origin and non-Muslim Asian women are more likely to be involved in paid work than their white counterparts. The low wages of Black men may be one of the reasons why a relatively high proportion of Black women take up paid work on a full-time basis. Certainly, Stone's research (1983) indicates that for both Black and white women the main motive for working is to provide an essential contribution to the family income. The relationship is, however, a complicated one since many Pakistani Muslim families, for example, have the lowest incomes and yet their women family members are less likely to take up paid work. Breughel's recent analysis (1989) strongly suggests that the under-representation of Black women in part-time work is a consequence of the racism faced in the labour market by both Black women and men, and their resulting vulnerability to family poverty (see also, Duffy and Lincoln, 1990). Full-time paid work outside the home or some form of homeworking are thus the most likely sources of income for Black women.

Both Black and white women are concentrated in certain sectors of the labour market where low pay and poor working conditions are prevalent. However, Black women's position is both different and less advantageous. Black women are much less likely to be in non-manual work than white women; and when they do move into non-manual work, they are less likely to be in professional or managerial jobs. Black women are as well qualified as white women on the whole, particularly below degree level. Nonetheless, many Black women (and men) are working in jobs below their qualification level. What Breughel (1989) calls racial exclusion and discrimination results in the over-representation of Black women in manufacturing and their under-representation in the high-pay sectors of banking, insurance and finance.

In the economy as a whole, Black women are concentrated in particular sectors of work. Women of Asian origin, for example, are more likely to be employed in manufacturing. Recent research conducted in Leicester confirms this picture (Duffy and Lincoln, 1990). Many Black women of Afro-Caribbean origin work in the public sector, notably in the National Health Service. Within all sectors of work, however, Black women are likely to be at lower status and lower paid levels of work (Breughel, 1989). The prevalence of low-status work and fewer training opportunities for Afro-Caribbean and other Third World women within the National Health Service is a case in point. As Bryan *et al.* express it:

> For many Black women who join the NHS with the intention of becoming nurses, this was to remain an elusive goal. Relegated to the hospitals' kitchens and laundries, or trudging the wards as tea-ladies, cleaners and orderlies, we were to have first-hand experience of the damning assumptions which define our role here. The patients saw it as fitting that we should be doing Britain's dirty work and often treated us with contempt. (Bryan *et al.*, 1985, p. 43)

Extreme exploitation faces the many women who have to take jobs as homeworkers with very low wages, job insecurity and many costs which are borne by the employee (see also Susan Lonsdale's chapter in this volume). The exact numbers of homeworkers generally and Black homeworkers in particular are not known. Although research such as that of Anwar (1979) indicated that most Pakistani women in Rochdale who worked were homeworkers, Allen and Wolkowitz (1987) warn against the routine linking of homeworking with 'Asian women' in any stereotyped way. Both Allen and Wolkowitz's work and that of Phizacklea (1990) underline the role of both racism and sexism in confining many Black women to homeworking and therefore to risk of poverty. Although cultural factors may well play a part in this process, they are by no means paramount in every case. For example, in Allen and Wolkowitz's admittedly small sample from West Yorkshire, none of the homeworkers were employed by their own relatives and over half were employed by firms owned by white people. A recent survey of Muslim homeworkers of Pakistani origin in a town in North-

West England underlines the exploitation experienced by this section of the workforce and the complex interaction of reasons involved in taking up homeworking. Financial necessity among this group was once again the main motivating force, as well as lack of alternative work and child care opportunities and family pressures against working outside the home. Wage levels were predictably low – one woman worked up to twelve hours a day, often for six or seven days a week, and never earned more than £50 a week. All the women had to supply their own sewing machines and most had to service them and supply their own needles (Price, 1991).

Central to the discussion of poverty and Black women has to be the issues of pay and resources. Data on pay are notoriously difficult to collect and analyse and become even more problematic when set in a context in which 'race' and gender are at the heart of the discussion. Brown's (1984) data suggested that pay levels were relatively similar for Black and white women in the labour market. However, Breughel's (1989) research review suggests that a more refined and sophisticated analysis of the data is necessary which takes into account such factors as the different implications for wage rates and working conditions of full-time and part-time work; the greater involvement of Black women in shift work; the relative youth of the Black female workforce; and the fact that many Black women work in London where pay rates are relatively high (but, of course, where living costs are also high). Breughel's analysis, based on the 1986 London Living Standards Survey, suggests that once these differences are taken into account, white women earn 23 per cent per hour more than Black women. A recent Leicester survey shows wide disparities in pay between Asian and white women – 55 per cent of white women but 86 per cent of Asian women earned less than £150 per week (Duffy and Lincoln, 1990).

A similar picture emerges from analyses of household resources. Black households are less well off than white households, even when women's earnings are taken into account (Breughel, 1989). To turn the point round another way, Black households are more in need of women's earnings than white households, even though these very earnings will contribute relatively less to the needs of the household. The force of racism can thus be seen in both the generation and perpetuation of poverty for Black women and their families.

The struggle to combine paid work with child care is one that faces almost all working mothers, but it is important to note that there is differential access by 'race' to scarce child care services (Parmar, 1982). The notion that some Black women, particularly women of Asian origin, have 'ready made' sources of child care among older female relatives has to be questioned. The Gujarati women in Warrier's (1988) study drew on a variety of informal child care support systems, which included grandmother care for pre-school children. None of the women in her sample used any formal systems such as childminders, day-care centres, private or state nurseries or creches. As early as 1975, the Community Relations Commission (CRC) produced a study which showed the way racism operated in formal child care provision. Black women were less able to find childminders to meet their needs (for example, long hours to cover shift work, childminders near home) and some childminders refused to take their children (CRC, 1975). The lack of flexible child care facilities persists, forcing many Black women into less desirable and less well-paid jobs (Bryan *et al.*, 1985). Recent initiatives to offer workplace nurseries are occurring in jobs, such as banking, from which Black women tend to be excluded and are therefore unlikely to help meet their child care needs to any significant extent.

Unemployment is a significant feature of the lives and experiences of Black individuals and communities in British society. The current recession and its associated rise in unemployment will repeat and exacerbate the well-documented differential effects on Black people which the recession of the early 1980s had. Indeed, for many Black people, particularly young people, the 'recovery' of the late 1980s has yet to impact on their job prospects in any significant way. Loss or failure to find a job, however poorly paid, clearly has an immediate effect on individual and family poverty. There are very few people who receive more in benefits than they previously earned – Smith's (1981) research has shown that only 3 per cent of white men, 5 per cent of minority men, 4 per cent of white women and 2 per cent of minority women were in that position.

'Race' has been shown to have a major bearing on people's chances of becoming unemployed, irrespective of other factors associated with greater risk of unemployment such as age, skill level or area of residence (Smith, 1981). Gender also plays a significant part, with Brown's 1982 figures showing that unemployment among white women was running at 10 per cent compared with 16 per cent for West Indian women and 20 per cent for Asian women. Black women were more than twice as likely as white women to be long-term unemployed.

Breughel's recent analysis (1989) using London data highlights a number of features of Black women's experiences of unemployment. She suggests that Black women have undergone a very significant decline in their living standards during the years 1981–6 primarily because of the impact of unemployment, but also because they have benefited least from increases in earnings in the 1980s. Her evidence suggests that the gap between Black and white women's incomes and living standards has been increasing more than that between Black and white men. Particularly hard hit have been Black women in manual occupations, who are more at risk of unemployment, and younger women, even when they have qualifications. Indeed, the 1985 Labour Force Survey figures show that Black women with qualifications are over twice as likely to be unemployed as white women with qualifications, irrespective of age group. The challenges that the Scarman Report (1981) and many other reports and commentaries have made to policy-makers about the long-term damage being done, particularly to young Black people, by allowing unemployment and poverty to become a chronic feature of their lives, have met with little response. All the recent evidence on policy interventions such as the Youth Training Scheme illustrates yet again the racist processes and outcomes of the schemes (Cross *et al.*, 1990).

Black women have not passively accepted the impact of unemployment, low wages and poverty on their lives or the lives of their families. Some Black women, few and far between so far, are achieving well-paid jobs (Orakwue, 1990), although this is often overlooked in the stereotyping of Black women as 'victims'. Some Black women are joining together in co-operatives, in various kinds of community employment initiatives or in self-employment (Bryan *et al.*, 1985). Black women are active union members (Brown, 1984) and have fought many campaigns for union recognition and union rights in both well-publicised cases such as the Grunwick dispute in the 1970s and in small clothing firms such as those in Coventry (Hoel, 1982; Phizacklea, 1983). They have fought for better pay and conditions in a wide range of workplaces, including the National Health Service. Paid work, however badly paid, does give many Black women a stronger position in their families and communities (Westwood and Bhachu, 1988a). There are also indications that some Black women are consciously and actively beginning to reject some of the 'traditional' work that the British economy has directed them into. 'The Black nurse – an endangered species?' is the telling title of a recent publication (Baxter, 1988). The experience of being a Black worker in the NHS has led many women as parents to express concern about their children repeating their work choices (Lee-Cunin, 1989). Will other occupational areas face a similar exodus in the future?

Black women and the boundaries of social security

Although there has been a growing concern and awareness of the inadequacy of service delivery from many Department of Social Security (DSS) offices, there has been little evidence gathered about Black people's experiences in particular. An internal DSS report in May 1988 specified general concerns as follows: 'The service provided to the public is too variable to be acceptable. In some places it is very good indeed. In some places it is absolutely unacceptable' (NACAB, 1991, p. 8). There is no explicit reference to Black claimants, but the implications are obvious.

Various studies have indicated that Black people are less likely than white people to claim the benefits to which they are entitled (Brown, 1984; Gordon and Newnham, 1985; Gordon, 1986). In her Leicester survey of Asian claimants, Gohil (1987) shows that, contrary to the DSS officers' beliefs that the failure to claim is due to language difficulties and lack of knowledge, many of the concerns of Asian people centre on the fear of unnecessary questioning about their status. Such anxieties are expressed by people whose presence in Britain is quite lawful. Earlier work by Gordon and Newnham (1985) also confirmed this view.

In addition to this, a study in Coventry indicated that many Asian families find out about their entitlements by chance (Cocking and Athwal, 1990). Most Black people are fully entitled to claim income support and other kinds of state benefits and they should therefore face no more difficulty in claiming than anyone else. In practice, this is not so and the policy of linking immigration status to benefit entitlement has had the effect of excluding some Black people from receiving benefits on grounds that are not always clear. For example, a small number of Black people are not entitled to income support if they are defined as 'persons from abroad' who are not supposed to have 'recourse to public funds', a term that has yet to be clearly defined. Furthermore, access to information about the benefits changes introduced under the 1986 Social Security Act was restricted by the fact that translations of leaflets and posters were only published fifteen months after the Act was operational.

The 1989 NACAB survey confirmed through evidence from Citizens' Advice Bureaux that Black claimants experience particular problems claiming social security benefits. The report (1991) summarises DSS responses to 252 Black claimants in different parts of England. Many cases are cited of excessive and undue delay in processing claims because of 'unnecessary and unreasonable demands for evidence to support a claim'; lost files; the incorrect use of Black claimants' names; requests for evidence of marriage licences; and requests for passports in order to establish Black people's identity. There is now considerable evidence that the 'checking of passports is not just common, but so common as no longer to be an issue which Black claimants complain of' (Gordon and Newnham, 1985, p. 24). None the less, the insecurity, anxiety and anger which such checking raises in Black people should not be underestimated. Furthermore, officials do not always accurately interpret stamps and other notes made in passports and as a result Black people may again be deprived of benefits:

A Black woman's application for income support was refused. A document from the Home Office which belonged to her dead husband and also had her name on it was 'not acceptable identity'.

A woman with 'settled status' since 1976 was asked to show her passport when she claimed income support. It took 4 weeks after submitting her passport for payment to be made. (NACAB, 1991, pp. 27–30)

These and other cases show clearly that some Black women claimants are receiving less than their entitlement in benefits and, in some cases, are being wrongfully refused benefit. Such situations cause financial hardship in addition to the stress, frustration and mistrust caused by DSS procedures and processes. These delays are exacerbated by staff who either have little or no time or inclination to take into account relevant aspects of Black people's circumstances or who, when under pressure, resort to racial abuse or harassment.

There are a number of issues which particularly affect Black women claimants and make their position problematic. In general women, particularly married women, are defined as the dependants of men in both the immigration and the benefit systems. Thus, for example, unless their husbands are settled in the UK, wives do not have an independent right to stay (WING, 1985). Sometimes Black women have had their benefits withdrawn because their husbands' status is questioned for reasons which they may or may not be aware of. Married women face other difficulties in establishing their rights to benefits such as widows' pensions, retirement pensions or death grants because the validity of their marriage has to be established. If the marriage took place in the UK, it is usually fairly easy to provide acceptable documentation. However, if the marriage took place overseas, difficulties can ensue. In one case, evidence was required from an Asian couple who had been married for thirty-nine years. Their passports were not deemed acceptable evidence. The husband's invalidity benefit was withdrawn while the case was investigated, and it took three-and-a-half months for his benefit to be reinstated (NACAB, 1991). In some cases, the rights of Black women to any benefit at all are questioned and Black women are thus sometimes deterred from making claims. For example, an Asian single mother was told to come back to the office to sort out her income support claim as there were no interpreters available at the time. In fact she did not need an interpreter, but the return bus fare costs were out of her reach (NACAB, 1991).

In view of the obstacles placed before Black claimants, it is perhaps not surprising that there is evidence of low take-up of benefits in Black communities. The issue of unclaimed benefits is one that affects many poor people, but the evidence shows that take-up is lower in Black than in white communities (Gordon and Newnham, 1985). For example, as a result of a take-up campaign in one part of Leicester, over a ten-week period in 1984 approximately £240,000 was paid out in previously unclaimed benefits (Leicester City Council, 1988). An attendance allowance campaign in Halifax in 1987/8 revealed considerable under-claiming by Asian people (NACAB, 1991). Lack of information and the complexities of the system have been found to be the main barriers to claimants, in addition to the racism of the benefits agencies themselves. In order to tackle some of these problems, new alliances are being developed between voluntary and community groupings in various parts of the country. For example, in the Midlands, the Service Delivery to the Black Community Group (SDBCG) was established in 1989 in order to challenge and improve the quality of services to Black people from many organisations, and in particular the DSS.

Social security reviews and appeals are, of course, very important safeguards for individuals' rights. However, some findings suggest that 'negative attitudes and racially stereotypical assumptions particularly to Black applicants are of grave concern and often lead to irrelevant lines of questioning' (NACAB, 1991, p. 46) and judgemental decisions. For example,

a Black woman attended an appeal about an overpayment of child benefit, after her son had withheld from her that he had left school. The chairman blamed what had happened on 'parental irresponsibility and poor quality parenting of a kind which is becoming increasingly prevalent in our society'. (*ibid.*)

Within DSS offices, Black members of staff are regularly mistaken for recipients of services, and negative attitudes from colleagues and claimants are a feature of their professional lives (Watt and Cook, 1989). When Black workers attend tribunals, they are often addressed by the appellant's name or asked what expenses they wish to claim (NACAB, 1991, p. 47).

Since October 1989, when the government withdrew entitlement to income support for most 16- and 17-year-olds, Black young people have been additionally affected. Of particular concern is the hardship experienced by young Asian women because of the lack of suitable provision on Youth Training Schemes. Young people who may have recently arrived in Britain are faced with complex benefit and training systems which may result in lost opportunities and increased financial pressures on families:

> A 19-year-old Asian woman was refused income support because she was not available for work as she did not speak English and would not attend a training course in another town. It had not been established that this woman spoke English and had had two job interviews. Eventually with CAB intervention the benefit was awarded. (NACAB, 1991, p. 59)

Finally, it has to be said that there are costs to claiming from the state for Black people, especially Black women, whose labour 'has propped up this country not only over the past four decades but for centuries. Far from draining its resources, we have been the producers of its wealth' (Bryan *et al.*, 1985, p. 111). The many campaigns and appeals on individual cases are testament to the determination of Black women to fight for their rights to state benefits should they need them.

Conclusion

The title of this chapter is, in effect, charged with political significance. For Black women, ideologies of racism and sexism are central to evaluations of their poverty. Individual households experience poverty, poor housing, unemployment and poor local facilities, but for Black households there is the added dimension of racism. Strategies for structural challenges to Black women's economic marginalisation must take account of the processes of poverty that deny them equitable access to economic and social institutions. Major changes are required to the fundamentals of social policy in order to develop and sustain such positive strategies.

Urban deprivation has been closely linked with race in all the various research data, but successive governments have sought to deal with the 'problem' of race by focusing on Black immigration. In so doing, governments (and other official agencies) reveal that the central issue is how Black people, their needs and concerns, are viewed in British society and are reflected in positions of power and authority. Black women in Britain have to face the dual oppressions of racism and sexism which impinge negatively on their opportunities and consign them to low-paid and low-status jobs. The major struggle for Black women is not just to challenge the oppressive nature of the society they live in, but to create and provide their own positive images of strengths, support and skills within the traditions of the herstory of Black people. It is within the context of supportive and self-help groups that Black women have been able to examine and address their own experiences of racism and sexism and develop their own political theory.

Notes

1. Defining terms such as Black, racism and sexism is a controversial activity. For the purposes of this discussion, we have formulated the following definitions:

(a) Racism is a process of systematic oppression directed against people who are defined as inferior, usually in pseudo-biological terms such as skin colour.
(b) Sexism is a process of systematic oppression directed against women, who are defined as inferior to men.
(c) Black is a political term used to refer to groups who have chosen to share their experience of racism (mainly) in British society, shifting that experience from a negative to a positive one. It is used as a powerful political focus around which to organise resistance to racism and at the same time to incorporate evolving debates about geographical, cultural, religious and historical issues. In the modern British context, Black refers primarily to people of African, Asian and Caribbean origin.

The discussion will focus primarily on family poverty rather than the very important wider aspects of poor housing, inner city poverty, under-resourcing of Black communities, etc. We shall therefore be concentrating on Black women who have sole or shared responsibility for family members (however defined) whether they are in paid work, unemployed, full-time housewives or heads of lone-parent families.

PART 2

Contexts and perspectives

3 *Women and poverty in the twentieth century*

Jane Lewis and David Piachaud

The number of elderly people, predominantly women, living on their own, is rising. One-parent families are increasing. Unemployment among women is growing. Not surprisingly, therefore, there has been a recent spate of literature on 'the feminisation of poverty' by, among others, Hilda Scott (1984) and Martin Rein and Steve Erie (1988). Yet the assumption that the feminisation of poverty is recent is misplaced. The simple fact is that throughout the last century women have always been much poorer than men. At the start of this century 61 per cent of adults on all forms of poor relief were women (GB, 1909, p. 16). Today 60 per cent of adults for whom supplementary benefit is paid are women. One hundred years ago women constituted a minority of the paid labour force, they were paid far less than men, they did most of the cleaning, cooking, child care and other unpaid household tasks, they lacked economic and political power . . . *plus ça change*.

In looking at poverty among women from an historical perspective, which is here confined to Britain over the last century, we have concentrated on the ways in which women's dependencies on the family, labour market and state have been and are interlocking, and how the relative importance of each has increased or diminished. We review how the command over resources has been differentially distributed between men and women and consider how the poverty experienced by women has changed. What we cannot do is to present a complete analysis of all the factors affecting poverty among women in the last century. When we discuss women's marginal position in the labour market or dependent children as causes of poverty, we are not implying that the solutions to female poverty lie in full employment for women and avoiding motherhood. We would argue that women's material poverty reflects the way in which society has persisted in undervaluing so much of the work that they do. Only a radical rethinking of our social and economic policies, such as that suggested by Anna Coote (1981), who suggested that we start thinking how best to provide for our children rather than how best to achieve full employment, will improve women's position in the long term.

It is impossible to draw direct comparisons between women's poverty in the late nineteenth and twentieth centuries. Maud Pember Reeves (1913) described the Edwardian working-class wife with five or six children living in a couple of rooms with no domestic water supply nor a cooker that turned on and off, struggling to balance an irregular income of 'round about a pound a week', undergoing frequent childbirth and more frequent pregnancy, standing at the wash-tub and mangle for long hours to earn an extra 1/6d a week (which would feed the family for a couple of days), or resorting to the pawnshop and, in final desperation, to the Poor Law Guardians for relief. Beatrix Campbell (1984) described life for a working-class wife in the late twentieth century whose family is on supplementary benefit: income may be regular, but an equivalent and largely unrecognised skill is still required to administer it; housing may now have 'mod cons', but how can we compare a tower block with running damp to an Edwardian walk-up with one tap per floor and shared lavatories? Elizabeth Roberts (1984) has suggested that despite the harshness of their environment and their desperate mutual poverty, many working-class wives in the period before World War I looked back on their lives with satisfaction – they took pride in what they had accomplished for their families. The mothers described by Campbell take little pride in their existence. The sense of social exclusion must necessarily be more complete in late twentieth-century society where there is so much more, so much closer, to aspire to. The overall improvements in living standards serve to emphasise the relative deprivation of the poor.

Comparing the circumstances of women over a long period clearly presents difficulties. The problems of definition that arise in assessing poverty at any one time – the poverty level to be used, the appropriate income unit, the measure of income, the work involved in paid and unpaid activities – are enormously magnified when we try to look at poverty historically. Nevertheless, the continuity of women experiencing an inferior economic position to men does stand out, whatever the definitions used. Over the past century women's command over resources has been lower than men's. It has also been to a large extent indirect, being a result of dependence on a father or husband.

Before examining this in more detail we first consider some of the demographic factors affecting the poverty of women. There have been marked improvements in female life expectancy at birth, from 51.6 years in 1901 to 76.2

Table 3.1 Composition of female population (excluding girls) by age and marital status: Great Britain, 1891–1981

			Age					
			Under 20	20–24	25–44	45–64	65 and above	All
1891	(a)	%	27.0	12.2	34.8	19.2	6.8	100
1921	(b)	%	18.5	10.9	38.0	24.2	8.4	100
1951	(c)	%	7.8	8.4	36.8	31.3	15.7	100
1981	(d)	%	8.1	9.0	32.4	28.2	22.3	100

			Marital status			
			Single	Married	Widowed and divorced	All
1891	(a)	%	47.8	42.3	9.9	100
1921	(b)	%	41.9	47.7	10.4	100
1951	(c)	%	25.5	61.0	13.5	100
1981	(d)	%	20.4	61.4	18.2	100

Notes: (a) Aged 10 and over; (b) Aged 12 and over; (c) Aged 15 and over; (d) Aged 16 and over.

Sources: Census of England and Wales 1891, Vol. III, HMSO, London, 1893; Census of Scotland 1891, Vol. II, HMSO, Edinburgh, 1893; Census of England and Wales 1921, Occupations, HMSO, London, 1924; Census of Scotland 1921, Vol. III, HMSO, Edinburgh, 1924; Census 1951 England and Wales, Occupation Tables, HMSO, London, 1956; Census 1951 Scotland, Vol. IV, HMSO, Edinburgh, 1956; Census 1981 Economic Activity, Great Britain, HMSO, London, 1984.

years in 1981, although women's life expectancy at age 21 has not increased as much (CSO, 1986). This, together with the falling fertility rate, has produced a growth in the proportion of elderly women from 7 per cent of those over school-age in 1891 to 22 per cent in 1981, as shown in Table 3.1. At the same time child-bearing patterns have altered markedly. Titmuss (1958) drew attention to the contrast between the average working-class woman of the 1890s marrying in her teens or early twenties, who experienced ten pregnancies and spent fifteen years of her adult life in either pregnancy or nursing, and her post-war counterpart, who spent four years either pregnant or nursing. The decrease in family size has meant not only that women have more time to engage in other pursuits, but has also resulted in improvements in their health status and arguably, therefore, in higher energy levels. The Women's Co-operative Guild Collection, *Maternity: Letters from working women* (Llewellyn Davies, 1915), testified to the high levels of morbidity experienced by many women as a result of childbirth, an issue that received medical recognition during the 1930s when one eminent obstetrician estimated that 10 per cent of all pregnant women were disabled by the experience of childbirth (Blair-Bell, 1931).

In terms of marital status the most marked change, shown in Table 3.1, is the decline in the proportion of single, never-married women and the growth in the proportion of divorced and separated women, many of whom have children –

although it should be noted that nineteenth-century marriages were as likely to be broken through death (usually of the husband and father) as are contemporary families by divorce (Anderson, 1985). The growth in 'female-headed' households has been even greater than Table 3.1 suggests, since most single women in the past were dependent on their parental household or were 'in service'. (The proportion of women in the labour market working as indoor domestic servants was 36 per cent in 1881 and 27 per cent in 1911; not until the post-war period did the proportion of indoor servants fall substantially, to 11 per cent in 1951 (James, 1962).) Changes in the age structure and marital status of women affect in turn their position in the family and labour market, to which we turn.

Dependency on family, labour market and state

This section describes the relationship between these dependencies, the next analyses the circumstances of each. Proceeding in this order needs explanation but does, we believe, make sense. To analyse, say, the labour market as a separate entity is to ignore the fact that women's opportunities within it are often shaped by family commitments. The experiences of Francie Nicol, a working-class woman from South Shields, at the beginning of the century provides an example of what we mean. She began her adult life by marrying, having children and relying on her husband for support, but his drunkenness and failure to provide forced her into the labour market. Here, by dint of Herculean effort, she managed to run a fish and chip shop and keep her family going, building the business up from scratch again after her husband returned to drink away the profits (Robinson, 1975). Many other women in such circumstances would have found themselves applying to the state for relief.

The gradual development of state benefits provided a means for some women of escaping from humiliating private dependency on the family (in the case of unmarried mothers, for example), as well as a more adequate level of income. But state benefits also served to structure and support female dependency in the family (as will be made clear in the next section). What is important here is to understand the way in which access to all resources in our society has been and is gendered, with the consequence that women found and find themselves enmeshed in a web of different dependencies. Dependency on the family, in effect on male relatives, whether father or husband, was more complete in the early twentieth century than it is today. This is because fewer women were active in the labour market; because what earnings they had fell below subsistence needs; and because state provision was less generous and access to it more restricted.

We shall examine first the nature of the options open to working- and middle-class women seeking to depend on the labour market for support rather than on men; and then look at the position of women, often with children, who became widowed or divorced, and of unmarried mothers. Single working-class women were as likely to work at the turn of the century as today, but marriage was for most an economic necessity. Social investigators of the Edwardian period calculated that a single woman needed 14–16 shillings a week to subsist in 1906. The average wage of female textile workers was 15/5d and of women in non-textile industries, 12/11d (Cadbury *et al.*, 1906; Drake, 1920). Thus a majority of women could not afford an independent existence. Contemporary observers remarked on the matter of fact nature of early twentieth-century working-class weddings. As Ellen Ross (1982) has remarked, marriage was not so much a matter of emotional and sexual intimacy as a contract between a husband who would bring home a wage and a wife who would manage household and children.

Thus it seems wrong to draw too stark a contrast between dependency on the family and dependency on the labour market. Marriage was to a large extent a labour 'contract'. Many forms of paid labour, such as the major occupation of domestic service, also involved a housing 'contract'. Most working-class women lived with their families of origin until marriage, because the cost of housing proved an intolerable strain on their budgets (Higgs, 1910). As long as employment possibilities were limited and wages provided little or no surplus over and above subsistence needs, employers in the retail trade found it easy to require their largely female employees to 'live in'. Similarly, many working-class women continued to enter domestic service, despite its low status, because it did at least provide board and lodgings and a measure of respectability, even if the fate of domestic servants in old age depended very much on the whims of their employers and on personal thrift. Marriage provided working-class women with the means, or hope, of escape.

In the case of the middle classes before World War I, single women were not expected to earn their own living at any point in the life cycle, which rendered them dependent on the good offices of their male relatives. Beatrice Webb recorded in her diary the misery that a 'surplus' (i.e. unmarried) daughter could experience, confined in later life to the meaningless rituals of her family home and, in the end, to the care of her ageing parents (Caine, 1982). Marriage was a means of livelihood for all classes of women, but a middle-class daughter who did not find a husband was more likely to be deemed to have 'failed in business'. The minority of single middle-class women for whom relatives failed to provide faced an extremely narrow range of options in the late nineteenth century, the most acceptable of which was that of governess. Such women often led as isolated a life as any working-class domestic servant and would usually look forward to an old age of privation, as the many benevolent societies for the relief of genteel female poverty bore witness to. The expansion of semi-professional employment for women during the early twentieth century, and its growing acceptability for single middle-class women in the inter-war years, marked a real advance for this group of women in terms of their income levels (both during their working lives and in old age), and in the degree of autonomy they were able to exercise over their lives.

Dependence on the family was thus reinforced for married women of all social classes by the lack of any alternative. Access to employment, especially in the professions, was largely controlled by men and in any case women's earnings could not support a family. Nor was the state any comfort. Married women had no separate personality in the eyes of the Poor Law and until World War I it was not uncommon for the authorities taking an able-bodied man claiming relief into the workhouse to require his wife and children to go too (Thane, 1978). Beveridge's National Insurance scheme reinforced the practice of making social benefits contingent in large part on labour market participation so that, for example, married women were dependent on their husbands for pension contributions. Feminists at the time criticised Beveridge for 'denying the married woman, rich or poor, housewife or paid worker, an individual personal status' (Abbott and Bompass, 1943). It is still the case that public law treats the couple as a unit for benefit purposes and aggregates their needs and resources. This contrasts with married women's position in private law (for example, in relation to marital property and divorce), which treats them as economic individuals (O'Donovan, 1985).

Changes in the relationship between dependency on the family, the labour market and the state have however been significantly different for particular groups of single women, namely widows, divorcees and single mothers. The history of their experiences highlights the way in which women's dependency is due both to child-bearing and rearing and to their lack of leverage on the labour market; how these reinforce one another; and how state policy plays its part in structuring the precise nature of women's dependency.

The 1909 Royal Commission on the Poor Laws showed that while more men received indoor relief (in the workhouse) than women, more women received outdoor relief than men. This was largely because of the numbers of widows with children drawing relief. However, women's relief payments were usually somewhat lower. Widows fared somewhat better than other lone mothers, but they were all regarded with suspicion and treated harshly; in 1871 for example, the Local Government Board issued a circular to the effect that outdoor relief should not be granted to the able-bodied widow – undoubtedly considered to be the most 'deserving' of the three groups – if she had only one child or none. In cases involving more than one child, the circular advised that it might be better for the local Board of Guardians to test the widow's need by offering to take her children into the workhouse rather than offering her outdoor relief. In practice, Guardians varied considerably in their treatment of widows, especially in regard to their willingness to grant outdoor relief and in the rates of relief they were prepared to pay. Deserted wives were regarded with more suspicion and the local Guardians were advised to deny them outdoor relief for twelve months to ensure that they were not colluding with their husbands to defraud the authorities. Unmarried mothers were invariably forced to enter the workhouse and, despite the insistence of the central Poor Law authorities that the function of the Poor Law was to relieve destitution and not to correct morals, they were often treated punitively (Thane, 1978).

The central issue for the state was whether to treat these groups of women as workers or as mothers. The early twentieth-century state proved reluctant to step in and play the role of breadwinner, preferring, at least in theory, to take the children into the workhouse and force the mother to work. There is evidence that large numbers of widows and deserted wives undertook sweated homework to make ends meet (Lewis, 1984). Those who were employed full-time rarely worked in insured trades and even in the inter-war years, when coverage under National Insurance expanded, women's needs were assessed as being less than those of men and they received lower benefits.

The pendulum swung in favour of treating women with dependent children and no husbands as mothers rather than workers at different times for different groups of women. As the most 'deserving', widows were granted pensions in 1925. Eleanor Rathbone (1925, p. 11) welcomed this as follows:

> When I think of its [the Widows, Orphans and Old Age Contributory Pensions Act] provisions, the faces which float before my mind are those of women whom I used to know 20–30 years ago, when running an Association of Homeworkers and The Association of Trained Charwomen, both under Liverpool's Women's Industrial Council . . . the lives they led were harder and drearier than anything we comfortable people have ever experienced for a week. Some had their children, others seemed to have nothing . . . nor hope of anything but to be able to go on stitching or scrubbing till they died.

Despite Beveridge's desire not to treat this group of women as automatically deserving of any state support, widows' pensions have proved resistant to erosion. After World War II the attention given to maternal bonding theory contributed to all women with children, including deserted wives and unmarried mothers, being treated as mothers first and workers second. Widows, divorcees and single mothers have clearly increased their share of state benefits, and in turn their dependency on the state since World War II. However, this does not mean that the pendulum could not swing in the opposite direction again. In some twenty-two states in the USA single mothers drawing 'workfare' must now put their children in day-care and work for their benefits (Nathan, 1986). Similar thinking has informed family legislation of 1984 in Britain which seeks to treat divorcees equally and encourage them to enter the workforce rather than be dependent on men's alimony payments. But when women's leverage on the labour market is poor, this is blatantly unequal treatment. Even if the state does not treat single mothers as workers plain and simple, it may try to return responsibility for their welfare to the family. Thus some Canadian provinces have decided not to give welfare to single mothers under 19, forcing them to rely on their family's generosity. The changes contained in both the British government's 1986 and 1991 social security legislation have been described as attempts to re-privatise women's welfare (Land, 1986 and Jane Millar's chapter here). In a male-dominated society in which access to resources is gendered, inequality between the sexes is likely to flourish if unregulated.

Thus women over the past century, and still to a great extent today, have found themselves faced with a dilemma of dependence on either the family, the labour market or the state – none of which offers much choice, control or a route to independence. Having briefly described the overall dilemma, next we shall analyse the different dependencies in more detail.

History of dependency

The family

In terms of women's economic status, the family has imposed both costs and benefits: costs in the form of work that had to be performed and opportunities that were forgone; and benefits in the form of a share in family resources. Historically, being single did not mean that there were no family responsibilities. At the start of the century the Fabian Women's Group estimated that half of all single women workers were wholly or partly responsible for someone else's maintenance, although Rowntree put the figure at only 12 per cent (Smith, 1915; Rowntree and Stuart, 1921). Eldest girls were least likely to marry, primarily because their labour was needed by their parents or other elderly relatives.

It was marriage, however, that brought the greatest family burdens with, in most cases, only a short period before the birth of the first child and then many years of child-rearing. The fact that families were much larger than now did not necessarily mean that proportionately more time was needed, since older children could and did care for younger children. But washing, cooking and cleaning in particular expanded with family size. In terms of overall workload, child-rearing must have been a greater burden to women in the past.

By contrast, the burdens carried by women caring for the growing number of elderly dependants is probably greater now than in the early part of the century. It is estimated today that there are 6 million informal carers in Britain, of whom 1.4 million are providing twenty hours or more a week. Female carers are more likely than men to be carrying the main responsibility for care-giving; to be helping for over twenty hours a week; and to be living in the same household as the person being cared for (Green, 1988; see also Caroline Glendinning's chapter). Because life expectancy at the turn of the century was shorter, it was less likely than now that daughters would face a prolonged period of caring for a frail parent. However, Jill Quadagno (1982) found that in the ribbon-weaving village of Chilvers Cotton in 1901, 84 per cent of those over 60 years old were living with a family member. Elderly women were more likely to find a place with relatives than were elderly men for, as the Royal Commission on the Poor Laws commented, women were more use to their children by contributing babysitting, sewing, etc. A much larger proportion of those caring for the elderly in the early twentieth century were single women, in large part a reflection of the fact that there were considerably more unmarried women in the population; although according to the 1985 GHS middle-aged unmarried women are still at very high risk of becoming heavily involved in care-giving.

While it is difficult to come to decisive conclusions about shifts in the burden of caring, it is clear that domestic technology has changed dramatically and has certainly eased the drudgery and hard labour that characterised early twentieth-century housework. Clothes must no longer be pounded in a dolly tub and mangled, nor floors scrubbed on hands and knees with minimal help from machinery and myriad cleansers. Nevertheless, it is not clear how far the time spent on housework has significantly changed. For example, when washing clothes or floors became easier, it was not only possible to do such tasks more quickly, but it also became expected that they would be done more frequently. In the case of a substantial number of middle-class women, it is likely that the burden and the number of hours spent doing housework increased after World War II. These women would have employed one general servant even during the inter-war period. After the war not only was this no longer the case but, increasingly, middle-class women went out to work as well. While a growing number of 'career' women married to professional men today hire nannies during their children's early days, if they still bear primary responsibility for home and family, their leisure-time may well be much more restricted than it was earlier this century.

In return for the burdens imposed by the family, there was the hope of an adequate income. This depended first on the husband receiving a 'family wage', which was an ideal rather than a reality for many (Land, 1980). As early as 1889, Booth's survey of London showed one-third of the population to be in poverty and hence incapable of earning a family wage. Rowntree's second survey of York in the 1930s showed that even in class E (the top third earning 63/6d or more a week) one-fifth of husbands did not earn enough to keep themself, wife and three children out of poverty (Rowntree, 1941, p. 161). Yet even if the husband's wage was adequate the problem for all married women, especially those in low-income households, was (and is) that they are in large measure financially dependent on their husbands. In her pioneering analysis of the family wage system, Eleanor Rathbone (1924) described women and children's status as that of 'male luxuries'. The contract whereby the husband brought home a wage and the wife managed home and children was by no means always kept. But whereas if women failed to do their part men could (and often did) enforce compliance by the use of violence (Ayers and Lambertz, 1986), women had no such recourse. Evidence throughout the twentieth century – Rowntree's study of York (1902), Caradog Jones' (1934) of Liverpool in the 1930s, Jan Pahl's (1989) recent research – shows that a large number of married women have not even known what their husbands earned. Housekeeping money tends to remain constant regardless of increases in prices, family size or husband's earnings. The well-documented result is that women, as the domestic chancellors of the family exchequer, put the needs of husband and children first and their own last. Working-class budgets of the Edwardian period show that even in respectable working-class households where the husband kept back only a small sum for personal items (chiefly tobacco and drink) his diet tended to differ significantly from that of the other family members. The worker expected and received 'a relish to his tea'. Furthermore, working-class women's struggles to make ends meet relied both on what Rowntree (1902, p. 43) called 'the mutual helpfulness of the poor' as well as a whole network of neighbourhood credit that varied in its degree of respectability. The closeness of many early twentieth-century working-class communities was, as Abrams has remarked (Bulmer, 1986), sustained largely by the mutual interdependency born of poverty. Women often ran up credit in the local shops, resorted to the pawnbroker or worse still to a moneylender without telling their husbands. (As Gillian Parker's chapter in this volume shows, this situation has changed little today.)

The labour market

Women's role in the labour market and the labour market's role in determining women's income levels will be considered in two stages: first, who has been economically active? and second, how have women's earnings altered relative to men's?

The trends of economic activity rates are shown in Table 3.2. Overall, women's activity rates rose between 1891 and 1987 from 35 to 51 per cent, but this total conceals important variations. Among married women, the activity rate rose from less than one in ten in 1921 to over half in 1987. Among single women, activity rates have remained around three-quarters of those of men.

By 1987 women had become 42 per cent of the economically active population and most of these women were married. By contrast, in 1891 only 4 per cent of the economically active population consisted of married women – indeed, 54 per cent of economically active women were then aged under 25 compared with 25 per cent in 1987, as shown in Table 3.3. The proportion of married women in the workforce has dramatically increased and the participation rate of married women aged 25–44 is now higher than that of younger married women. This reflects women's greater attachment to the labour force throughout their adult lives. They no longer tend to leave the workforce permanently on marriage as they did prior to World War II, nor to leave on the birth of their first child and return only when their children are grown up – the characteristic pattern of women's labour market behaviour during the late 1950s and 1960s.

The economic activity figures from the Census are subject to two limitations. First, casual employment undertaken by married women in the past was largely ignored, as officials were often not sure how to categorise it. Married working-

Table 3.2 Economic activity rate by age, sex and marital status, 1891–1981

		All women %	Married women %	All men %
Under 20	1891	43.7	na	59.0
	1921	48.4	14.6	63.2
	1951	78.9	38.1	83.8
	1981	56.4	45.5	64.5
	1987	71.0	55.0	73.0
20–24	1891	58.4	na	98.1
	1921	62.4	12.5	97.0
	1951	65.4	36.5	94.9
	1981	69.3	54.6	89.1
	1987	72.0	63.0	91.0
25–44	1891	29.5	na	97.9
	1921	28.4	9.1	97.9
	1951	36.1	25.1	98.3
	1981	59.4	55.7	97.5
	1987	na	na	na
45–64	1891	24.6	na	93.7
	1921	20.1	8.0	94.9
	1951	28.7	19.0	95.2
	1981	51.9	51.7	90.3
	1987	na	na	na
65 and over	1891	15.9	na	65.4
	1921	10.0	4.2	58.9
	1951	5.3	2.7	31.1
	1981	3.7	4.2	10.7
	1987	5.0	3.0	8.0

		All women %	Single women %	Married women %	Widowed/ divorced women %	All men %
All ages	1891	35.0	na	na	na	83.9
	1921	32.3	60.8	8.7	25.6	87.1
	1951	34.7	73.1	21.7	21.1	87.6
	1981	45.5	60.8	47.2	22.9	77.8
	1987	51.0	na	55.0	na	75.0

Sources: As Table 3.1; and *Labour Force Survey, 1987.*

class women undertook casual work to supplement the family income – charring, sewing, hawking fruit, etc. – especially when the wage-earner was ill, unemployed or otherwise unable or unwilling to provide. Little of this highly irregular work was recorded in the Census and few of its rewards were consumed directly by women themselves. Secondly, most of the recent increased

Table 3.3 Composition of economically active women by age and marital status, Great Britain, 1891–1981

		Age					
		Under 20	20–24	25–44	45–64	65 and over	All
1891	%	33.8	20.3	29.3	13.5	3.1	100
1921	%	27.7	21.1	33.5	15.1	2.6	100
1951	%	17.7	15.9	38.2	25.9	2.4	100
1981	%	10.0	13.7	42.3	32.2	1.8	100
1987	%	10.3	14.2	na	na	1.2	100

		Marital status			
		Single	Married	Widowed and divorced	All
1921	%	78.9	12.9	8.2	100
1951	%	53.6	38.2	8.2	100
1981	%	27.2	63.6	9.2	100
1987	%	na	66.8	na	100

Sources: See Table 3.2.

economic activity by women has been in part-time work and women remain unequal participants in the labour market.

Next we turn to women's earnings relative to men's. Ideally, we should like to look at hourly earnings, but historical data on this are limited. Therefore we compare in Table 3.4 the average wages of full-time workers in a number of industries in 1886, 1906 and 1990. It will be seen that women's wages remain far below (in most cases around two-thirds) men's, although there have been some relative increases over the last century.

In 1886 the average wage of male manual workers was 25 shillings a week; only one in a thousand women earned over the men's average (Department of Employment and Productivity, 1971). In 1990 the comparable proportion had risen – but still only 7 per cent of women manual workers earned over the male manual average (Department of Employment, 1990a). In both 1886 and 1990 less than 5 per cent of men earned less than half the male average, but over one-third of women did so in each year. Thus low pay has been, as it is now, a problem for the majority of women.

The state

The state's lack of neutrality in respect to social policies affecting women is well documented (Land 1978, 1983; David, 1983, 1986). There is considerable evidence to support the idea that state policy has consistently been framed with the intention of sustaining the traditional family form of breadwinning husband

Table 3.4 Women's wages as percentage of men's wages: average of manual workers

	1886	1906	1990
Woollen and worsted	57.2	51.6	66.3
Hosiery	47.1	45.4	60.7
Footwear	51.5	45.6	64.1
Textiles	na	54.9	64.2
Clothing	na	44.8	73.3
Food, drink and tobacco	na	43.4	66.5
Paper and printing	na	35.4	63.5
Metals, engineering and shipbuilding	na	37.3	63.1
All industries	51.5	na	61.1

Sources: *British Labour Statistics, Historical Abstract 1886–1968*, Department of Employment and Productivity (London: HMSO, 1971), Tables 35 and 37; *New Earnings Survey, 1990* (Part C), Department of Employment (1990a).

and dependent wife and children. However, policy outcomes have not necessarily been consistent with these aims. Furthermore, policies in areas not directly concerned with the family – for example, in health or education – have often been contradictory in terms of their effect on women's position.

Social security law has from the first merged the identities of husbands and wives. In practice this means that successive schemes have been administered through the spouse with the greatest attachment to and the most secure position in the labour market – the husband. The first National Insurance Act of 1911 essentially excluded married women, who could only join the scheme if they were insured workers in their own right. The Fabian Women's Group (1911) pointed out that such a scheme of contributory insurance was bound to exacerbate problems concerning women's economic position, dividing those living as their husband's dependant from what was before World War II the small minority of married women who worked full-time. The Women's Industrial Council (1911) regretted the fact that National Insurance intensified the tendency 'to consider the work of a wife and mother in her home of no money value'.

These early critics were correct in their perception that any social security scheme administered on a contributory basis through participation in the workforce would always be of limited use to women because of their marginal position in the labour market. Assuming in his turn that married women's proper place was not in the labour market, Beveridge perpetuated the idea of women's double dependency on husbands – both for day-to-day maintenance and for state benefits – and summarised his views thus: 'on marriage a woman gains a legal right of maintenance by her husband as a first line of defence against risks which fall directly on the solitary woman' (Beveridge, 1942, p. 49). The assumption that married women should be financially dependent on their husbands has meant that state policy has been used further to restrict their access to benefits, thereby reinforcing the role of men as breadwinners and marginalising women as earners. Thus in 1931, in the depths of the Depression, the Anomalies Act assumed that any married woman who had left the labour force for whatever reason had effectively retired and was therefore ineligible for benefit. This legislation finds a parallel in recent changes in the regulations for unemployment insurance which, as Claire Callender describes in Chapter 9, now insist that married women claiming benefit must be able to demonstrate that they have made child care provision and are thus effectively available for work.

While women's primary responsibility for home and family has been emphasised, state policy has shown meagre financial recognition of the time costs and forgone earnings involved. Statutory maternity provision in Britain is one of the lowest in Europe and child benefits fall far below those of many countries (Bradshaw and Piachaud, 1980). Thus unpaid work in the home is inevitably associated with women's poverty.

In some areas women have positively gained from direct access to services such as the National Health Service. Nella Last, recording for Mass Observation during World War II, felt that the NHS would prove the greatest boon to married women (Broad and Fleming, 1983). The contributors to the Women's Co-operative Guild's collection of letters (Llewellyn Davies, 1915) on maternity a generation before would surely have agreed. Indeed, women have used the NHS more than men because they become mothers. Yet, while this may be interpreted as women gaining more than men from a state service, it is also not inconsistent with state policy to encourage women's maternal role.

State policy continues to treat the household as a unit for benefit purposes, aggregating the needs and resources of its members and paying scant regard to the contribution made by married women in particular to the family economy. In many areas of state provision there is now a formal equality of opportunity but outcomes remain highly unequal. In general, state policy has accommodated rather than attacked the structural causes of women's inferior economic position.

Measures of inequality and poverty

Here we draw together the quantitative evidence that is available on the effects which the changes described above have had on women's economic status relative to men, and we examine how the nature of poverty among women has altered. As we have said, comparisons of the extent of poverty among women present many problems – different concepts of poverty, changing poverty levels, the paucity of data on the poverty of households and the virtual absence of data on women's share of resources within households. On many matters of importance there is simply no comparable quantitative data going back any length of time.

Changes in women's participation in the labour market may be summarised as follows:

	1890s	1980s
Women as proportion of economically active population[1]	31%	42%
Women's earnings as proportion of total earnings[2]	19%	26%

Turning to social security benefits, in the past women were treated almost entirely as dependants so that benefits were paid to husbands for their spouses or to widows on the basis of their husband's contribution record. We may therefore distinguish between, first, that part of benefits which was paid *for* women, even if much of it was paid to their husbands, which in 1989 amounted to 51 per cent of social security;[3] and second, that part of benefits paid *to* women, including benefits paid for children and other family members, which in 1989 amounted to 44 per cent of social security.[4] Data on rates of poor relief and the marital status of recipients do not allow comparable estimates to be made for the past, but it is possible to compare numbers of recipients (though not the amounts received):

	1908	1989
Proportion of poor law/income support recipients who were women[5]	61%	60%

Combining earnings and social security benefits and payments of rents and dividends, we can estimate the share of income directly paid to women – *direct* income. We distinguish this from *total* income calculated on the dubious assumption that household income is shared equally between household members. It would appear that, whereas women's share of *total* income has changed little, women's share of *direct* income has increased – although women still receive directly only a quarter of all income. (The figures for the 1890s are only approximate.)

	1890s	1989
Women's share of direct income[6]	15%	22%
Women's share of total income[7]	45%	44%

Finally we examine the changing composition of poverty among women. We do this by re-analysing the results of the earliest systematic study of poverty carried out by Rowntree (or, more accurately, largely by his predominantly female staff) in York in 1899, and comparing these with recent government statistics on low incomes (Rowntree, 1902). The data for the 1980s are for Great Britain, but York was (and is) sufficiently representative for the comparison to be of interest. We make no attempt to compare the poverty levels used; rather, we have for 1899 used Rowntree's 'primary' poverty level and for 1987 treated as poor those on or below the supplementary benefit level. The proportion of the

Table 3.5: Comparison of causes of poverty, 1899 and 1987

	Among persons		Among women	
	1899	1987	1899	1987
Old age, sickness and disability	12%	32%	22%	49%
One-parent family	9%[a]	15%	18%	14%
Unemployment	5%[b]	31%	6%[b]	23%
Large family (see notes)	22%[c]	14%[d]	14%[c]	6%[d]
Low wages	52%	8%	40%	8%
All causes	100%	100%[e]	100%	100%[e]

[a] Widows plus deserted and separated women aged under 60.
[b] Chief wage earner out of work and irregularity of work.
[c] Five children or more.
[d] Three children or more.
[e] Omitting other causes, which amount to some 5 per cent of the total.

Notes: For 1899, based on those in 'Primary poverty', Rowntree's classification has been largely followed save for separating widows under and over age 60. Chief wage earners have been assumed to be male, spouses to be female and other adults to be divided equally between women and men.

For 1987, based on those in receipt of Supplementary Benefit or Housing Benefit Supplement or with Relative Net Resources below Supplementary Benefit level. The DHSS division by economic status has been largely followed. It is assumed large families are distributed equally among the other types of families under pensionable age. Estimates of numbers of women have been based on proportions of women in each category among SB recipients in May 1987.

Sources: Rowntree, B.S., *Poverty: A study of town life*, Chapter V (Longmans 1902); Johnson and Webb, 1990; *Social Security Statistics, 1988* (DHSS, HMSO, 1988); and authors' calculations.

population below the two levels in each year were 9.9 per cent in 1899 and 18.8 per cent in 1987. The results are shown in Table 3.5.

The causes of poverty among women have shown major changes. Most notably there has been a growth in the extent to which poverty is associated with old age, sickness and disability. There has also been a growth in poverty associated with unemployment. On the other hand, the proportion of women's poverty associated with low wages (predominantly of husbands) has declined. Predictably, large families are a smaller component, even using a lower definition of 'large' in 1987 than 1899; but more surprisingly, women in one-parent families now represent a lower proportion of poor women than in 1899, primarily because of the decline in widowed women below pension age.

Conclusions

On the issues we have discussed we are severely constrained by limitations of data; for example, changes in marital status are a poor indicator of changes in patterns of living, cohabiting and sharing. Many important developments have not been considered, such as changes in training, promotion and occupational welfare in employment, patterns of inheritance, or treatment by the tax system. Our discussion has been generalised and has concealed many important changes. We do not distinguish the circumstances of ethnic minorities even though unemployment rates among women of West Indian and Asian origin are roughly twice those of white women (Brown, 1984); Black women in Britain experience poverty much more than white women as Juliet Cook and Shantu Watt show in Chapter 2.

The evidence we have examined shows clearly that the idea that poverty has only recently become 'feminised' is wrong. Women constitute a roughly similar proportion of the poor today as in 1900 and this reflects the position of women in society more generally. Paid employment is for the vast majority the main way of avoiding poverty; the nature of women's work, both paid and unpaid, and the undervaluing of both, lead in our social and economic system to women's relatively greater income insecurity throughout the life cycle. While there are of course exceptions, it remains true that the great majority of women are trapped in a vicious circle of domestic responsibilities and low-paid, low-status employment.

While female poverty has been a constant fact, its composition has changed substantially. In the early part of the century, married women were the largest group of women in poverty because of the low wages paid to husbands and because of large families. Widows and elderly women were the next largest group. Today female poverty is concentrated among lone women, especially among the elderly. The balance of dependency has also shifted. Married women now have fewer children and higher material standards than their great-grandmothers, which means that potentially they have more leisure (subject to housework and child care expanding to fill the time and little changing in the domestic division of labour between the sexes). Nor are married women as financially dependent on the generosity of husbands. Their share of direct income has risen, largely due to their increased labour market participation, and they have individual direct access to many social services such as the NHS – although not to social security. Lone mothers are more likely to be wholly dependent on the state than were their foremothers. The early twentieth-century state could not decide whether to treat lone mothers as mothers or workers; more recently the social security system has been prepared to support motherhood – however exiguously. In the case of the elderly, before 1948 the legal obligation to maintain covered three rather than two generations, so families were legally obliged to support elderly relatives (Crowther, 1982). Now state support has increased, but with the growing number of elderly dependants the work of caring, which falls largely on women, has probably increased rather than decreased.

The persistence of female poverty can only be explained in terms of women's position in society. Women's work is rewarded less than men's and this affects their well-being throughout their lives. That work now includes a large proportion of so-called 'economic activity' which is rewarded with earnings, but it still includes a wholly disproportionate share of unpaid work in the home, raising children and caring for husbands and other dependants. The latter, unpaid, work has a direct effect on the former, paid, work, contributing to inequalities in pay.

There is, of course, no reason why women should accept the ethos of the market-place and wish to maximise income or aspire to male models of full employment; women are not 'economic men'. Yet with existing child benefits and child care facilities and the existing division of labour in society, whatever the personal rewards of unpaid work such as rearing children, it undoubtedly increases female dependency on men within the family or on the state. Children have, since Eleanor Rathbone (1924) wrote, been recognised as a source of poverty in families; they are, as things stand, above all a source of female poverty.

Poverty has been a central issue in social policy over the last century, but female poverty has been of only tangential concern. Poverty in old age and child poverty have received far more attention, with little recognition of their links with women's position in society. To a limited extent, a shift towards more collective responsibility for the elderly and towards recognition of changing family structures has led to developments that have allowed some women more autonomy. But for the most part social policy has assumed, or presumed, that women would continue to carry the burden of caring and remain unequal in the economy. It has therefore ignored the structural causes of female poverty. It is not surprising that women remain the principal victims of poverty.

Notes

1. Calculated from Censuses of England and Wales and of Scotland for 1891 and Labour Force Survey, 1987.
2. 1890s based on Census return of occupied populations in 1891 and average wages of manual workers in 1886; *British Labour Statistics, Historical Abstract 1886–1968*, Department of Employment and Productivity (London: HMSO, 1971), Table 35. 1980s based on number of employees and mean earnings in *Family Expenditure Survey, 1983* (Department of Employment, 1984).
3. Based on *Family Expenditure Survey, 1989* (Department of Employment, 1990b), Sources of Income. For each type of household the social security income for women = total social security income × W/W + M + 0.5C (where W is number of women, M is number of men and C is number of children).
4. Based on *FES, 1989* (see note 3) calculated on the basis of social security payments to female heads of household and to wives (with pro rata estimates for other household types).
5. 1908 figures from GB, 1909, Vol. I, Pt II, paragraph 17. 1989 figures calculated from *Social Security Statistics, 1989* (DHSS, 1989b).
6. 1890s based on the proportion of earnings to women (19 per cent) and the

fact that women's share of salaries (which constituted 17 per cent of income from employment in 1891; Feinstein, 1972) and of rent were small. 1989 figures based on *FES, 1989* (Department of Employment, 1990b).

7. 1890s calculated on the assumption that the great majority of women were living with their fathers or husbands and that income is shared equally between adults, with children getting a half-share, i.e. women's share = W/W + M + 0.5C (as in note 3 above). 1989 based on *FES, 1989* on same method as in note 3 above using gross weekly income.

4 *Whatever happened to the social wage?*

Hilary Land

> What matters to women even more than the cash wage increases they or their husbands may get is the standard of publicly provided services which mean so much to the family – health care, education, housing and a good environment. In other words: the social wage.

Thus wrote Barbara Castle in 1981 reflecting on her time in the mid–1970s when, as a Secretary of State for the Social Services, she had fought hard for the social wage (Castle, 1981, p. 21). This was not just because at the Department of Health and Social Security she was its 'largest custodian' but because she believed 'the battle for the cash wage increase is a masculine obsession' and that to her 'socialism is not just militant trade unionism. It is the gentler society in which every producer remembers he is a consumer too' (Castle, 1980, p. 309). For a time in the early 1970s it had looked as if voluntary wage restraint might be acceptable to the trade union movement in exchange for a Labour Government's commitment to implementing a package of measures which included increases in the social wage. Statutory policies had failed to curb trade union bargaining power, as Edward Heath had found to his cost, so

> the only way was to turn that power into something more positive by involving unions in the responsibilities of economic management in return

for involving them also in the choice of social policy. It was from this approach that the concept of the social contract emerged. (Castle, 1980, p. 9)

However, the social contract in Britain was too fragile to bear the weight of the repercussions of the steep oil price rises, the failure to achieve economic growth, continuing inflation and growing unemployment. The rescue package which the Labour Government negotiated with the IMF in 1976 involved cuts in public expenditure on the social services. When these were followed by more cuts and, in 1978, an attempt to keep pay increases well below the rate of inflation as well, the social contract was totally discredited. Then followed the 'winter of discontent' in 1979 involving large numbers of public sector workers. The image of irresponsible, over-powerful trade unions whose wage claims fuelled inflation and whose work practices, particularly in the public sector, encouraged overmanning, inefficiency and waste was one which helped Mrs Thatcher to power and gave her government the licence to reduce the rights of trade unions. Rolling back trade union power became one of the first targets of the new Conservative Government.

The residual model of welfare

However, the aim of the first Thatcher government was not only to reduce state intervention in the market but also to reduce the role of the state in the provision of social services. At first this took the form of direct cuts in public expenditure. Public expenditure, particularly on social benefits and services, had to be reduced because it was believed that the high levels of taxation required to sustain it stifled initiative and enterprise at the same time as creating apathy and a culture of dependence among the claimants and recipients of these services. A strong and growing economy could not be achieved while public expenditure levels remained high. Later on in the 1980s it became much clearer that the old universalistic model of the welfare state which had underpinned much social welfare provision in the 1950s and 1960s, and which made it hard to cut benefits and services substantially, was being abandoned and replaced by what Richard Titmuss has called the residual welfare model (Titmuss, 1974, p. 31). This is based on the view that state welfare provision should only come into play when the private market or family breaks down and fails to meet an individual's needs. Access to, and the use of, social services and benefits was no longer an unqualified right. Those using state welfare services acquired the status of a 'dependant' who is a second class citizen: the social wage is inferior to the money wage. However, money wages must not become or indeed remain 'too high' otherwise workers will price themselves out of the labour market. Only a deregulated labour market can ensure that this will not happen. The government's attitude towards wages and social welfare is well summed up in its evidence to the House of Lords' Select Committee on the European Community, when explaining its opposition to the Community Social Charter which is concerned with establishing 'fundamental social rights' in the Single Market. The Under-Secretary of State for Employment said:

> What we have done quite deliberately as a government has been to try to minimise the tax burden on businesses and individuals and leave them as free as possible to make up their minds about how they make their arrangements either as employers or indeed as individuals. (House of Lords, 1990, p. 26)

With this individualistic, *laissez-faire* philosophy informing economic and social policies, it is not surprising that in the 1980s both money wages and the social wage came under attack. In this chapter, I want to look at what this has meant for women, because although the attack on the social wage was not part of a deliberate policy to reduce the well-being of women or to drive them out of the labour market and back into the home, in general the social wage is of greater significance in the lives of women than of men, as Barbara Castle recognised. Women are also, as other contributors to this book show, more vulnerable in the labour market. Before looking at the impact of cuts in particular social services and the greater reliance on private provision and how this relates to women's position in the labour market, I want first to look at how the government undermined those institutions which historically fought to establish and defend the social wage. For in weakening those who opposed these attacks on the welfare state, the government has reduced the opportunities of men and women, but particularly women, to participate in the processes which shape the content and the form of the social wage.

Changing political processes

Central government

In Britain in the 1980s there was not the institutionally entrenched resistance at the centre to the political attack on the welfare state which seems to have succeeded in protecting social policies in some other countries, such as Scandinavia for example. In Britain corporatism had been tried and seen to have failed in the 1970s; and the demise of the social contract had reawakened long-held suspicions within the labour movement that welfare provision could be used not just as an alternative to wage *increases* but as a means of *cutting* wages. These suspicions are not always without foundation, as I have argued elsewhere (Land, 1975, 1990).

The government's substantial majority in the House of Commons throughout the 1980s (won on only 43 per cent of the vote in 1987) has meant that it has been possible to make major changes to welfare legislation with little fear of defeat, in spite of the fact that public opinion polls show that the majority of the British electorate would support *more* spending on health and education and give a higher priority to reducing unemployment than to low inflation (Brook, Jowell and Witherspoon, 1989). As the political journalist Hugo Young wrote:

> The absence of an effective parliamentary opposition was central to a great deal of what happened. For the whole decade the government enjoyed immunity from at least half the customary pressures of political life . . . But it was the failure of the non-Conservative opinion to modernise and organise itself, rather than the impossibility of such opinion ever speaking for a British majority, which enabled the Thatcherite experiment to turn, in the course of three terms, into the new orthodoxy. (Young, 1989, p. 21)

It should also be noted that accountability to Parliament itself has been eroded in the past decade. Much of the legislation has been drafted in unspecific terms, with the detail settled *after* the Bill has been passed. These take the form of regulations which have to be laid before Parliament but which are very unlikely to be debated and therefore subject to the same scrutiny they would have had, had they been incorporated in the Bill itself. Bills have become what Lord Mishcon called the Child Support Bill, 'legislative skeletons' (H. of L. Debate, 25 Feb. 1991, col. 780). For example, the 1986 Social Security Act gave enormous powers to the Secretary of State for what was then the Department of Health and Social Security (DHSS). Clause 50 of the Act allowed that regulations made within a year of its enactment need not even be referred to any advisory body (there are in any case only two left) and Clause 51 enabled 'statutory instruments to provide for a person to exercise discretion in any matter'. In a recent case in which the decision of a Department of Social Security (DSS) adjudicating officer, to exclude a disabled person from a benefit using a criterion unrelated to disability, was challenged, the Appeal judges, although clearly shocked, had to uphold the Department's decision, for it was in accordance with the provision of the Act. Even worse, against decisions made in some parts of the social security system, notably the social fund, individual claimants have *no* right of appeal.

Local government

Not surprisingly, therefore, it was from *local* government that much of the resistance to the attack on the welfare state came. After all, local authorities were responsible for the delivery of education, housing and social work services (but no longer for any of the health services: these had been removed from them in the early 1970s). Local authority expenditure accounted for nearly 30 per cent of public expenditure in 1979. Local authorities were also closer to the social and economic circumstances of the local community. Many of their elected representatives did not share the political views of the Conservative Government in Westminster and were strongly committed to universal, good quality welfare provision. During the miners' strike and in its aftermath, some local authorities in the mining areas incurred the wrath of the government by providing free school meals to miners' children, thus cushioning the impact of the strike. The most successful opposition came from the Labour-controlled Greater London Council; it was so successful that the government had to abolish it in 1986, along with the five other large metropolitan authorities. (Paradoxically, it was the un-elected House of Lords which almost defeated the Bill to abolish this tier of government which stood between the smaller local authorities and central government.)

However, the government has done much more to weaken local authorities, for if public expenditure was to be reduced, they had to be forced to make cuts. To quote Hugo Young again:

> Institutionally, the key target was local government. Wave upon wave of assaults on the financial independence of local authorities weakened their power and cast doubt on their point. Education and housing, its core activities, were both reorganised in ways calculated to reduce or even exclude the concept of local democracy. (Young, 1989, p. 21)

As well as having far less control over their finances, local authorities now also have far less control over how their services are delivered. Under the 1988 Local Government and Finance Act, all local authorities must put more of their services out to tender and accept the cheapest contract. Contract compliance, which has been used with some success in the USA and Sweden, for example, to improve employment opportunities for women, ethnic minorities and disabled people, became illegal in 1988, except in Northern Ireland. Instead of being direct providers of services, local authorities must increasingly manage services provided by others, for example community care. Finally, perhaps the most important attack on local democracy, which attracted very little comment at the time, is embodied in the 1989 Local Government and Housing Act. Under this legislation, any local authority employee earning more than £13,500 per annum is disbarred from standing for election as a councillor either in their own *or* in a neighbouring authority. The majority of local authority employees are women and the threshold applies on a pro-rata basis to part-time workers. When the Act was passed £13,500 was approximately the average (mean) male wage, but there is no mechanism built into the legislation to ensure this is revalued as earnings rise, so over time more and more women will be disqualified. Women and ethnic minority groups are grossly under-represented in Parliament (only 9 per cent of Members of Parliament currently are women) but more (albeit not enough) have been able to find a voice in local government. At the time this Act was being debated in Parliament, about 20 per cent of local councillors were women. Often, experience in local government has been a stepping-stone to Parliament. This will be harder in future.

This profound attack on local government bodes ill for the future of the social wage. As the novelist Winifred Holtby wrote, dedicating her novel *South Riding* to her mother who was a county alderman:

> When I came to consider local government, I began to see how it was in essence the first-line defence thrown up by the community against our common enemies – poverty, sickness, ignorance, isolation, mental derangement and social maladjustment. The battle is not faultlessly conducted, nor are the motives of those who take part in it righteous or disinterested. But the war is, I believe, worth fighting, and this corporate action is at least based upon recognition of one fundamental truth about human nature – we are not only single individuals, each face to face with eternity and our separate spirits; we are members one of another. (Holtby, 1936, p. 6)

Winifred Holtby was writing in the 1930s before the British welfare state had been consolidated. Nevertheless her analysis still stands, for the opportunity provided by local government (with all its limitations) for taking collective action and exercising collective responsibility has not been replaced by other opportunities. The proposed 'Citizens' Charter' will enhance the rights of individuals as consumers, but it remains to be seen whether it contains a real potential for anything other than an individualistic reaction to poor and inadequate services.

The labour movement

The commitment to good quality social provision by the public sector workforce associated with the health, education and welfare services, in other words the producers of the social services, has also been weakened as trade union power has been eroded. Despite its reservations at times, the labour movement has fought hard to establish health, education and welfare services. High levels of unemployment always weaken the bargaining power of organised labour, but government legislation in the early 1980s, by removing rights won decades earlier, considerably curtailed its power. Trade union membership reached a peak of 13.3 million in 1979, representing over half the civilian workforce in employment. By 1988 it had fallen to 10.2 million, representing less than two-fifths of the workforce (CSO, 1991a, p. 192). Public opinion polls now show that the view that trade unions are too powerful is considerably weaker than it was in the early 1980s.

Of particular significance to women, both as workers in the public sector (women comprised 45 per cent of the public sector workforce in 1981 and over 80 per cent of those worked in health, education and welfare) and as recipients of the social services, has been the curb in the rate of growth of public sector unions such as the National Union of Public Employees and the Confederation of Health Service Employees. The membership of these two unions alone doubled during the 1970s to over a million between them. Both unions had made an effort to recruit more women members. In 1981, 30 per cent of the workforce in employment was in the public sector but this had fallen to 23 per cent by 1989. 'Most of the decrease in public sector employment since 1981 has been accounted for by a fall in employment in public corporations, partly due to privatisation' (CSO, 1991a, p. 72). Privatisation, involving contracting out such services as hospital catering and cleaning, refuse disposal and school meals to the cheapest tender, has resulted in the increased use of non-unionised labour. Such labour has lower wages and poorer conditions of work. Moreover, the standard of service provided has fallen, sometimes to levels which endanger health and safety, as shown when, from time to time, scandals over the lack of cleanliness in hospital wards and operating theatres surface in the press.

The professions have not been immune either from changes which have altered their working environments and working practices. The style of management in the health services and, to a lesser extent, the personal social services has changed from one based on achieving consensus among all those involved in providing the service to one based on a top-down decision-making process dominated by financial targets. Under the National Health and Community Care Act, those in the health and personal social services must be adept at purchasing the most 'cost effective' package of services for their patients or clients. Their financial accountability has certainly been increased but this does not necessarily increase their accountability in the broader sense. Again it remains to be seen whether or not the 'Citizens' Charter' will achieve this and give the lay person a real voice in decisions about how policies are developed *and* services delivered. Meanwhile the voice of the professionals has been weakened without strengthening that of the patient or client. While all the professions can be criticised for acting in their own self-interest rather than in the interests of their patients or clients, they are nevertheless important mediating bodies standing between the individual and the state. They are also an independent source of wisdom and advice, which competes with the other sources on which governments depend. This is something which is very important to sustain in a democratic society.

Looking back, then, over the past decade, not only has the value of the social wage declined, as will be shown below, but the mechanisms available to people to defend and improve the services which make up the social wage have deliberately been rendered less effective. Certainly, those involved in the *production* of the social wage now have a weaker voice. The strengthened rights of *individual* consumers to receive more information about the standards achieved by these services and the right to seek compensation for failure to achieve certain standards are no substitute for the loss of those mechanisms, which depended on what Winifred Holtby called 'corporate action'. A great deal depends on the adequacy of resources made available for the various services and who has the power to determine these. If resources are perceived and experienced by consumers to be grossly inadequate *and* they remain so, then the positive advantages of greater individual consumer participation may be largely negated. As Tawney wrote over half a century ago:

> No individual can create by his isolated action a healthy environment, or establish an educational system with a wide range of facilities, or organise an industry in such a manner as to diminish economic insecurity, or eliminate the causes of accidents in factories or streets. Yet these are the conditions which make the difference between happiness and misery, and sometimes, indeed, between life and death. In so far as they exist they are the source of a social income, received in the form not of money, but of increased well-being. (Tawney, 1964, p. 127)

The social income in the 1980s

In the debates about the social wage in the 1970s, its value was equated with public expenditure on government social welfare programmes. Barbara Castle estimated that in 1975 60 per cent of public expenditure was going on the social wage and this was worth £20 a week to a family comprising a couple and two children (Castle, 1981, p. 21). At the time, the average male wage was £50 a week and in his Budget speech that year, Denis Healey observed 'the social wage has been increasing very much faster than ordinary wages – much faster than prices too' (House of Commons, *Hansard*, 15 April 1975). (Of course, if the social contract were really working, this should have been the case, but Denis Healey was implying the social wage was too high – see Barbara Castle, 1980, p. 353.) Such a measure of the social wage, however, can be misleading because, as Paul Adams has argued, government social welfare expenditures

> support a wide range of activities which may have either a 'social control' function (helping to police the existing social and economic order) or a social wage function (providing real benefits to workers and their families which improve their standard of living); or they may combine both functions. (Adams, 1981, p. 233).

Moreover, the increased cost of a service may be accounted for entirely by increases in the number of recipients due to unemployment, for example, or because of demographic changes. Changes in interest rates, levels of inflation, and the salaries and wages of those working in the public sector are also key determinants of the cost of a service. In other words, increases in the level of expenditure may not mean there has been any real improvement in the level of provision made to individual recipients. It can therefore be misleading to discuss the value of the social wage in terms of global public expenditure figures. This is particularly so in the 1980s, when there was an increase in expenditure on what

Paul Adams has called the 'social control' functions; unprecedented levels of unemployment which increased the costs of the social security system (despite major reductions in the rights of unemployed people to claim benefits coupled with cuts in the value of benefits); and demographic changes, such as an increase of 20 per cent in the numbers of people aged over 75 years. More revealing is to examine in detail the impact of cuts in particular social services.

Within the space of a short chapter it is not possible thoroughly to review the different components of the social wage across all the social services. In any case some, particularly those concerning social security benefits, are discussed elsewhere in this book. Instead, I shall focus on two: housing and child care provision, for in both these services there have been major shifts in the boundaries between the public and private sectors. Furthermore, while child care services have never been regarded as a major social service, they are of vital importance to women. Indeed, according to the results of a survey commissioned by the European Commission's Director General for Employment, Industrial Relations and Social Affairs, 'if governments are genuinely concerned to improve the quality of family life, they should make housing and child care provision their top priority' (Family Policy Studies Centre, 1991, p. 12). Moreover, in ways which have yet to be thoroughly documented, the role of employers has become more important. This has not necessarily taken the form of direct provision; indeed in the public sector pressure has been on health authorities, for example, to sell off nurses' homes. Instead, in the case of housing, individual employees have received tax-free cash subsidies either in the form of reduced interest rate loans or substantial allowances for moving location. Most of these employees are already among the more highly paid and more secure workers, unlike those who are losing their tied accommodation in the public sector. In other words, the erosion of the social wage is deepening inequalities and exacerbating the difference between the well-being of those in the growing 'flexible' labour market in which women outnumber men by two to one; and those in the shrinking core where the permanent, full-time, highly paid jobs held predominantly by white men are found.

Housing

Public commitment to state provision of good quality housing has never been as strong as in the other major social services, in particular health and education, because the private sector has always remained significant. Moreover, public housing has been harder to defend because responsibility for its provision has remained at the lowest and therefore weakest tier of local government. In the 1970s some local authorities, including some Labour-controlled authorities, had allowed council tenants to purchase their homes. However, during the 1980s 'the right to buy', accompanied by substantial discounts, encouraged many more council tenants to become owner-occupiers. In 1979 in the United Kingdom there were 6.8 million dwellings owned by local authorities or New Town

Table 4.1 Annual house-building completions (England and Wales)

Sector	1975–9	1980–4	1989
LA/New Town Corporations	103,000	44,000	14,000
Housing Associations	18,000	15,000	9,000
Private Sector	126,000	117,000	148,000

Source: Department of Environment (1991), *Annual Report*, Cmnd 1508, London, HMSO, p. 85.

Corporations. By 1990 the number had fallen by 1½ million, representing a reduction of 20 per cent of the stock. Unlike the policies of the 1970s, local authorities were not free to use the money released by the sale of council homes to build new dwellings or to repair and refurbish existing stock. There is now strict government regulation of the use of the receipts from council home and residential land sales. As Table 4.1 shows, there has been a dramatic decline in the number of dwellings built by local authorities during the 1980s. Moreover, this reduction in public sector home-building has not been compensated for by either housing associations or the private sector.

The government's White Paper on housing, 'Housing: the government's proposals', published in 1987, foresaw a future in which local authorities will not provide housing: 'There will no longer be the same presumption that the local authority itself should take action to meet new and increasing demands. The future role of local authorities will be essentially a strategic one identifying housing needs and demands' (DoE, 1987, p. 14).

At the same time, the private rented sector has declined. Between 1979 and 1987 the number of rented homes fell by 1.3 million (Raynsford, 1990, p. 194). Government attempts to halt this decline will not, even if they succeed, ensure an increase in the availability of cheap rented accommodation. 'Fair rents' have been abolished for all new tenancies, security of tenure has been restricted and there is no right of succession to a new 'Assured Tenancy' except for spouses. This will affect those, particularly daughters, who have cared for elderly and infirm parents. Tenants may be entitled to compensation for illegal eviction but there is no longer any right to reinstatement. Section 71 of the Race Relations Act 1976 required every local authority 'to eliminate unlawful discrimination and to promote equality of opportunity and good relations between persons of different racial groups'. Under the 1986 Housing Act this does not apply to individual housing associations, approved landlords or Housing Action Trusts, although the Housing Corporation, which oversees housing associations, must observe Section 71.

Therefore, those sectors of the housing market on which lower income households depend, has shrunk; rents have risen and are likely to rise further; and the rights of tenants have diminished. This particularly affects women and

Table 4.2 Annual number of households who are homeless and living in bed
and breakfast or temporary accommodation

Year	No. accepted as homeless	No. in bed and breakfast	No. in temporary accommodation
1978	53,110	1,260	2,400
1983	78,240	2,700	7,140
1989	126,680	11,480	28,420

Source: Department of Environment (1991), *Annual Report*, Cmnd 1508, London, HMSO,
p. 94.

Black people because they rely heavily on these sectors. Altogether in 1987, 40
per cent of female-headed households were renting their accommodation from a
local authority, 9 per cent from a private landlord and 4 per cent from a housing
association. The dependence of divorcees and separated women on the rented
sector was even higher: 60 per cent in total, including 49 per cent from local
authorities (OPCS, 1989, p. 114). Throughout the 1980s, women became more
dependent on local authority housing. In 1981, 31 per cent of householders
renting from local authorities were women; by 1988 this had increased to 41 per
cent (OPCS, 1990, p. 236).

The number of homeless households grew dramatically in the 1980s (see
Table 4.2). The Department of the Environment explains this by saying: 'A
major cause [of homelessness] has been the increase in the number of
households *wanting* to live separately due to relationship breakdown and the
younger age at which people *choose* to leave home' (DoE, 1991, p. 93, emphases
added). It would be more accurate to say 'needing' to live separately, for many of
these breakdowns involve domestic violence and to protect themselves and their
children women are driven to leave their homes. Similarly, some young people
have no choice about living at home – on leaving care they have no home or
family to go to. (It has been estimated that a third of homeless young people were
formerly in care. See, for example, Newman, 1989.) Nevertheless, policies
concerning homeless people are informed by the view that these are largely
people who have wilfully chosen homelessness in order to gain access to rented
accommodation and housing benefit. Mrs Thatcher said in an interview in *The
Times* that there was a problem of 'young single girls who deliberately became
pregnant in order to jump a housing queue and get welfare payments' (quoted by
Forest and Murie, 1988, p. 90). In 1989, 35 per cent of new tenants accepted by
local authorities were homeless households, compared with 23 per cent in 1984.
Such figures taken out of context of declining numbers of local authority
dwellings feed such prejudices. Official policy has therefore been to broaden the
definition of 'intentionally' homeless, thus relieving local authorities of taking
responsibility for them.

Homelessness particularly affects women. It has been estimated, for example, that in London women make up two-thirds of all those accepted as homeless by local authorities (Ginsberg, 1989, p. 58). Most homeless households have children, for it is extremely difficult to be accepted as unintentionally homeless unless children are involved and the 1988 Homeless Persons Act has made it more difficult even if they are. In 1989, 67 per cent of homeless households had dependent children and in a further 13 per cent the woman was pregnant (DoE, 1991, p. 11). The health of children in bed and breakfast accommodation is giving health visitors, and those doctors willing to take them onto their lists, grave cause for concern.

Local authorities rarely take responsibility for homeless single men or women and the withdrawal of benefits from young people in the late 1980s, together with the reduction in availability of cheap rented accommodation, has increased the numbers of young people sleeping on the streets. In other words, those who do not live in 'normal' families are finding it harder and harder to find and keep a roof over their heads and it is left to the voluntary sector to attempt to make provision for them.

While government expenditure on bricks and mortar has decreased, expenditure on housing benefits and the cost of tax relief on mortgage interest has increased. During the 1980s owner-occupation grew, so that by 1990 two-thirds of all dwellings were owner-occupied. The cost of tax relief in real terms nearly doubled from £3.5 billion to £6.9 billion (CSO, 1991a, p. 144). Over 9 million taxpayers benefited from this relief in 1989–90. Housing benefit paid to nearly 4 million households, half of which were pensioner households, cost just over £4 billion in 1989–90 and rate rebates cost a further £1.5 billion.

Some of the rules concerning income support and housing benefit have changed in ways which particularly affect women whose relationship with their partner or husband has broken down. Their opportunities to remain or become owner-occupiers on their own have diminished. Under the 1986 Social Security Act, for the first six months of receiving income support, only half the interest element of the mortgage is paid by the DSS (formerly the whole was paid from the outset). Often in the early months of separation or divorce, women depend on social security benefit while they adjust to their new situation and find employment. During this time, therefore, their financial resources are likely to be very stretched. Those who do succeed in getting a job and coming off income support will find that they are no longer eligible for any housing benefit if they are owner-occupiers, as housing benefit is only available to low-wage earners in rented accommodation. In future there may be even fewer lone parents who are owner-occupiers because the Child Support Agency, by insisting on the payment of maintenance by absent fathers while their former partners are in receipt of income support, may make men think twice before agreeing to their former wife staying in the matrimonial home in return for waiving maintenance payments (see Jane Millar's chapter in this volume).

The overall impact of the changes in the amount and pattern of housing subsidies is complex. The poorest households gain from housing benefit –

provided they can find and keep a roof over their heads. Mortage interest tax relief (MITR) benefits those with middle incomes and above, although there are signs that this may become less advantageous to the higher income groups. It seems unlikely that the £30,000 limit on MITR will be raised and the recently-introduced rule that relief be limited to the standard rate of tax looks as if it will stay. However, as mentioned above, some employers are providing substantial subsidies to their employees. This provision may take the form of low-interest loans and these benefits are found predominantly in banking, insurance and finance. These are sectors in which there are few manual workers and although all employees, male and female, are usually eligible, the more highly paid derive the greatest benefit as do those who stay longest with the same employer. Unlike other fringe benefits or other low-interest loans for other purposes, they are exempt from tax. It is difficult to know how many employees benefit from such schemes; Ray Forest and Alan Murie suggest a figure of 800,000 (Forest and Murie, 1988, p. 89).

The other form of help which is associated with senior, high status, well-paid jobs held mainly by men is generous assistance with relocation costs, including compensation for moving into an area where housing costs are higher. Again relocation payments are exempt from tax. (It should also be remembered owner-occupiers do not have to pay capital gains tax on their principal residence. In 1989–90 this cost £7 billion in forgone revenue compared with £1.5 billion in 1978–9 – HM Treasury, 1990.) As Forest and Murie conclude:

> In the past, council housing and to a lesser extent MITR softened the connections between bargaining power in the labour market and access to housing . . . Should MITR become a less prominent part of the structure of housing finance, it may be that other forms of occupationally related assistance will develop. These forms of assistance are likely to be at least as regressive as MITR but certainly more complex, fragmented and covert. What is clear is that it is not only those in receipt of welfare benefits who are receiving assistance with housing costs. (Forest and Murie, 1988, p. 92)

What is also clear is that for women without either a satisfactory male partner with reliable earnings or a highly paid job of their own, the chances of keeping a roof over their own and their children's heads has declined in the 1980s. There is no sign that this trend will be reversed, despite the growing evidence of the extent of domestic violence and child abuse occurring within the home.

Child care

Public sector involvement in the provision of day-care for children under 5 years of age is low and is falling. Fewer than half of the children who receive some form of education or day-care provision attend publicly funded services provided by local education authorities in nursery schools (in which much provision is

Table 4.3 Change in numbers of places in different under-5 services: England
1979–89

Year	1979–84	1984–9	Number of full-time equivalent places
LA nursery education			
– children attending	+23%	+14%	
– full-time equivalent places	+18%	+11%	167,496
LA receptions places			
– children attending	+ 8%	+ 7%	
– full-time equivalent places	+ 9%	+ 6%	241,472
LA day nurseries			
– children attending	+17%	– 4%	
– places	+ 2%	0.5%	28,789
Private nurseries			
– places	+ 3%	+95%	46,589
Childminders			
– places	+23%	+60%	186,356
Registered playgroups			
– places	+ 6%	+ 4%	162,662

Source: Peter Moss and Edward Melhuish, *Current Issues in Day Care for Young Children*, London,
HMSO, 1991, p. 88.

part-time) and reception classes in infant schools, or by social service
departments in day nurseries. Private provision is growing, as Table 4.3 shows. It
should be noted that these figures exclude the number of nannies and au pairs
who look after pre-school children.

Children attending local authority day nurseries are almost entirely children
considered by social workers to be 'deprived' or 'at risk'. The direct cost to
parents is small because, although fees are charged, they are means-tested. The
care provided is, however, full-time. The most common form of child care
provision, which is only *regulated* by social services departments, are childminders. Childminders' fees are not subsidised at all. Local authorities have no
responsibilities for regulating either the pay or working conditions of nannies or
au pairs, neither have the Department of Health or the Home Office, which
issues work permits to those recruited overseas. Indeed, because the Home
Office issues permits to work only with a particular employer, it can be very
difficult for a nanny or au pair to escape from an exploitative employer. In every
sector of child care, most of the workers are badly paid. Control over the quality
of care provided by nannies and au pairs is left entirely to the parents.
(Mrs Thatcher always had an English nanny because she 'wouldn't have been
quite certain whether the au pair could speak English or knew how to ring the
hospital if anything happened' – quoted in Webster, 1990, p. 44.)

Employers' nurseries, which are few and far between, charge fees which may or may not contain an element of subsidy. In the 1991 Budget, the Chancellor of the Exchequer removed the tax charged on the subsidy. This tax had only been introduced in 1984 and its removal is a tiny token gesture in support of employer-based nursery provision. The Department of Employment is looking to employers to make more child care provision, but it places greater faith in flexible working hours which would enable women to combine paid work with child care. After all, employers

> will need women employees, and must recognise both their career ambitions and domestic responsibilities. This will involve broadening company training policies, much more flexibility of work and hours and job-sharing, to facilitate the employment of women with families and help adapt to their needs. (DoE, 1988, p. 8).

Some employers have introduced child care vouchers which can be used to pay for *registered* day-care, thus ruling out the majority of working women who rely on their own mothers or other relatives to provide child care. Mrs Thatcher summed up the government's attitude towards child care provision in the 1980s when she said: 'women make their own arrangements now and they can carry on doing so' (*She*, February 1989, p. 54).

In Britain, then, state policies with respect to child care derive from a residual welfare model. State maternity benefits have been cut and maternity grants, once universal, have been means-tested since 1988 and even the poorest mothers now get a grant worth only *half* its value twenty years ago. Only a minority of mothers qualify for unpaid, let alone paid, maternity leave. Moreover, the problem of child care does not end when children start school, because local authorities have no responsibility to provide after-school care and only very few do so. Indeed, when the 1989 Children Act was going through Parliament, the government introduced an amendment *removing* the duty placed on local authorities by the 1948 Nurseries and Childminders Regulation Act, to regulate child care provision for the over-5s. Deregulation was required, it was argued, to encourage voluntary and private sector involvement in providing schemes.

A minority of well-paid women with scarce skills will be able to negotiate assistance with child care costs from their employers in the same way as we have seen a minority of already-advantaged employees acquire assistance with their housing costs. Alternatively, they can afford to purchase help at home. The tax system does not provide further subsidies – yet. There is pressure to introduce tax relief on child care expenses but since the majority of mothers in paid employment do not pay tax, this would be of no benefit to them. Moreover, two-earner couples with high incomes have already benefited substantially, first, from separate taxation and, more recently, independent taxation. When separate taxation was introduced, those couples who chose to be taxed separately had to forgo the married man's tax allowance. The cost in forgone revenue in 1978–9, five years after separate taxation was introduced, was £90 million. By 1989–90 this had increased to £410 million (HM Treasury, 1990, p. 102). The introduction of independent taxation in 1990 has meant those couples have continued to enjoy the advantage of being separately taxed, but the husband has had the married man's allowance (now called married couple's allowance) restored to him. By refusing to develop child care services as part of the social wage, and instead relying on an increasingly deregulated labour market in which tax subsidies go to those already privileged in that market, the government is not only failing to meet the needs of many women and their children but is widening inequalities between them.

Conclusions

The British government has been actively opposed to any proposed EC directive which would enhance the social wage and thus reverse a decade of policies designed to reduce it. The draft EC directives on parental leave and on part-time workers, as well as the Social Charter, have been opposed and so far blocked by this government. When they justify this in terms of protecting 'freedom' and 'choice' they would do well to remember something which Tawney wrote fifty years ago:

> In so far as the opportunity to lead a life worthy of human beings is needlessly confined to a minority not a few of the conditions applauded as freedom would more properly be denounced as privilege. Action which causes such opportunities to be more widely shared is therefore twice blessed. It not only subtracts from inequality but adds to freedom. (Tawney, 1964, p. 235)

5 Women and poverty: The European context

Gill Whitting

The prediction that the 1990s will be the decade in which women in Europe will realise substantial gains is becoming popular. Typically, this prediction draws on the analysis of particular trends which are perceived to favour women, especially women of working age. The ageing of the European Community (EC) labour force and the reduced numbers of young people entering the labour market each year are two of the most significant trends. Statistics for recent years show increasing female labour market participation rates in the EC and this appears to support the positive view. However, there is no guarantee that these gains will penetrate the deep-rooted inequalities which women face in employment and access to employment and thereby improve their overall position in the labour market. The estimated 44 million people in poverty in the EC (O'Higgins and Jenkins, 1989) include large numbers of older, disabled and migrant women, women who are lone mothers, carers, unemployed or marginalised citizens. The prediction that women stand to gain as a group therefore needs careful examination.

First, women will not benefit evenly because of differing economic, social and political circumstances and potential. Secondly, women are vulnerable to geographical inequalities in the distribution of economic prosperity. The latter factor is especially pertinent given the EC Internal Market programme which aims to reduce regional disparities and improve social cohesion in Europe, but which at the same time is likely to result in some disbenefits. It cannot be assumed therefore that women living below the poverty line in Europe will automatically benefit from any economic and social restructuring in the post-1992 era. But at this stage one can only speculate about the losers. Nevertheless research is underway to identify those sectors and regions of the economy which are weakest, in order to bring to the attention of policy-makers the likely problems for regions, communities and social groups.[1]

Women in poverty in the UK share common experiences with women in poverty in other Member States. Throughout Europe, women's poverty is a largely invisible phenomenon, although various research and other actions instigated by the Equal Opportunities Unit of the European Commission are improving the availability of data and knowledge. The Commission's programmes on poverty have in the past neither sought to identify women as a target group nor debated the special circumstances for women in poverty arising from discrimination and disadvantage, although many of the local projects have worked closely alongside some groups of women. The Second Programme to Combat Poverty focused attention on single parents as one of the target groups and this provided considerable material on the poverty of lone mothers throughout the EC (Robbins, 1989). Like lone mothers in the UK, the experience of lone mothers in other parts of Europe shows how multiple discrimination in training, access to jobs, pay and housing combine together to consolidate their poverty. The Second Programme to Combat Poverty drew to a close at the end of 1989; a third follow-on programme 'to foster the economic and social integration of least-privileged groups' is now in operation (*Official Journal of the European Commission*, 1989).

Within different countries of the EC there are, of course, specific cultural and political traditions and trends which may account for differences in the way that poverty is manifest. For example, in Ireland the role of the Catholic Church crucially affects the lives of women; in the UK it is the government which is tending to reassert the domestic responsibilities of women, especially their role as primary carers; in the Mediterranean countries the position of women in the family is undergoing significant and rapid change. There are other important variations between the Member States, especially in the institutional structures of welfare agencies and departments and the regulations which allocate welfare benefits. Informal mechanisms for welfare and support also vary considerably. For example, the family networks associated with farming communities in rural areas in the south of Europe contrast sharply with the more formalised and institutionalised provision typical of many urban communities. However, comparisons *between* rural areas can also be drawn, particularly between isolated rural communities, whether they are in Wales, Northern Ireland, or on the islands of Greece.

The Second Programme to Combat Poverty also drew attention to women migrants. The particular problems of economic and social integration which women migrants experience depend on how they relate to the migration process. For example, there are women who emigrate alone or with their husbands and who seek employment in the new country. There are women who join husbands who have already emigrated. The continued residence of these women in the new country is very often dependent on their husband's work and the marriage relationship. There are migrant women who are not able to or choose not to work and who face cultural and social isolation in the new environment. There are local women who marry migrants and who face the problems of cross-cultural marriages; new problems are added if the migrant decides to return to his home country. There are also women who are left behind with the responsibility of children when husbands decide to emigrate abroad (Hadjivar-nava, 1988).

The vision of Europe as a supra-national region where the opportunities for women will flourish is thus an optimistic one. Certain questions need to be raised. Are the new employment opportunities for women likely to be sustained or are they a short-term response to a temporary shortfall in the labour force? Are women again fulfilling a role as a reserve army of labour which, in the UK, was a feature of wartime and post-war employment? How will the pattern of women's work break away from the traditions of low pay and insecurity? What reforms are necessary to ensure that the obstacles which face women in combining jobs inside and outside the home are removed? To what extent can European Community institutions influence both the direction of reforms and the implementation of EC laws and recommendations in Member States?

Part of the positive prediction for women living in Europe rests on high expectations of the development and application of EC legislation and actions. This is particularly the case for the UK where the current government's views on women's roles mean that policies tend not to be progressive for women. Some EC intervention is directly targeted at women (for example, the Equal Treatment legislation, the Community Action Programmes and the Promotion of Equal Opportunities and research on child care), whilst some has considerable indirect potential for benefiting women (for example, the Community Charter of the Fundamental Social Rights of Workers [the Social Charter] and the reform of the Structural Funds[2]). These and other actions involve considerable resources at the European level which, if mobilised, could make a significant impact on the terms and conditions of the jobs that women do, their access to training and employment, levels of pay, levels of taxation and access to child care.

This chapter attempts to explore these arguments and questions with respect to women in Europe. Although current European debates emphasise the interdependence of social and economic growth and cohesion, the EC's potential to influence the situation for women is greatest where the links to the economy are closest. Arguments for reducing women's poverty are also more powerful in the EC context if they are located in the wider debates of achieving economic integration. The prospects for women in poverty in Europe therefore look brightest in relation to paid work: improving pay and conditions, increased access to jobs, better prospects for promotion, more opportunities for training, greater support especially in child care, adequate social protection and so on. This chapter therefore focuses on issues of employment and on the extent to which EC action might help to improve the situation of women in the labour market, hence reducing their risk of poverty. After examining the evidence on women's poverty in Europe, the next section of the chapter describes the recent trends in women's employment and evaluates the legislative powers and other actions of the EC. The final section concludes by examining some of the potential implications for women and poverty in the UK.

European trends and issues

As noted above, it has been estimated that 44 million people in Europe live in poverty. How this is divided between men and women is unknown. Statistics are not readily available and recent studies on poverty have not investigated the particular circumstances of women (for example Room, 1990). O'Higgins and Jenkins (1989) also excluded questions relating to women from their otherwise excellent study of poverty statistics. The significance of poverty for women in the EC can, however, be inferred from three main data sources:

1. Data on the incidence of poverty in households.
2. Data on lone-parent families.
3. Data on poverty and elderly people.

Household poverty

Recent calculations (Eurostat, 1990c) show that in 1980 female-headed households had poverty rates well above the national average in five out of the eleven Member States studied (Luxembourg excluded). Poor households were defined as those spending less than 50 per cent of the national average household expenditure per adult equivalent. In Ireland and the UK, the poverty rate for female-headed households was more than 150 per cent of the national rate; in Belgium, Spain and France, the equivalent poverty rate was between 125 and 150 per cent of the national rate. Moreover, all Member States studied (with the exception of the Netherlands) had poverty rates for female-headed households which were higher than the national average.

Eurostat research also shows that the differences in the incidence of poverty between male- and female-headed households are very high in the UK, Ireland, Portugal and France. And over the period 1980–5, the relative disadvantage of such households grew in the UK. In contrast, France was especially successful between 1980 and 1985 in reducing poverty in households headed by a woman (Eurostat, 1990b).

Although gender is clearly a significant differentiating factor in poverty, the data from the EC are not a comprehensive source for revealing the differences in poverty between men and women. This is primarily because the use of the *household* as the unit of analysis obscures the circumstances of the vast majority of women who live in households headed by a man.

Poverty and lone-parent families

It is highly significant that lone-parent families are a rapidly growing family type in the EC. A study of seven countries, including the UK, illustrated the rapid growth in lone-parent households during the 1970s, with the pace of growth quickening in many countries as the decade wore on. At any given point of time in most of the countries, more than one in ten families were lone-parent households, with the vast majority headed by a woman (O'Higgins, 1987; Roll, 1989). The analysis showed that the growth in one-parent families is more dramatic in the UK than for the other countries for which data were available (see also Jane Millar's chapter here). Many lone parents throughout the EC have very low incomes and live in, or on the margins of, poverty (Roll, 1989).

Poverty and elderly people

Recent Eurostat analysis (1990c) on inequality and poverty in Europe during the period 1980–5 makes reference to households with a head aged 65 and over as being at high risk of poverty. In 1980, seven countries, including the UK, had a poverty rate for this group of more than 150 per cent of the national rate. In 1985, the position had improved somewhat, although nine of the eleven countries studied had a poverty rate higher than the national average.

What is particularly significant is the increasing proportions of women in the population of elderly people in Europe, and the changes in demographic structures. From the age of 60 upwards, there are more women than men in the population in all Member States. Elderly people over 60 will also assume a greater significance in the population of Europe as a whole, with 23.6 per cent of men and 29.2 per cent of women 60 or over in 2020, compared with 16.5 per cent and 22.3 per cent respectively in 1988 (Eurostat, 1990a). More and more elderly women throughout Europe are likely to be living alone and are less likely to have a spouse than elderly men, thereby increasing their dependency and heightening their risk of poverty (Laczko, 1988; Millar, 1991b).

Employment trends

Thus women in Europe, as in the UK, are likely to have a higher risk of poverty than men. However, in the EC as a whole, the trends which might in the future favour at least some groups of women include higher levels of economic activity for women, technological innovation, and an increasing imbalance in the demand and supply of skills.

Women make up 51 per cent of the EC's population and 40 per cent of its workforce. Between 1985 and 1990, the number of people in paid employment in the Community increased by an average of 1.5 per cent a year, resulting in a net addition of over 9 million to those in work during these five years. Women's employment increased at twice the rate for men between 1985 and 1990, yet the proportion of women of working age in employment is still under 50 per cent as against 75 per cent for men and is considerably lower than this in many parts of Southern Europe (CEC, DGV, 1991).

Over the period 1979–89 female employment grew by an average for the EC of 13 per cent.[3] The greatest increase was in the Netherlands (up by 32.7 per cent) followed by Luxembourg (31.5 per cent) and Greece (29.8 per cent). The lowest increases were in Ireland (up by just 5.9 per cent), the Federal Republic of Germany (FRG) (7.4 per cent) and France (8.2 per cent). The figure for the UK was 16.5 per cent.

Member States with the highest proportion of women in the employed labour force in 1989 were Denmark (45.3 per cent), the UK (43.8 per cent), Portugal (41.9 per cent) and France (41.3 per cent). The lowest proportions were in Spain (30.7 per cent), Ireland (32.1 per cent) and Greece (32.2 per cent). Thus women typically make up between a third and a fifth of the employed labour force.

Throughout the EC the vast majority of single women are economically active (employed or unemployed), but there are substantial variations in the activity rates of married women. In 1988 high figures were recorded for Denmark (66.7 per cent) and the UK (55.6 per cent), whilst exceptionally low activity rates were found in Spain (26.9 per cent), Ireland (29.1 per cent) and Luxembourg (29.9 per cent). Comparisons are complicated, however, by the high numbers of essentially unpaid family workers in some countries, who are not always included in the activity rate calculations.

In the Community as a whole in 1988 almost three-quarters of women were employed in the service sector, with only around one-fifth in industry. Luxembourg and the Netherlands show the highest proportions in the service sector, with Greece and Portugal by far the lowest. As would be expected, employment in these latter two countries is proportionately higher in agriculture.

Around 28 per cent of all women in employment in the EC in 1989 worked part-time (according to national definitions of part-time work). The Netherlands had the highest proportion with 60 per cent, ahead of the UK (43 per cent) and Denmark (40 per cent). Lowest figures were found in Greece (10 per cent), Portugal (10 per cent) and Italy (11 per cent). The vast majority of women in employment work as employees (83.3 per cent in the EC as a whole), but family employment and self-employment are quite strongly represented in Greece and Spain.

A comparison of the average number of hours worked by women shows that in 1988, for the Community as a whole, women worked 34.6 hours compared with 42.5 hours for men. This to a great extent reflects the higher incidence of part-time working among women. The differences between Member States are nevertheless quite marked with, for example, women in the Netherlands working on average 26 hours and in the UK 30.6 hours, whilst in Greece the corresponding figure is 40.6 hours and in Spain 38.6 hours.

In the Community as a whole, the rate of registered unemployment among women has altered little between 1985 and 1989. Whilst there has been a general downward trend in the majority of Member States, two have seen increases over the period. In Greece, the rate increased marginally from 11.7 per cent to 12.7 per cent and in Italy the increase was more substantial, from 15.5 per cent to 17.0 per cent.

In terms of numbers of women unemployed, again there was little change for the Community as a whole between 1984–9. However, within it Belgium, Luxembourg, Portugal and the UK all saw decreases in excess of 30 per cent. By contrast, in Italy the number of women unemployed increased by around 22 per cent and in Greece by 14 per cent. However (as discussed in Claire Callender's chapter here), unemployment rates are not an accurate indicator of women's non-participation in the labour market.

Thus while there are substantial variations across the EC in the labour market activity of women, especially married women, in general women's employment has been rising. Women are more likely than men to be working part-time and the majority of women are in service sector jobs (or in family employment in more agricultural countries).

Technological change

Innovation is occurring in many sectors of production and technological skills require renewal or updating. The implication for the European workforce, which has fewer young people joining it, is to attract new entrants who can be trained or retrained to fulfil the tasks. There is a debate, however, about what the precise demands are of future methods of production: some commentators see a need for very specific skills; others a need for multi-skilling and adaptability (IRDAC, 1990; Whitting, 1991; CEC, DGV, 1991). Whatever the outcome of these debates, women are rightly seen as an important resource to meet Europe's future economic demands. Given that many of the technological changes will have an impact upon key parts of the service sector economy, it may be necessary for women to acquire new skills in order to retain their current positions, as well as to move to other existing posts or fill newly created jobs.

In addition, employers are voicing their concerns about skill shortages. Research has shown that in all Member States, but to different degrees, a problem with skills exists. Different sectors or occupations are experiencing recruitment problems and these apply to some countries more than others, for example nurses in the Netherlands and engineers in Italy. Despite the problems of accurately measuring skills shortages, there can be little doubt that the problem is of sufficient size and duration to be an important issue for women who are looking for work (IRDAC, 1990; Whitting, 1991; CEC, NEC, 1991).

Emerging issues

We can now begin to identify some of the issues for women in the EC. Compared with previous decades, demographic and economic trends have combined together to create opportunities which certain groups of economically active women will be able to seize. Considerable potential remains. With 21 million currently economically inactive women in the Community in the 25–49 age group, a sizeable resource is still untapped (CEC, DGV, 1991). The women who would like to work tend to fall into two main groups: those seeking to return to the labour market after an absence of several years or more; and those seeking to combine their jobs with family responsibilities which require absence or leave of varying duration.

Circumstances vary between countries. For example, in Greece, workers who have in the past been economically active as family helpers are now seeking guaranteed paid employment. However, gaining access to employment in Europe brings to the fore those obstacles with which women in the UK are all too familiar. The problems are common (child care, other caring responsibilities, training, working time, social security structures, maternity and paternity leave, transport to work) although the importance of the different obstacles to women's labour force participation varies widely between Member States.

It is not insignificant that the gap between male and female wages remains. In 1989, the ratio between female and male earnings in industry varied between 1:1.18 in Denmark and 1:1.58 in Luxembourg. In the distributive trades, the range of this ratio between female and male earnings was higher, ranging from 1:1.28 in Greece to 1:1.81 in the UK. On the other hand, for credit institutions and insurance, the ratio is less unfavourable towards women, except in the UK, where there is great disparity (1:1.90) (Eurostat, 1990d). The exceptionally poor figures for the UK demonstrate the low pay which is typical of so many women's jobs, particularly in the expanding service sector, and is one of the reasons why women in the UK, even while in the labour force, are still below the poverty line or at risk of poverty (see Susan Lonsdale's chapter here).

The continuing pay differentials between women and men (which are substantial in all EC countries, though with some variation) mean that women, even in employment, remain more susceptible to poverty than men. Furthermore, the problem of low pay, already affecting many women, is likely to be exacerbated by an increase of 'atypical' jobs in Europe. Meulders and Plasman (1989, pp. 1–2) define 'atypical' as 'forms of employment which are distinguished from traditional occupations by characteristics as diverse as the number and distribution of hours worked, the organisation and localisation of production, wage determination and statutory regulations or conventions'. Atypical working includes part-time employment; temporary employment such as fixed-term contracts; interim employment; seasonal employment and casual employment; self-employment and subcontracting; assisting relatives; homeworking; and hidden or illegal employment. This is not an exhaustive list. The main point, however, is that women are largely over-represented in the sphere of atypical employment. These forms of employment have traditionally allowed women to combine family and paid work responsibilities and activities, especially because of the concentration of work in the tertiary sector. As a consequence, the development of atypical working has facilitated the entry of women into paid employment (Meulders and Plasman, 1989). The development of atypical working has, however, generated a considerable debate. One of the questions is whether this form of employment constitutes a genuine choice for women, especially those with domestic responsibilities. The Women in Employment Network, for example, at a recent meeting, emphasised that social protection was required to cover all forms of employment, particularly atypical forms of employment.

In addition, it is justifiable to ask whether the existing labour shortfall in Europe will gradually be absorbed by internal migration within the EC, migration from central and eastern Europe or from elsewhere, including the possible arrival in the EC of citizens from the Soviet Union.

EC developments

The EC developments which may benefit women fall under three headings: the Internal Market, the Social Charter and equal opportunities legislation and other EC actions.

The Internal Market (the Single European Act)

The Single European Act (the Act) aims to remove all remaining barriers to free trade between the twelve Member States of the EC in order to achieve economic integration on a scale which would allow the European market to compete more effectively with its Japanese and American counterparts (Cmnd 372, 1988). The Act is primarily concerned with economic and monetary change.

References to other policy sectors focus on the health and safety of workers, recognising the need to harmonise conditions across the EC and the promotion of the dialogue between management and labour at the European level. Social cohesion features within the spirit of the Act. This relates to the strengthening of economic and social cohesion within the Community and, in particular, to the reduction of regional inequalities. For this purpose, the Act specifies reforms to the way in which the Structural Funds are allocated and managed. The European Social Fund (ESF), one of the Structural Funds which provides essential financial resources for training, has considerable potential for improving the training opportunities for women (Whitting and Quinn, 1989). Since the Act was passed, a new programme called New Opportunities for Women (NOW), which operates under the rules of the Structural Funds, provides resources directly for women to promote their vocational training.

The Commission recognises that the social implications of the Internal Market require the active participation of both national authorities and Community institutions. A number of priorities have been identified, for example the social policy contribution to establishing a single European labour market; the scope and financial cost of providing social security; action in the fields of education, training and job creation; and legislation relating to working conditions and industrial relations. Women's poverty is not identified as a priority, although many of the existing and proposed measures may improve the situation for at least some groups of women.

The Social Charter

The adoption of the Social Charter by the European Council in December 1989 was a landmark in the further development of EC social policy. The Commission has also now introduced its Action Programme relating to the implementation of the Social Charter. There are twelve main sections of the Social Charter, all of which could directly or indirectly affect the lives of women. The section dealing specifically with equal treatment for men and women calls for intensified action

> to ensure the implementation of the principle of equality between men and women as regards in particular access to employment, remuneration, working conditions, social protection, education, vocational training and career development ... Measures should also be developed enabling men and women to reconcile their occupational and family obligations. (CEC, 1990, p. 17)

Other sections, especially those dealing with employment and remuneration, could, if implemented, have a profound impact on the many women part-time workers. The Charter states that 'workers should be assured of an equitable wage, i.e. a wage sufficient to enable them to have a decent standard of living; workers subject to terms of employment other than an open ended full-time contract shall benefit from an equitable reference wage ...' (CEC, 1990, p. 14).

Equal opportunities legislation and other EC actions

In legal terms, the EC's commitment to equal opportunities is founded upon three main equality Directives (Szyszcack, 1987; Meehan, 1987; Docksey, 1987). These are the Directives on Equal Pay for Work of Equal Value (10 February 1975); Equal Treatment for Men and Women in Access to Employment, Vocational Training, Promotion and Working Conditions (9 February 1976); and Equal Treatment for Men and Women in Social Security (19 December 1978). The UK government alone has opposed and prevented the adoption of various other draft Directives, including a Directive on Parental Leave and Leave for Family Reasons. The European Parliament is also discussing European

Commission proposals for three Directives on atypical work. These Directives cover access to training, social security benefits, pensions, holiday pay, health and maternity benefits. Rights in these areas would be extended to part-time and temporary workers working more than eight hours per week.

The Commission monitors existing legislation and develops policy through the establishment of Community Action Programmes on the Promotion of Equal Opportunities for Women. The Third Programme has just commenced (1991) and runs until 1996 (CEC, Equal Opportunities Unit, 1991).

There are also networks of independent experts from all Member States which monitor the practical and legal implementation of Directives, and note obstacles and cases of discrimination. There are now five networks covering the application of the Equality Directives, women in the labour force, the diversification of vocational choices, child care and women in local employment initiatives.

In order to benefit women, it is necessary first to continue to develop equal opportunity legislation and action at the level of the Community and, second, to assist the full implementation of these Directives and Programmes within Member States. The implementation of equal opportunities legislation relies primarily on the powers which the EC has to influence practices in the Member States. This is particularly so for policy areas such as income maintenance, which remain the responsibility of national governments. Where there is pre-existing legislation, as is the case for equal treatment between men and women, the EC is able to exert greater influence over Member States primarily through the work of the European Court of Justice (Meehan, 1987). But even with this assistance, implementation is a complex, slow and frustrating process. Thus 1992 presents a prime opportunity to review the scope of legislation and the content of plans, and to expand policies and programmes to counter discrimination on the grounds of sex.

Training

Training will play a vital role in the success of the new, enlarged market because women's participation in the more secure and better paid jobs will depend on their ability to acquire the necessary skills. Within the EC, the major resource for funding vocational training is the European Social Fund (ESF), which has recently been doubled in size to support the Internal Market programme. With this change, the allocation of ESF resources has moved away from priorities determined by eligible population groups on the basis of submitted projects. Priorities are now determined at the level of regions, on the basis of programmes which specify labour market priorities. The recently introduced NOW programme is, however, a welcome addition which enables women to be more visible in the allocation of resources for training. Women who are disabled may also be provided for under the new HORIZON programme. EUROFORM, the third measure in this series of new human resource initiatives, focuses on new skills and qualifications. NOW, EUROFORM and HORIZON also serve as a useful bridge between the Structural Funds and the Equal Opportunities Action Programme.

However, one problem is the difficulty in ensuring the funding available under the ESF, NOW, HORIZON and EUROFORM filters down to those women in the community most in need. In the UK, there is an ESF programme which focuses specifically on women's training. Other countries, especially the newer members of the EC, are less experienced in obtaining European funds. The organisation and development of women's groups also varies between countries; not all Member States have women's organisations which can initiate and sustain training which is geared to women's needs (Whitting and Quinn, 1989).

One of the results of the EC's Second Programme to Combat Poverty demonstrated how projects could successfully meet the training needs of lone mothers (Whitting, 1988; Robbins, 1989). In many countries, projects had initiated training schemes which were tailor-made to the lifestyles of lone-parent families. For example, schemes provided child care for participants and they were sensitive to the restrictions on a lone mother's time. But more than this, the approach to training and the organisation and direction of courses required careful thinking, in order to avoid situations where women felt put off, unable to participate, or were even made to feel failures. The example of training also emphasises the need for proper monitoring and evaluation of social policy so that initiatives, particularly of the innovative kind referred to here, can be evaluated and replicated in order that other women stand to benefit from the experience.

Child care

The European Child Care Network, established as part of the Second European Equal Opportunities Programme, has undertaken a study of child care policy and provision throughout the Community, and has made proposals for action to the Commission which in turn is committed to put forward its own proposals for action (CEC, 1989). The Childcare Network proposals envisage a three-part European Strategy consisting of legislation, with Directives on Childcare Services and Employment Rights for Parents; funding for the development of services, primarily in less developed regions, possibly through the use of the Structural Funds; and a European Action Programme on Childcare, involving collaboration and exchanges between Member States. The co-ordinator of the network emphasised that the issue of child care and, more broadly, the issue of reconciling work–family responsibilities are assuming greater importance in the Commission (Moss, 1988). This reflects an increasing realisation that discussions of the implementation of the Internal Market have been hitherto gender-blind. For example, the free movement of labour needs largely uniform and high levels of child care services and parental employment rights in all countries, if it is fully to benefit women with children.

Although there is a serious lack of child care provision in the majority of the

Member States, a number of Member States are responding innovatively to the new opportunities for women in the labour market. In the UK, however, the position is far from favourable; current developments in child care which consist entirely of exhortations to employers may well fail to address adequately a labour market opportunity of major social and economic significance.

Europe: The consequences for women's poverty in Britain

The influence of the EC on the nature and extent of women's poverty in Britain is likely to be more indirect in its impact than direct. The term indirect is used here to emphasise the accidental or secondary nature of the outcomes of many of the trends and policies emanating from Europe as they affect women. However, any benefits for women in poverty in Britain are likely to be contingent upon the successful development and application of EC Equal Opportunity legislation, the implementation of the Social Charter and the targeting of policies and programmes such as those related to training.

Although women as a group are benefiting from the demands of the economy through increasing participation in the labour force, this is an accidental outcome wrought by particular demographic developments. Women are also likely to be affected by the secondary consequences of economic integration on employment and labour market trends. Research which is underway to identify those sectors and regions of the economy most sensitive to the Internal Market has now been extended to identify what this means for the jobs in which women's work is concentrated (Conroy-Jackson, 1990). For example, a predicted decline in the clothing and textile industry, which accounts for 21 per cent of women's industrial employment in the Community, is likely to result in redundant and unemployed women who do not have skills which are easily transferable. In banking, where the competitive demands of the Internal Market are leading to considerable restructuring and important technological and human resource changes, women will need to gain access to highly skilled jobs where previously easy entry for women has been denied. At a more general level, the concentration of women's employment in the service sector renders them vulnerable to the precarious and atypical character of some service jobs. Thus, as far as men and women are concerned, the short-term consequences of the Internal Market on mobility are predicted to benefit only well-paid professionals, such as those already able to migrate.

In summary, the women who are benefiting from European economic and employment trends are those who are economically active, or who are able to participate in the labour market. In the UK, the prospects for women are further complicated by the attitude of the UK government towards Europe, the uncertainty which currently prevails and the strong stand adopted by the UK on the issue of sovereignty. This resistance has seriously affected European policy regarding, for example, parental leave and the conditions of part-time work. Progress in the UK towards equal treatment has relied on the intervention of the European Court of Justice, which has been able to enforce social policies over the head of a reluctant national government.

Thus, there is likely to be a differential impact on women's poverty in Britain. The most likely to benefit from EC actions are those who are currently in the labour market or who want and are able to participate, especially well-qualified women with transferable skills, permanent jobs, good job conditions and some mobility. Those least likely to benefit are women who are outside existing EC legislation because they have no rights of citizenship. Migrant women fall into this group because their rights, in the majority of cases and the majority of countries, are derived from their husbands. While migrant workers are protected, women migrants are usually defined as family members and dependants and so are very vulnerable to exploitation (Prondzynski, 1989). In between, the women who might benefit, on the most optimistic scenario, are those who are on the edges of the labour market and those who are not in the labour market and who have no, or reduced, capacity to participate. The former include low-paid, redundant or unemployed women with few or no skills, and those living in remote areas. The latter include women who care for dependent relatives or small children, those who have ill-health and elderly women.

The likelihood of advantages filtering down to women in poverty in the UK is contingent upon a number of factors. Principal among them are:

1. Improvement in the global economy and the continuation of current demographic trends which lead to both economic and employment growth and new demands for skills. The evidence shows that some women gain through their increased labour market participation.
2. Restructuring of sectors and overall labour market expansion which favours women and thereby presents new opportunities for work by women, albeit supported by training and other support programmes such as child care.
3. The development and application of equal opportunity legislation and programmes on equal pay for work of equal value, child care, taxation; the implementation of legislation and actions under the Social Charter, especially the emphasis paid to the dialogue between industry, government and trade unions; and an enhanced and targeted allocation of resources for the training of women from the European Social Fund.

To conclude, none of this suggests any certainty of a beneficial impact on women living in poverty in the UK. The benefits are dependent on a number of contemporary developments and other contingencies. In fact, these arguments draw attention to one of the most fundamental criticisms of existing EC legislation, that is, the restriction of equal rights to the sphere of work (Meehan, 1987; Luckhaus, 1990). However, the context of change and the potential legislative framework emerging from the EC, together with the many actions of the Commission referred to here, offer more in the way of prospects for women than the predilections of recent British governments.

Notes

1. See, for example, 'The cost of non-Europe' research (twenty-four separate studies) and 'The impact of the internal market by industrial sector: the challenge for the member states', available from the Office for Official Publications of the European Community, L–2985, Luxembourg. See also SYSDEM Bulletin, *Journal of the European System of Documentation on Employment*, available from ECOTEC Research and Consulting Limited, 28/34 Albert Street, Birmingham B4 7UD; and Conroy-Jackson (1990).
2. The Structural Funds are substantial expenditure programmes of the EC and the key instruments for tackling regional inequalities and unemployment. The three funds are the European Regional Development Fund (ERDF); the European Social Fund (ESF); and the European Agricultural Guidance and Guarantee Fund (EAGGF). Recent reforms to the Structural Funds have improved the integration and coordination of the three Funds and targeted the resources more directly on the priority regions of the EC.
3. The data were a special calculation provided by Eurostat originally for a feature on female employment and unemployment which appeared in SYSDEM Bulletin 3 (see note 1).

PART 3

Women, paid work and poverty

6   *Training girls to be low-paid women*

Carol Buswell

Since 1983 in Britain youth training has developed from a voluntary one-year system (the Youth Training Scheme – YTS) introduced with official rhetoric which in a period of unprecedented youth unemployment maintained that young people needed to be trained in 'skills' for such jobs as were available, to a virtually compulsory two-year system (the Youth Training Programme) which now absorbs approximately one-quarter of all 16-year-olds (Training Agency, 1990). The compulsory element has been achieved by changes in social security regulations resulting in the denial of benefit to young people under 18 years who decline to enter training programmes on leaving school. This important shift in the status of training programmes makes examination of them, and the labour market for which they are training, imperative for an understanding of the kinds of jobs for which girls are being trained and their likely futures as women, especially as the first job a young person enters has an important effect on their subsequent employment (Payne, 1987). The government's own Youth Cohort Study also shows that more young people (36 per cent) enter employment from training schemes or programmes than enter straight from school or further education (Training Agency, 1990). This is not surprising as employers have had no need to pay wages to young people since the inception of YTS and are now unlikely to do so except in unusual circumstances.

The Sex Discrimination Act 1975 not only outlawed discrimination in education, training and employment, but also specifically mentioned the responsibility of the Manpower Services Commission (MSC), then running the YTS, to help redress existing imbalances. The MSC was therefore committed, by law, to provide equal opportunities within training programmes. Even though, from the outset, approximately 64 per cent of girls were on clerical schemes, the MSC did not make it easy for schemes to obtain legal exemption to run girls-only courses in non-traditional areas and offered trainers no guidance at all on implementing equal opportunities. In fact, their complacency on the subject was breathtaking and revolved around the assumed culpability of everyone except themselves and their training schemes. The principal training officer of the MSC articulated their view: 'The problem is further back. The major influences on youngsters' choices are parents, teachers and careers advisory services' (Wilce, 1985, p. 11).

Sex segregation within training has not declined since then. Although the recently formed regional Training and Enterprise Councils (TECs), who now administer youth training, do not yet seem to be in a position to provide overall figures based on sex, it seems that at any one time 11 per cent of trainees are in retail training, 7 per cent hairdressing and personal services and 30 per cent in clerical training (private communication). Other studies (for example Hollands, 1990) indicate that approximately 80 per cent of trainees in these sectors will be girls. Hence girls are currently being trained for shop and office work and personal services.

The importance of sex segregation on programmes has both an immediate and a long-term consequence for girls. Some trainees start training with an 'employment contract' which allows them to be paid more than the basic training allowance. Of trainees in 'engineering' (mainly boys), for example, three-quarters are likely to have such contracts and have twice as much chance as non-contract trainees of being offered a job at the end. By contrast the 10 per cent of trainees in community care (mainly girls) have no employment contracts and only half the chance of being offered a job on completion of the training (*Times Educational Supplement*, 1989). Additionally, the training allowance, currently £29.50 per week in the first year, has shown only an 8 per cent increase over the last six years – which is, in fact, a net loss in real terms for those who are paid only this amount.

The introduction of youth training in Britain has involved not only an extension of vocational training and education but also has antecedents in nineteenth-century education which for girls was shaped by an ideology of domesticity which embodied notions of femininity. This ideology, as will be illustrated, still underpins both current vocational initiatives and the present restructuring of the labour market. Case study material will illustrate how girls' experiences during their training year conditioned their expectations not only about future wages but also about the nature of the jobs they might expect to obtain. Service sector employment is currently being restructured to provide predominantly part-time work for older women and low-paid full-time work for young people. This will have far-reaching consequences beyond the individual and it is in this context that youth 'training' for girls is occurring.

Vocationalism

In the nineteenth century the emphasis in education on 'useful' knowledge was, for working-class girls, not a vehicle for social mobility but a means of maintaining the *status quo* (Purvis, 1981). By the end of that century grants were being made available for the teaching of domestic subjects in elementary schools and it was argued that girls might be more attracted to 'going into service' if domestic duties were respected (Dyhouse, 1977). Vocational education for girls, with its emphasis on domestic skills, was important both for unpaid family duties and for the waged sector of the labour market which working-class girls entered. In the twentieth century all recipients of vocational education became redefined as 'less able', but the extension of different kinds of waged work took gender-specific paths and the nature of 'women's employment' then contributed to notions of femininity (Marks, 1976).

Working-class education for both girls and boys has, historically, been vocational education; but for girls the vocationalisation was imbued with a domestic ideology which attempted to teach them to be good wives and mothers if they were middle-class, and to fit them for domestic occupations and be 'good women' if they were working-class (Purvis, 1983). The domestic ideology, in this sense, served both their home and labour market positions, although not without tensions. The ideology also served that stage of capital accumulation characterised by the separation of home and work, by male occupations which required a great deal of domestic servicing and by a cheap pool of local labour. It is crucial in attempting to understand current developments in education and training not only to consider the social positions for which different classes and genders are destined but also to remember that class divisions exist *within* gendered groups. This is a truism when applied to men; but the 'myth of female classlessness' (Arnot, 1983) both gives primacy to a domestic ideology which homogenises women and also does not facilitate consideration of the very different nature of working-class girls' education and training.

During the 1980s the Youth Training Scheme gave employers crucial power over the vocational education of 16-year-old trainees. The whole system was dependent on the willingness of individual employers to accept trainees, and to judge their competence and the worth of any qualifications they might have obtained during their training. The right of the 'employment market', and those who controlled it, to dictate the educational and training needs of young people, seen in relation to their immediate needs as employers, gained in momentum with the insertion of the Technical and Vocational Education Initiative (TVEI) into school-based education. In spite of the rhetoric that the vocationalism was 'for all' – with useful, transferable and objective skills – it has, in fact, signalled a return to an earlier era of a more limited form of education and training for working-class young people and girls in particular. Further, the direct labour subsidy given to employers who have taken trainees has been significant in the service sector of employment which has provided a pattern of training provision which does not address 'skills shortages' but prepares many girls for low, or no, skill occupations. The new vocationalism emphasises the preparation of young people primarily for the social aspects of the job, at the expense of technical knowledge and qualifications necessary for real career advancement, hence the emphasis on 'personal effectiveness' and 'social development'.

Now that the TECs administer training, the aims and emphases have shifted in a way that should cause further concern on equal opportunities grounds. One of the aims now is that trainees will achieve qualifications equivalent to National Vocational Qualification (NVQ) Level 2 as a minimum. (This in turn is said to be equal to five passes at GCSE.) This means that 'less able' youngsters may be at a disadvantage in obtaining training places as employers may be more interested in young people who can reach that level with the minimum of time and help, especially as achievement of their qualification 'target' is to be a performance indicator for employers and managing agents. NVQ itself is based on 'skills standards' and is an employer-led assessment of skills and not a useful guide to training quality. This compounds the effect of the existing greater educational and social selectivity that employers apply to girls compared with boys (Lee *et al.*, 1990). Young people as a whole, and girls in particular, have now disappeared from official consideration in a manner that replicates the nineteenth century: 'By increasing employers' responsibility for local training arrangements and enterprise support and development, TECs will ensure that training provision is more relevant to employers' needs and so improve the skills and enterprise of the workers' (Department of Employment, 1988, p. 43). The government equates employer behaviour with the public good but it is, in fact, based on a rationale of short-term, competitive individualism. The gendered nature of training, though, is important precisely because it stands between a gendered educational system and a gendered labour market – leading girls from one to the other. Along with vocationalism goes the 'personality package' (Brown, 1987) where young people's subjective attributes are assessed on a subjective basis; the whole person is sold in the market-place.

Femininity

Currently over 30 per cent of women in employment are in clerical work (*Employment Gazette*, 1991). The fact that the same proportion of girls in training are being prepared for this work is, therefore, congruent with the labour market as it exists. Girls are encouraged to enter certain areas of the labour market by the fact that the occupations in question are often presented with a glamorous image. 'Service sector employment is characterised by trim surroundings, neat dress or prestigious uniform, constant exposure to "clientele", coffee breaks, telephone calls, culminating – no doubt – in promotion to the Board of Directors or marriage to the boss' (Kumar, 1978, p. 206). Griffin (1985), in fact, found that the distinction between office and factory work was the crux of the difference between a 'good' job and a 'bad' one for girls in her study. Not only are the conditions of office working thought to be better; but it is also a site where an idealised form of femininity is represented. Griffin concludes that it is also a setting where girls think they might meet the 'right sort of man', and that it holds the illusion of upward mobility.

Office work can, of course, accommodate a wide range of girls and the skill of typing is only part of the requirement for the job. Griffin quotes a survey of male managers who looked for 'personality, good grooming, clear speech and a sense of humour'. A study of employers in the Thames Valley has also recently shown that they considered 'personal qualities' to be as important as academic achievements (Training Agency, 1991). As Curran (1985) notes, however, it is difficult in our society to disentangle notions of personality from those of gender; and where employers have an 'embarrassment of choice' with regard to workers the situation may facilitate the operation of personal preference and social stereotypes more than under conditions of low demand for jobs.

There are currently approximately two million workers in retail distribution. About 64 per cent of these are women, the majority being shop assistants (*Employment Gazette*, 1988).

> Shop assistants are expected to possess these characteristics (efficiency, patience, submissiveness and pleasantness), in order to provide the customer with a specific kind of experience. A certain standard of appearance and grooming is important for representing the store and selling the merchandise. Perhaps the worst expectations are those placed on assistants in cosmetic departments. Just in case the message was not firmly conveyed one store provided a booklet to employees explaining exactly how a woman should prepare for work. Female assistants were told to try and get up a little earlier each morning to ensure that their hair was neat and tidy, to leave enough time to apply make-up carefully ... and to decide on their outfit the night before. (Broadbridge, 1991, p. 42)

Shop work can also be seen as an appropriate work setting if the shop concerned sells fashion goods or expensive items, where dealing with the commodities at a service level has higher status than manufacturing them. The public presentation of the secretarial image and 'boutique' assistant through the media and advertising is one that defines the elements of work in close connection with the expectations about stereotyped female behaviour and appearance. As Brown points out, 'The ideal shopworker becomes a simple extension of the goods for sale. Job satisfaction for the new model worker, especially in the feminine version, is measured by the work image one can project and the profit one creates for the company' (Brown, 1987, p. 25). Such expectations will not only be a powerful determinant over which particular girls obtain such jobs as exist, but also influential over the girls themselves.

In order to consider the place of girls on youth training programmes and their likely futures with regard to employment, it is necessary to take account of social processes that occur prior to this. It is well known that option choices in secondary schools serve largely to divide pupils by gender during the last couple of years of compulsory schooling; and that these choices are activated partly by assumptions concerning 'appropriate' studies for both boys and girls, partly by gender-typing of subjects themselves, and partly by pupils' own self-identification and assumptions about their eventual place in the adult world. Many of the processes which occur during schooling to reinforce and maintain gender divisions are, however, both subtle and complex.

Girls' 'choices' both at school and within training are sociologically problematic (Buswell, 1991). If certain subjects, for example science and technology, have a masculine image then boys will be motivated to achieve in them as part of their masculinity and, conversely, girls will see success in them as being incompatible with their emerging femininity. School subjects can only be gendered when 'femininity' and 'masculinity' are active social processes affecting the whole of people's lives and life chances.

Processes of gender relations within education help to explain not only girls' 'choices' but also how the cultural ideas of masculinity and femininity are transmitted. Girls accommodate to the contradictory messages they receive, both to 'achieve' and to be 'feminine', by using strategies such as invisibility/quietness (Stanley, 1986), or ultra-femininity (McRobbie, 1978). Girls also learn to 'manage' their interpersonal relations with male teachers who, in turn, may 'nurture' the girls in a patriarchal fashion (Buswell, 1984). The coping strategies that girls learn, however, both legitimate the unequal gender structure and serve to locate them in subordinate positions, when the 'feminine' attributes take on a different meaning in different settings. These coping strategies are also useful in fulfilling the requirements of employers in the service sector at a lowly and badly paid level. School subjects are also associated with different occupations, which are gendered, and girls' 'choices' have to be considered in this light.

Thus, besides the actual subjects studied at school many girls, like boys, leave with certain behavioural skills which are gender-specific. It is not so surprising, then, that when given a choice of future training for particular occupations predictable patterns emerge. This is not to minimise the fact that some careers officers, teachers, employers and training officers undoubtedly do make sexist assumptions and channel girls along particular routes, but also to suggest that girls themselves are not always open to other suggestions. These girls, though, in choosing traditional paths have a grasp of the reality of the labour market and of their future position within it. This is shown by one study (Lee *et al.*, 1990) which illustrated that even whilst on training programmes many girls saw marriage and children as an attractive alternative to the kinds of work, if any, they were likely to obtain at the end. 'Women', as Griffin (1982) points out, 'are simultaneously positioned in the labour market and the sexual market place.'

However, while traditional forms of femininity are often encouraged within schools and sought by employers in service sector jobs, some girls may resist these even to the detriment of their own job-seeking attempts. In a study of girls on retail and clerical youth training schemes in a North of England city in 1985/6, this resistance was most marked among retail students for whom, in addition to the expectation of traditional female dress that pertains in offices, there is often the added dimension of more general 'appearance', whereby not only dress but every aspect of the person is expected to conform to a particular stereotype. The following comments by retail students not only illustrate this but are also significant in as much as they were unsolicited and emerged during general discussion regarding the search for work:

> I was going to [national chain of chemist shops] but I changed me mind 'cos you've got to go with your hair all done up and make-up plastered on your face. I wouldn't do that – it's just selling yourself to them.

> I was going to write away for that job in [franchise cosmetic firm] but they wanted a photograph of you. I thought 'No way am I going to do a job like that.'

> I had an interview for a scheme at [national shoe chain] but before me interview I changed me mind 'cos I didn't like the uniform! Me mam was going mad, she said 'You can't pick your uniform' – but it was a dead flarey blue skirt, a blue waistcoat, a white blouse and a big white tie thing. It was smart, like, but I didn't want to wear it.

While the definition of femininity that contains prescriptions regarding dress and manner is an element of service sector jobs that appeals to some girls, with current levels of unemployment it is possible for it to be made virtually compulsory, to the detriment of girls who do not, or do not want to, subscribe to that definition. The definition may be endorsed by some women and girls but it is generated and maintained by men. This is particularly obvious in certain chain stores where individual managers – usually male – have the authority to decide what form of matching dress 'their girls' will wear for the coming season. Complaints by some girls about blouses that are hard to wash and the requirement to wear 'heeled' shoes indicate the discrepancy between the appearance they would choose and the one that is chosen for them in a direct and compulsory way to endorse the form of femininity which appeals to white, middle-aged, middle-class men.

The changing labour market

It is well known that over one-half of the total employed population currently works in the service sector of the economy; that clerical and administrative workers make up 45 per cent of the total British workforce, and that one-quarter of all employment is in distribution, banking and finance, personal services and hotel and catering occupations (*Employment Gazette*, 1991). Disproportionately, three-quarters of all employed women work in the service sector and 45 per cent of all employed women are employed on a part-time basis (Training Agency, 1991; see also Susan Lonsdale's chapter in this volume).

Within the service sector, retailing employs more than twice as many people as any single manufacturing industry and accounts for 15 per cent of women's employment (Lewis, 1985). Just over half of these jobs in 1981 were part-time and almost all the part-time jobs were held by married women (OPCS, 1984). A continuing increase in the ratio of part-time to full-time employees is a feature of this sector, encouraged by the fact that it is cheaper to employ two part-time workers than one full-timer, as employers are not liable for national insurance contributions for low-paid workers.

In terms of the domestic ideology which, in the past, underpinned both working-class women's vocational education and their labour market positions, it is clear that the consequences of such an ideology have not only been a constant thread but, more recently, have actually been 'capitalised' on (in the literal sense of the term). The regions which earlier this century offered mainly single industry employment for a male workforce, in which long hours and shift-work were the norm, depended upon the domestic servicing provided by women. The subsequent introduction of 'female' part-time, badly paid employment rests on the same premise (although differently articulated) since part-time work is seen to be more 'compatible' with modern domestic commitments. But the incomes of the new 'female' jobs are still seen as secondary in the household economy, the labour market is structured to be part-time and the assumption is that workers can enter and leave easily – as women are not considered to be full-time, life-time workers. During the 1980s the occupational growth that has occurred has been in banking, finance, business services and retailing. However, this growth has been in the number of part-time, as opposed to full-time, jobs. Approximately a quarter of the total employed workforce is now part-time, some 6½ million workers (Training Agency, 1991).

In fact, women's pattern of working tends to change from being full-time before childbirth to a mixture of part-time and full-time after the first child. Approximately two-thirds of women first return to work after childbirth to a part-time job and, at this point, there is a great deal of downward mobility (Dex, 1984; see also Heather Joshi's chapter here). This move to part-time employment after childbirth is coinciding with, or being used to shift, the female workforce not only out of full-time into part-time employment but also from manufacturing to the service and distribution sectors. These sectors are therefore *relying* on women having to take time off work during a certain phase of their life-cycle and 'the shift from manufacturing to services is being built, to some extent, upon elements of women's experience – domestic responsibilities, break for childbirth and consequent loss of earlier jobs' (Dex, 1984, p. 106).

Working-class girls live in families where this pattern of working is part of life. The fact that shops and offices tend to recruit young people full-time and adult women part-time is a factor that might make these jobs 'attractive' in the light of assumed futures, if their expectations are that their lives will eventually be similar to their mothers'. But this future attractiveness may well initially be culturally disguised by the fact that these occupations are presented with a glamorous image for young full-time workers. So the labour market offers badly paid full-time jobs for young women, which adult women can also do part-time. The 'desirability' of these occupations is emphasised for young women primarily through the ideal of femininity; and for those same women after childbirth as a 'convenient' job which is congruent with domestic ideology. Current ideologies of femininity and domesticity, therefore, far from being historical hangovers, are actually *central* to the restructuring of the economy, labour force and work processes.

Young people are conscious of the reality of job markets and tailor their choices to real possibilities; girls are aware of the occupations to which they will be permitted access and consider how they may survive within them. Cockburn (1987, p. 199) succinctly sums up the relationship between girls' educational and training choices and the wider labour market:

> Women know what trouble lies in store for those who defy the rules of gender. If they are the 'wrong' gender for the job they will meet with discomfort, isolation and even harassment in the place of training. They will also have difficulty in obtaining work afterwards.

The occupations in the tertiary sector for which young women are being trained are badly paid. The 'decency threshold' as specified by the Council of Europe was £178 per week or £4.76 per hour in 1990. In that year, within the hotel and catering industries, 88 per cent of manual and 70 per cent of non-manual women workers earned less than the threshold; 83 per cent of manual and 34 per cent of non-manual women workers in 'other services' (shops, hairdressers, etc.) and 40 per cent of women in the banking and finance sector also came into this category. Thus, over a half of the women working full-time and 81 per cent of those working part-time in Britain are officially 'low paid'. The lowest 10 per cent of women employees earned less than £100 per week. It is worth noting that in 1990, 60 per cent of full-time and 80 per cent of part-time women in the North of England earned less than £4 per hour (Northern Region Low Pay Unit, personal communication). Moreover, the percentage of workers coming into this low-paid category has shown an increase in every year since the mid-1980s. An USDAW (Union of Shop, Distributive and Allied Workers) survey showed that shop workers' wages are so low that basic living requirements amounted to 99 per cent of their monthly wage (quoted in Broadbridge, 1991).

The official aim of youth training – 'to provide opportunities for young people to learn not only job related skills but also to learn about the world of work in general' (*Youth Training*, 1984) – might be considered to have been met successfully if young women learn something of these aspects of work while they are training.

Learning dependency

Forty girls on retail and clerical schemes were observed and interviewed in the course of research conducted in 1985 and 1986. At that time, young people on youth training schemes received an 'allowance' of £27.30 a week plus any travel expenses over £2.50 a week. The terminology is important because it justifies the negligible amount by assuming that the training being received is the prime goal. Young people, however, only participate in 'off-the-job' training for thirteen weeks, with the remainder of the time being spent 'on the job'. In effect, the youngsters work full-time. One of the consequences of this is to introduce them to the *experience* of having too little money to participate fully in the adult working life they are pursuing.

Of the forty girls who were observed and interviewed, the average amount of 'board' paid to parents was approximately £9 per week. After having paid travelling expenses most girls were left with about £16. They were therefore still dependent on their families for most things other than pocket money and some clothes. This dependence has consequences for whole households when, as in this sample, more than a quarter of them lived in single-adult families. Additionally, almost half of the girls were in households with only one adult wage, almost a quarter had no adult or only one part-time wage, and only a quarter lived in families with two full-time or one full-time and one part-time wage. Put another way, three-quarters of the young women were dependent on adults who had one wage or less to support the family. Thus the adults supporting these youngsters were themselves in households that were not the most affluent. In the Northern Region, where this study was conducted, government spending on unemployment benefit is higher per head than elsewhere – £41 compared with the UK average of £27 (Department of Employment, 1990d) so these young people are more likely to come from households in poverty. Furthermore, as the amount of board paid did not fully cover their children's support, these parents were a fundamental part of the operation of the training schemes. Many parents, conscious of their children's circumstances, nevertheless did more than the minimum:

> Mam lends us money for clothes – but half the time when I go to give her the money back she'll say it doesn't matter.

> Mam gives us 50 pence a day back for me lunch and she lends me the money for me clothes.

> I only pays me mam £5 board. I was going to give her ten but she says

'It's only a scheme so I'll just have the five' – and she pays for me dinners as well!

This dependency also, for a few girls, extended beyond the family:

Me boyfriend pays for everything when we go out – he earns £60. I get paid to go out by me boyfriend.

One consequence of training, therefore, is to enmesh young people in a web of dependency and obligation to individuals and families which, for some girls, has the added dimension of an early dependency on a wage-earning male. This is not to suggest that the girls themselves regarded this with equanimity, as economic independence was also valued. One girl explained this in relation to her divorced mother:

I would've have stayed at school if I'd got paid – but I would've felt stupid at Christmas with people giving me presents. I mean, I *like* giving presents, so I went crazy this year and bought everybody nice presents although I had no money for three weeks. I'd never *ever* been able to afford anything nice for me mam so I bought her something nice – she never expected it. Me mam's a one-parent family and we haven't got a man in the house to support us, so me mam can't afford anything nice – so I needed the money really.

Another girl explained her presence on a scheme in similar vein:

I didn't go to college to do a secretarial course because of the money. If you went to college you'd have no money and I'd have to have lived off me mam and dad and I didn't want to do that – I wanted to be independent but, I mean, £27 – it doesn't go anywhere.

While the meagre amount of money paid to these young people is officially regarded as a training allowance they experience it as low pay. Although trainees are intended to be 'extras' to their employers they are nevertheless present and correct for a full working week:

The other people in the office say the money we get on schemes isn't worth it – they say it's slave labour, when I have to stay behind late me mam says that as well. (Clerical trainee)

I know people say 'money isn't everything' – but you work nine till half five and come out with £27 – it really annoys us. You work so hard you're collapsing at the end of each day. The part-time people only work 15 hours and get more than I do. I'm the only full-time person there except the supervisor. (Retail trainee)

You'd get £10 for a Saturday job and that's only one day. I get less than a pound an hour – I think that's dreadful. (Clerical trainee)

In a few instances the young people were not, in fact, extras and they were aware that they were being employed to do a proper job.

> Somebody has to do the job I'm doing. The reason I got the job is that the girl who used to do it has left to have a baby and they haven't bothered replacing her, well – they've replaced her with me! If I wanted to take a holiday or anything I'd feel more dubious about taking it – especially if it was a busy time – rather than if I was just an extra, then I wouldn't be bothered. (Clerical trainee)

> There used to be a woman there before me doing the job I'm doing but they made her redundant because they couldn't afford her – so I type everything that goes out of the office. (Clerial trainee)

The demoralisation associated with the lack of money is highlighted for many girls on placements in offices and shops where particular kinds of dress are required and the youngsters have to comply – at their own expense. It costs to be 'feminine':

> It's terrible – every place you go to you've got to buy a new uniform. It's so stupid when you're on a scheme . . . Fair enough if you're gettin' their wage – but otherwise there's no way. Then you have to wear tights all the time – and in a shop you're running around like a lunatic and always laddering your tights. Even if you buy cheap ones it still runs expensive. (Retail trainee)

> I was always gettin' wrong for wearing skirts that she thought were too short – but, I mean, we couldn't afford to go out and buy a whole new wardrobe. I've got more trousers than skirts and she wouldn't let me wear them. (Clerical trainee)

The girls' marginality also often seemed to be reinforced in offices where it is usual for employees to wear different clothes each day. The girls sometimes commented on their embarrassment at having to wear 'the same old thing'.

Some girls increased their incomes by doing other jobs as well. The traditional pocket-money source of babysitting was fairly common; one clerical trainee kept the Saturday shop job she had done whilst at school; and another clerical girl worked as a waitress after work two nights a week until 10 p.m. and for up to ten hours on a Saturday – in total a fifty-seven-hour week. Discussions about money peppered many of their conversations throughout the day, as this exchange between retail trainees illustrates:

> Marie: I can't have lunch today – I've only got 12 pence to last until we get paid tomorrow.
> Kirsty: I can't afford to go out at all now with Christmas presents and that.
> Tricia: I only go to the disco on Tuesdays now, when it only costs a pound. I think we should get £37 over Christmas time.

Marie: Around £40 would be all right!

Experiencing relative poverty at the age of 16 or 17 for a year or two might not be considered to be too damaging in itself. A more important consequence, though, is that *expectations* are based on this experience, because future earnings are seen in relation to the baseline of the £27 which they regard as their 'pay'. Most of these young people had applied for, and seen advertised, jobs in offices and shops where a wage, for their age, of about £40 was usual – and in relation to £27 seems quite good:

> The people where I work get £30 and over you know, I wouldn't mind that. (Clerical trainee)

> My friend got an office job and gets over £50 – so she's very well off. If you're permanent where I work you get between £40 and £60 – that's good compared to what we get now. (Clerical trainee)

> They say they don't get very good pay where I am – I think it's about £60. That would do me! (Retail trainee)

Besides having lower expectations about what a 'proper wage' should be, there are even more serious consequences for these girls' views on what a 'job' should be. During her training year one retail girl was offered a part-time job in the shop where she was placed, and left the scheme to take it:

> He's offered me a 20-hour contract for £29 with the promise of overtime. That's pretty good because a lot of people who've been there quite a while have only got 15 hours.

This girl, perhaps contrary to first impressions, is acting rationally in the light of the labour market conditions that prevail in much of retailing and certainly in the firm she worked for, where the main city centre shop employed only the manager and supervisor on a full-time basis and all the other employees were on part-time contracts ranging from ten to fifteen hours. These part-timers were not all older women, as there was at least one 18-year-old who had not been able to obtain a full-time job. A twenty-hour part-time contract was, therefore, as this girl pointed out, a better deal. This particular girl also said she might be in line for a 'trainee supervisorship' and she took that into account. The corporation for which she worked prides itself on the fact that 'Saturday girls' and part-timers can become supervisors and managers and, indeed, this is sometimes the case. What is not so obvious is the fact that 'supervisor' is merely the term used for the full-time employee who has charge of all the part-time employees, but who probably earns only the basic full-time wage. These supervisors, usually women, have responsibility but often no real prospects, as managers are more often men, yet this spurious 'status' is presented as a future prospect. This girl has got the measure of this labour market and, incidentally, the labour process:

> If your face fits you're OK. It's all down to personality and if he [the manager] likes you.

Clearly not all part-time workers are going to become full-time in this sector of the labour market. Nevertheless, part-time work is being accepted by some young people as a possible route to a full-time job. Besides being an accurate assessment of these particular sectors of the labour market, some young people in small firms identify the wages paid by their employers as a 'cost' that is high, relative to *their* understanding of wages. For example, the clerical girl quoted previously who was doing all the typing since her middle-aged predecessor had been made redundant said:

> When I was sorting out the filing cabinet I came across the old wage sheets and she earned £100 a week. I'm not surprised they couldn't afford her!

In addition to the experience of poverty and the conditioning of future expectations is the development of a fatalistic attitude among some young people. With regard to the £27 'allowance', comments like 'It's better than nothing and more than the dole' and 'What you haven't got you're not missing' were fairly common. It has to be remembered that many of these young people experienced a few months of unemployment before starting training schemes and their present income position was, at least early on in the scheme, seen in relation to that:

> When I was on the dole I only got £17.30. I was bored and just doin' housework for me mam all day.

Now that youth training is virtually compulsory, with the withdrawal of benefits to young people, there should be concern regarding the fact that a large proportion of the country's young people – and girls in particular – are receiving training in dependency, low expectations and fatalism to prepare them for an unpromising future.

The future

The service sector of the labour market, for which most girls are being trained, has increased rapidly but technical developments and restructuring are likely to make this sector problematic in the near future. With regard to office employment, it is now estimated that word processors can do the work of two-and-a-half to five traditional typists – and the estimated loss of 40 per cent of clerical jobs actually means between 400,000 and 700,000 people (Littler and Salaman, 1984). Resistance in this sector has been muted, not because of the passive nature of women workers, but because the occupation is characterised by high turnover and the widespread use of temporary and part-time workers. The introduction of equipment such as word processors is also likely to result in a change of office hours, with more shiftwork. Indeed, some large British companies have already introduced a 'twilight shift' for clerical workers to enable women to work part-time while still fulfilling their domestic duties, a pattern which has hitherto been confined to factory work using local labour. The lack of employment protection for part-time workers, moreover, has been described as constituting a 'legalised black economy' (Rubery and Tarling, 1988). Technical change in tertiary employment is therefore being introduced with reference to the ideology of domesticity which characterised women's work in the past. Littler and Salaman (1984, p. 99) maintain that in the twentieth century 'office service replaced domestic service for working-class (and some middle-class) girls'.

The banking and finance sector is another area where the impact of new technology has fallen primarily on low-level, mostly female, staff. Child *et al.* (1985) report that senior bank officials freely admit that they have been introducing new technology within an unpublished dual employment policy, in which the stereotype of the female worker as a non-career-seeking, short-term employee has justified a lower tier of routine jobs.

With regard to retailing, a statement made in Australia in 1907 (quoted in O'Donnell, 1984, p. 128) seems equally pertinent today: 'The futility of shop work as a life work for a woman is self evident. At its best it can only be a stop-gap between girlhood and matrimony for the majority. As means of livelihood it is hopeless . . .'. Changes in this sector of employment are proceeding rapidly as the average size of outlets increases, as diversification needs more sophisticated control and with larger shares of the market going to multiples. These circumstances are extremely favourable for the adoption of new technology (Marti and Zeilinger, 1985).

In order to respond to increasing competitiveness, attempts to decrease labour costs in retailing have therefore resulted in a pool of cheap labour – married women and young people – and it is these workers who are likely to be affected by the current phase of investment growth and microelectronic equipment. In these developments the multiples lead the way; their market power can be illustrated by the fact that in 1980 multiples had a 45 per cent share of the retailing market in Britain. In 1982 Sainsburys and Tesco accounted for 30 per cent of the *total* grocery market. However, the introduction of new technology in retailing has hardly started for, despite the fact that 'electronic point of sales systems' have been on the market for over a decade, only 6 per cent of cashpoints in retail outlets had these systems installed by the mid-1980s. But investment is speeding up at a tremendous pace (Lewis, 1985).

Labour markets which recruit cheap full-time youth labour and part-time female labour are actually structured around the assumed dependency of both these groups within a family context. It is assumed that both belong to households where the main expenses are borne by a higher earner. Changes in the labour market, therefore, are not simply about employment but about the connections between employment, home, class and gender. The occupations for which girls are currently being trained not only offer, in practice, low pay whilst they are young and full-time but are also being restructured to operate with part-time adult women workers.

Their training, as has been illustrated, also gives young women first-hand experience of dependency, low pay and 'realistic' – in the light of the actual labour market – expectations. The future looks bleak in regions such as the North of England where the collapse of traditional male occupations and the possible consequent increase of men into such service sector full-time jobs as may exist will push women further to the margins (Buswell, 1985). If these girls eventually, as adults, form a traditional family unit – with one full-time service sector wage, one part-time wage and a couple of young people on training allowances or very low pay – they will experience not only individual, but also household, poverty. As Lee (1991) points out, the rise of the service sector with its relatively lower wages and career structures implies that young people, especially girls, will in future find themselves permanently trapped in 'poor work'.

Acknowledgements

I am grateful to my colleagues Tony Jeffs and Jan Smith for their advice during the preparation of this chapter.

7 Patterns of paid work

Susan Lonsdale

An important cause of poverty in Britain today is low pay, and the large majority of low-paid workers are women. The meaning and experience of work is quite different for most women than it is for men. Women not only undertake a great deal of unpaid work in the home, but their domestic circumstances have a profound effect on their ability to take up paid employment outside the home. As a consequence, their patterns of paid work are singularly different to those of men. Women tend to be concentrated in lower status and lower paid jobs. They constitute the majority of paid homeworkers and part-time workers – work which is often inferior in rewards and conditions of service and geared more towards the requirements of the company or firm than women's own needs for flexible hours of work. In general, women's participation in paid employment is of a kind that accommodates their domestic commitments.

The differences in their patterns of work are due largely to a division of labour which separates women and men into gender-specific areas of work. The structure of this division of labour is underpinned by an ideology regarding the roles which women are expected to perform in society. Both significantly affect women's access to income. This chapter will look at the role the sexual division of labour plays in characterising women's work as significant inside the home but of less value outside it. It will show how women's patterns of paid work affect their earnings and conditions of employment. It will suggest that certain patterns of work which appear to give women relative autonomy in reality often bear a heavy cost. Finally, it will evaluate policy measures designed to improve the situation of women in the labour market.

The demographic time bomb

The number of young people entering the labour market has been falling since the middle of the 1980s. This has meant that the labour market for young people has become much more competitive at a time when there is a need for a more highly trained and educated workforce, a phenomenon often referred to as the demographic time bomb. The main alternative sources of labour to 'defuse' this time bomb are women returning to work after child-bearing and groups among whom there is a heavy concentration of unemployment such as ethnic minorities or people with disabilities. Women 'returners' are generally perceived to constitute the main labour pool for the 1990s and into the next century, although there is little evidence that employers are adapting their recruitment, training and employment practices to take this into account.

In 1988, 3.7 million women who were reported in the Labour Force Survey as being economically inactive[1] quoted domestic commitments involving the care of family or homes as their main reason for not working or looking for work. Despite this, a survey of nearly 2,000 employers in the same year found that fewer than one in three employers were considering practices such as job-sharing, career breaks or child care schemes (NEDO, 1989). Much of the rest of this chapter will show that these types of initiatives are necessary not only to attract women back into the labour force, but also to bring them into parity with their male counterparts.

The great divide

Women's employment patterns are largely determined by beliefs about their role in society and by a structure of employment which subordinates them and uses their labour less to their own advantage than to the advantage of their employers. The sexual division of labour refers to the different tasks undertaken by women and men in society. It is buttressed by a belief that women must give precedence to their homes and families over work and the world outside. In simple terms, this can be described as an expectation that men will fulfil the role of breadwinner, employed in the public sphere outside the home, while women will be held responsible for domestic or household work and child-rearing within the private sphere. These expectations are upheld largely because the nature of paid work reinforces them, as does much else in the social, economic and political fabric of industrial society (Lonsdale, 1985, pp. 64–71).

The sexual division of labour and the ideology of sex role differentiation that goes with it affect employment in many ways. The paid jobs that women do outside the home tend to be very similar to the unpaid jobs they do inside the home, such as cooking, sewing, cleaning and washing. For instance, 'catering, cleaning, hairdressing and other personal services' is the industrial group with the second largest concentration of women. Four out of five jobs in these industries are done by women. Consequently, these industries effectively set women's rates of pay in manual jobs. However, skills that are associated with the home do not tend to command good wages. Wages in industries such as catering, clothing, cleaning and laundry are generally very low. In addition to underestimating their skills, the dominance given to women's domestic life affects how they are regarded in the workplace. By suggesting that paid work is secondary to women's role in the home, women are characterised as lesser workers eligible for a lesser wage.

Separate but unequal

The sexual division of labour not only divides work into paid and unpaid labour. It also influences what kinds of jobs women and men do when both are in paid employment. The degree to which women and men are segregated into different occupations is crucial to an understanding of women's position in the labour force and the wages they receive. Occupational segregation is measured by the proportion of women who work only with other women doing the same kind of work. Studies have shown that there is a marked separation between the kinds of paid work which women and men do and that this has hardly changed throughout this century (Hakim, 1978, 1981; Martin and Roberts, 1984). The jobs women do are not only different to those that men do, but tend to be at a lower level and lower paid. Regardless of occupation, women are also much more likely to work only with other women if they work part-time (Martin and Roberts, 1984). They are, therefore, segregated both horizontally and vertically from male workers.

The sex structure of jobs has remained fairly constant since 1970 with about one-quarter of all jobs being typically female and three-quarters being typically male. This has had a significant effect on women's earnings and the impact of equal pay legislation (see below). According to the 1989 Labour Force Survey, about four out of five (81 per cent) working women are to be found in service industries and just over half (52 per cent) are in clerical, catering, cleaning and hairdressing occupations compared with just over a half (52 per cent) and one in ten (10 per cent) men respectively. Five out of the sixteen listed occupations had less than 1 per cent of women in them (*Employment Gazette*, 1990).

The significance of job segregation is threefold. It has allowed a different wage structure to develop for women and men, keeping women's wages low. Secondly, it has removed women's jobs from the reaches of equal pay policy and legislation for a long time. Thirdly, it has resulted in women and men making quite different judgements regarding their relative status and abilities in the occupational and income hierarchy (Hakim, 1981). For instance, in 1990 a woman working full-time on adult rates would have had to be earning more than £8.80 an hour to be in the top 10 per cent of female earners whereas a man would have had to be earning more than £11.60 an hour to be in the top 10 per cent of male earners (Department of Employment, 1990a, Table A1). This might go some way to providing a more satisfactory explanation of why women consistently accept less pay than men than the more common suggestion that women only work for pin money and, therefore, do not expect or need higher wages.

It could be argued that occupational segregation is developing new dimensions which have not traditionally been thought of as part of occupational segregation. Two recently expanding types of work are now almost exclusively female: homeworking and part-time work. Homeworking refers to people working *at* home rather than *from* home, for a wage, usually at piecework rates, and for only one employer. Most surveys show that virtually all this kind of homeworking is done by women (Hakim, 1984; Bissett and Huws, 1984; Allen and Wolkowitz, 1987). Part-time work is now a major feature of women's employment. In recent years, the number of part-time jobs has increased, mirroring the increase in married women's participation in paid work. In the 1989 Labour Force Survey, 42 per cent of women of working age in employment were in part-time jobs, compared with only 4 per cent of men. Before considering the effect of this on women's jobs and pay, we need to look at women's earnings generally in relation to men.

Slim pickings

Their actual and perceived domestic and child care responsibilities have limited the availability of most women to work the same hours as men. Whether women are economically active or not, and whether they work full- or part-time, is largely determined by their age and the age of their youngest dependent child. Women with young children are least likely to be economically active or working full-time, especially if they are under 25 years of age. According to the 1989 Labour Force Survey, 71 per cent of women of working age are economically active compared with 88 per cent of men of working age. However, women's participation in the labour market drops dramatically when they have young children. Only 48 per cent of women whose youngest dependent child is of pre-school age are economically active and only 12 per cent are in full-time jobs. Much of the increase in women's participation in the labour market has been in

Table 7.1 Women's earnings[1] relative to men's
between 1970 and 1990
(percentages)

	All employees %
1970	63
1975	70
1980	72
1985	74
1990	77

[1] Average gross hourly earnings including overtime of full-time adult employees whose pay was not affected by absence (1970–80 refers to men aged 21 and over and women aged 18 and over; 1985–90 refers to women and men aged 18 and over).

Source: *New Earnings Survey, 1990*: Table 16A (Department of Employment 1990a).

the area of part-time work. Between 1951 and 1989, the number of women working part-time has increased sixfold from ¾ million to nearly 5 million.

Women's earnings are significantly lower than men's. According to the 1990 New Earnings Survey, the average gross hourly wages of women working full-time on adult rates was 71 per cent that of men when comparing manual employees and 64 per cent when comparing non-manual employees (Department of Employment 1990a, Table 26). These are likely to underestimate the differences between women's and men's earnings as the New Earnings Survey does not include those earning below the National Insurance threshold, namely women who are more heavily concentrated at the lower end of earnings (see below).

It is interesting to note that these figures were collected twenty years after the Equal Pay Act was passed. The male/female earnings gap has been very slow to narrow since the early part of this century when, in 1913, women's earnings were 53 per cent those of men's (Routh, 1980). Table 7.1 shows women's earnings relative to those of men's between 1970 and 1990.

As well as earning less on average, women are heavily concentrated at the lower end of the earnings league. According to the 1990 New Earnings Survey, three times as many women as men working full-time on adult rates earned less than £3.00 an hour gross – 12 per cent of women compared to only 4 per cent of men. The difference increases when restricting the comparison to manual rates of pay. In full-time manual jobs, women were five times more likely to earn less than £3.00 an hour than men – 30 per cent as against 6 per cent (*ibid.*).

The differences between women's and men's earnings become most glaring at the level of specific jobs. For instance, in 1990 a woman working full-time on adult rates as a salesperson or shop assistant earned on average £125.20 gross per week compared with a man in the same situation who earned £177.40. Likewise, the average gross weekly wage of a woman working full-time on adult rates as a hairdresser was £139.40 compared with £183.50 for a man and £117.20 for a barmaid compared with £158.10 for a barman (Department of Employment, 1990a, Tables A8/9).

A clear pattern of earnings differentials can be seen in Figure 7.1, where women overwhelmingly earn the lowest sums of money. There is a clear hierarchy of employees with men working full-time in non-manual jobs at the top of the earnings league, followed by women working full-time in non-manual jobs and women working part-time at the bottom. These inequalities between women's and men's earnings create an incentive in two-earner households for the woman rather than the man to leave employment to bring up the children. Even without an ideology which contributes to pushing women out of the labour market, economic sense would dictate that the lowest earner should be the one to go. The impact of this on her future career and earnings forgone will be critical, as Heather Joshi shows in her chapter here and elsewhere, where she has estimated the opportunity costs of child-rearing (Joshi, 1984, 1989).

Certain industries are notable as low-paying employers. These industries are covered by Wages Councils, which each year set minimum rates of pay for the industry known as statutory minimum remuneration (SMR). The Equal Opportunities Commission estimates that three-quarters of all workers in the Wages Council sector are women (MacLennan, 1980). The SMR constitutes a form of minimum wage and tends to be set at about 30–60 per cent of the level of average earnings, although employers can, and sometimes do, pay above them. They also sometimes illegally underpay their workforce. In 1990, just over 5,000 firms covered by the Wages Councils were found to be underpaying their staff.

There is some evidence that women's earnings are less likely than men's to exceed the minimum rates. MacLennan (1980) found that the actual earnings of women in the Wages Council sector exceeded the average SMR by around 25 per cent while those of men exceeded the SMR by nearly 100 per cent. The Department of Employment Wages Inspectorate does not collect data separately on the underpayment of women and men. However, there is some evidence from studies of particular industries which suggest that women are more likely than men to be underpaid. The Commission on Industrial Relations (1974) found that in retail distribution, 2 per cent of men working full-time, 10 per cent of women working full-time and 36 per cent of part-time workers (mainly women) were paid below the SMR. In 1990, the retail industry was still the one most likely to be underpaying its staff (Low Pay Unit, 1991, pp. 6–7).

In 1990, only 25 per cent of male manual workers in Wages Council industries earned less than £130 a week compared with 66 per cent of female manual workers (Department of Employment, 1990a, Table B34). Since 1970 there has been little improvement in the earnings of Wages Council workers relative to the

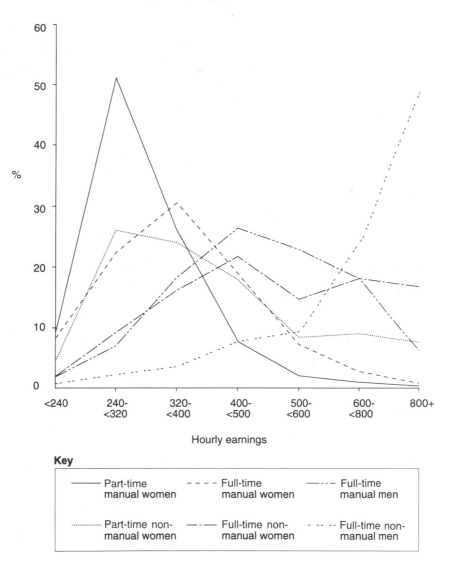

Key

—— Part-time manual women	– – – Full-time manual women	——·– Full-time manual men
············ Part-time non-manual women	—·— Full-time non-manual women	- ·· ·· Full-time non-manual men

Notes:

(i)   Since the NES only covers earnings above the lower earnings level for National Insurance contributions, those earning less than £46.00 a week (the LEL for 1990/1) are not included in this distribution. If they were, they would be likely to fall in the category of part-time worker, increasing the inequality illustrated here.

(ii) Intervals are not equal.

Figure 7.1 Distribution of gross hourly earnings of different types of workers according to hours of work, occupation and sex, 1990

(Source: *New Earnings Survey, 1990*, Table A 26.3 and Table F 173.2)

rest of the workforce. The increase in average weekly earnings between April 1989 and April 1990 in all Wages Council industries for full-time, adult, manual workers was 10.8 per cent for men compared with 9.9 per cent for women. This means that the earnings of large numbers of women are falling even further behind those of most men.

The main characteristics of Wages Council employment are that it tends to be done in small firms, by women, by part-timers, and has a high level of labour turnover. All of these features make it difficult to police or for trade unions to organise. They also explain the low rates of pay. Many of these firms are competing with each other for an uncertain market. They rely on low wage bills and a flexible labour force. In many instances, these factors lead to illegal underpayment and, as already shown, women are particularly vulnerable to this.

The Department of Employment uses a Wages Inspectorate to police those establishments covered by Wages Council Orders, although few prosecutions are undertaken. The Low Pay Unit regularly monitors and documents the work of the Inspectorate. In 1990, only 7 of the 5,200 firms found to be illegally underpaying their employees were prosecuted. A reluctance to prosecute has been the pattern of policing for many years, particularly recently when a number of attempts have been made to abolish the Wages Council system. The 1986 Wages Act removed Wages Council protection from those under 21 years and in 1988 a proposal was made but subsequently withdrawn to abolish Wages Councils altogether. Not taking action tacitly accepts the legitimacy of illegally low rates of pay for people such as women and young workers who are predominant in these industries.

The 'pin money' approach to women's wages (i.e. that their wages are less important to the household than are men's) is open to serious doubt. It is questionable whether this view has ever been a realistic one. Many women work out of economic necessity, either to increase the low wage of a partner or as sole breadwinner. First, an increasing proportion of families seem to be dependent on two wages. In addition, the presence of dependent children in a family leads to additional costs which are not met by child benefit (Walsh and Lister, 1985). Therefore, the presence of a second earner in a family can have considerable financial advantages at certain stages.

Secondly, the view that families predominantly consist of a breadwinner father and a housewife mother is no longer appropriate. One in eight households is now headed by a lone parent and 91 per cent of these are women. As Jane Millar's chapter in this volume shows, the financial circumstances of lone mothers are usually very strained, with fewer opportunities for employment and a restricted earning capacity. Should these mothers be in paid employment, their earnings will clearly be vital to them. However, Bradshaw and Millar's (1991) study of a representative sample of 1,820 lone parents found the earnings of lone mothers in full-time employment to be just over three-quarters of those of all women in full-time work. Lone mothers in part-time work were found to be in particularly low-paid jobs.

Thirdly, in a number of families, women are the sole breadwinners because their partners are unemployed. A study of people signing on as unemployed in 1987 found that half the partners of men who were unemployed were in either full- or part-time work (Erens and Hedges, 1990). It is unlikely that the earnings of these women would be 'pin money'. Therefore, although culturally there is a division of labour between women and men which determines existing patterns of paid work and wages, it does not reflect the real material needs which make women work.

Footing the bill of flexibility

Women with children face many constraints when taking on paid work. This section will look at different working patterns which, for women, represent responses to the problems of combining paid work with family responsibilities: part-time working, working unsocial hours and homeworking. These patterns of paid work are often perceived to be convenient for women, giving them greater flexibility and fitting in with primary domestic commitments. It will be argued that, in reality, they are neither. They often disrupt family life and are primarily suited to the requirements of employers. Far from accommodating family life, they often take little account of it, while paradoxically reinforcing the ideology behind the sexual division of labour. The needs of women with children do not fit neatly with the needs of industry. What often takes place is a complicated balancing act by women between the need for money and a deep sense of responsibility towards the care of children and male partners.

In the face of declining profitability, companies can resort to a number of strategies to reduce costs, one of which is reorganising employment. One way of doing this is to replace full-time jobs with cheaper, part-time ones which are more amenable to fluctuating orders and the use of capital-intensive processes. Another is to put work out to people in their own homes. For management, a flexible workforce has great advantages. Part-time workers are malleable in terms of hours of work; homeworkers are useful in terms of savings in overheads and wages. The final expedient is to shift whole areas of production out to sub-contractors and there is growing evidence that this has led to a new structuring of the labour market. It is argued by some that the labour market is divided in such a way that there now exists a core or primary sector of stable and well-paid jobs alongside a peripheral or secondary sector which is characterised by low wages, poor working conditions and job instability (Wilkinson, 1981; Gordon *et al.*, 1982 and Carol Buswell's chapter in this volume). The supply of labour to fill these jobs comes from marginal workers like immigrants, women, Black workers, older workers. Highly disposable workers such as women are particularly suited to the secondary sector because of the instability of the work involved.

Part-time work

The growth of part-time work represents a long-term change in the composition of the labour force, but this has been almost entirely restricted to female employment. The expansion in part-time employment is unlikely to be a consequence of constraints in the supply of labour, since it has coincided with an increase in rates of unemployment. Neither is it likely to be a response to demands by women for employment that is more suited to their needs. Most part-time jobs have as their starting point a firm's desire to save money or maximise productivity without incurring extra costs. Robinson and Wallace, in a number of case studies, found that the demand for part-time labour was seen to be 'essential to the adoption of more cost-effective employment policies dictated by pressures to improve efficiency in highly competitive conditions' (Robinson and Wallace, 1984a, p. 396). Most importantly, they found that part-time jobs existed in their own right and were not regarded as fractions of full-time jobs. In manufacturing, employers preferred part-time labour because it meant they could make maximum use of capital equipment and keep production continuous without overtime or shift premium costs. In the service sector, part-time labour allowed firms to meet irregularities in trading patterns by taking on additional labour for peak periods, for example, in catering.

While the consequences of part-time employment for firms may be increased efficiency, greater productivity, more competitiveness and, therefore, greater profitability, the consequences for the women concerned are somewhat different. One such consequence may be a reduction in employment rights; another is the lowering of pay. A working week of at least sixteen hours (or eight hours for someone with five years' continuous employment) is necessary to qualify for cover under the 1975 Employment Protection Act. These are the thresholds required for protection against unfair dismissal, entitlement to maternity benefits, rights to reinstatement after maternity and redundancy payments.

The thresholds effectively create two classes of part-time workers, the protected and the unprotected. There are different ways of defining part-time work. The standard definition used (for example, by the General Household Survey and New Earnings Survey) tends to be 'working up to thirty hours a week'. In 1990, 10 per cent of part-time workers worked less than eight hours a week, 27 per cent worked from eight to sixteen hours a week and 63 per cent worked between sixteen and thirty hours a week (Department of Employment, 1990a, Table F183). Those working less than eight hours typically were in catering and cleaning jobs such as school helpers and school assistants. Robinson and Wallace's study (which has the advantage of not excluding women below the National Insurance threshold and, therefore, not underestimating the numbers of very low-paid workers) found that over a third and one-quarter of local authority manual workers worked for less than eight hours and eight to sixteen hours respectively. This suggests that, in some areas, the proportion of unprotected part-timers is even higher.

Part-time work can also reduce a woman's earnings. The hourly earnings of both manual and non-manual part-time women are less than those of full-time men and women (as shown in Figure 7.1). Furthermore, the hourly earnings of women in part-time employment are declining relative to the hourly earnings of men and women working full-time in the same industries. In addition, by reducing the part-time working week, employers can keep wages below the threshold at which they become liable for National Insurance contributions (£52.00 in 1991), thus keeping down their total wage bill. The consequences for employees will not immediately be apparent, but will subsequently affect their entitlement to a range of social security benefits.

Part-time work may reduce not only current earnings, but also deferred earnings such as pensions and earnings replacements such as sick pay. An employee's remuneration package is made up of both wages and occupational benefits, such as occupational sick pay and pension schemes. Part-time workers, mainly women, form one of the largest groups excluded from occupational pension schemes. In 1987, only 11 per cent of part-time workers were in such schemes and well over twice as many male as female employees were members (Government Actuary, 1991; see also Dulcie Groves' chapter in this volume). Similarly, fewer women than men are members of occupational sick pay schemes, particularly among manual employees (Lonsdale and Byrne, 1988). Employees in those industries in which women are concentrated also tend to have lower coverage than other industries (Brown and Small, 1985, p. 40). In general, a principle seems to operate whereby the more tenuous the link between employers and employees in terms of hours of work and, therefore, hours of contact, the fewer obligations an employer has towards the workforce. It is a theme in employment protection legislation and is manifest in occupational benefits and pay.

Working unsocial hours

Part-time work is sometimes synonymous with systems of shift working. Shift work includes a number of different working patterns such as double-day shifts, part-time shifts, split shifts, alternating day and night shifts, night shifts and so on. Like part-time work, it has been increasing for similar reasons of increased efficiency and productivity. Much shift work takes place in unsocial hours such as evenings or early mornings and allows intensive use of some machinery. There is some evidence that the proportion of women working shifts is rising faster than that of men (EOC, 1979). Working shifts is another way in which women try to accommodate the pressures of child care. Before 1986, women's hours of work were restricted, but with the passing of the Sex Discrimination Act 1986, all restrictions on shift working, night working, overtime and the maximum number of hours contained in various pieces of legislation were abolished. There are conflicting views about the effect of shiftwork on health and safety, but much of the evidence seems to indicate that it is harmful.

Homeworking

Another form of work which, like part-time work, could be perceived to offer women greater flexibility is homeworking. This is probably due to its incorrect association with people who are self-employed or freelancing from their homes. It is more useful to analyse homeworking as work done at home, for a wage, usually at piecework rates and for a single employer. In this way, the starting point to understanding homeworking is to see it as part of the productive process rather than simply defining it by its location. At the same time, however, homeworkers are different from employees working on company premises. They are subject from different legislative coverage than other employees and different working conditions, rates of pay and control over their work.

The scale of homeworking in Britain is not large. A reasonable estimate of the numbers of homeworkers, as defined above, is 300,000 (Bissett and Huws, 1984). Virtually all these homeworkers are women and many are from ethnic minority communities. Factors influencing the decision to do homework have been found to be mainly child care responsibilities, but also ill-health, financial difficulties, language problems and the need to complement husbands with irregular work patterns such as shiftwork (Hakim, 1980). Most homeworkers probably go into the work because of the autonomy and flexibility which they believe it will give them to combine paid work and family commitments. The reality of homework is that it leaves little scope for women to work to suit themselves. A number of studies show that homeworkers work to tight deadlines, with little control over the amount and type of work they do or over when they do it (Leicestershire CPAG, 1983; Bissett and Huws, 1984; Allen and Wolkowitz, 1987). A common issue for homeworkers, for instance, is the irregularity of the work they do, ranging from meeting very short deadlines to going without work for lengthy periods. Women in this work situation are adjusting to the requirements of those who supply them with work rather than working to suit their own needs.

The significance of homework lies in its extremely poor rates of pay, its hidden costs and the hazards for the women who do it and their families. Most studies of homeworkers have found evidence of extremely low rates of pay (Cragg and Dawson, 1981; Leicestershire CPAG, 1983; Allen and Wolkowitz, 1987). Approximately 10 per cent of homeworkers are covered by Wages Councils and should receive some protection because of this. However, illegal underpayment often persists because of lack of knowledge about their rights and fears that they might lose what little they have. Payment in manufacturing homework is almost always on a piecework basis and this is often used among clerical homeworkers too. Piecework introduces considerable pressure into the task, with whole families helping at times in order to guarantee earnings and meet deadlines so that future work is ensured.

In addition to low rates of pay, homeworkers face additional expenses which other workers do not. Working at home uses heating, lighting and electricity (when industrial or other machines are used) and has the inconvenience of noise and loss of space. These costs are rarely reimbursed, but when taken into account in calculating real wages, reduce low rates of pay even further. A disabled homeworker known to the author took telephone calls responding to a finance company's advertisement for personal loans. Her pay did not include reimbursement for her telephone calls relaying the information back to the company in another town. The telephone calls came at all hours of the day and night and were very disruptive. This was only one of a number of jobs she was doing and the effect of the telephone calls on the pace of her other piecework was substantial.

Inconvenience and disruption can become health hazards. Although home-workers are included in the provisions of the Health and Safety Act 1974, no procedures have been established for dealing with the particular circumstances of homeworkers. Homeworkers can face a wide variety of different health hazards. Machinery has dangers ranging from actual injuries to badly mounted machines causing vibrations and the need for women to stretch uncomfortably to reach the equipment. Chemicals and other materials causing fumes and dust require additional ventilation that few homes can provide and, even if they can, homeworkers may be tempted not to ventilate properly in order to save fuel bills. Fire is always a hazard which can arise from storing large quantities of materials or using domestic wiring for industrial machines. While the impoverishment of homeworking lies primarily in its very low rates of pay, it also imposes on family life and causes a very real threat to the health of many women and children.

The elusive goal of equality

The evidence that is available suggests conclusively that women's average earnings are well below those of men's in virtually all industries and occupations, and have been so for some time. Despite increases in their participation in paid work, women's earnings have, on average, only reached just over three-quarters those of men's, due largely to the sexual division of labour which pushes women and men into different patterns of paid work. However, the social pressures which generate this supply of labour also respond to economic and industrial forces for certain types of labour at certain times. The most important factors determining the differential in women's and men's earnings are the following:

1. The *type* of jobs they do and the segregation of women into lower paying occupations.

2. The *hours* they work and the concentration of women into part-time, lower paid jobs.

3. The *location* of their work with some women working for very low wages and in poor working conditions in the home.

It is these factors which have made women's equality at work such an intractable goal. The segregation of different groups of workers into different labour markets, in separate industries with different occupations, different workplaces and working different hours, has meant that women and men are rarely in sight of one another, let alone in competition with each other. At least part of the wages differential also has to be understood by reference to women's and men's different relationship to working time and the different commitments each has outside of paid work. However, job segregation and its roots in the sexual division of labour is crucial to an understanding of the failure of social policy measures designed to improve the situation of women in the labour market. It is increasingly clear that, as instruments of social policy, the Equal Pay Act (EPA) and the Sex Discrimination Act (SDA) have been unable to overcome job segregation and the forces that make it so attractive in the pursuit of profitability.

Under the EPA, a woman must be paid the same as a man if she is doing broadly similar work, work which has been rated as equivalent by a job evaluation study or work which is of equal value in terms of effort, skill and decision-making. The latter condition was only introduced in 1984, nine years after the Act came into force. Its exclusion allowed many inequalities to remain unchallenged because job segregation made many comparisons impossible. Under the SDA, a woman can take her case to an industrial tribunal if she is being discriminated against contractually, whether this is discrimination by intent or effect. When both pieces of legislation first came into force in 1975, 1,742 applications were made under the EPA and 243 under the SDA. These then fell dramatically in the case of the EPA where only 397 applications were made in 1989/90 and increased in the case of the SDA to 1,046. Tribunal applications are either settled through ACAS or withdrawn. In 1989/90, just under one-third of EPA cases and over one-quarter of SDA cases reached a hearing. Of these, 27 per cent of the EPA and 29 per cent of the SDA hearings were successful.

The extra costs arising out of making wages non-discriminatory may well reinforce the existing processes of labour rationalisation referred to above. By and large, the legislation rests on the assumption that the problem is one of equal opportunities. It accepts practices in industry which do nothing to break down, but instead reinforce, the division of labour between women and men both in paid work and at home.

Equal opportunity legislation will be further undermined by policies of deregulating the labour market, such as the abolition of Wages Councils and the lowering of employment protection. Both are likely to affect women disproportionately. However, the goal of equality at work cannot be achieved through equal opportunity policy alone. It requires a fundamental restructuring of our private and public worlds.

Note

1. The term 'economically active' will be used in its traditional sense of referring to those in or seeking paid employment, but it is unsatisfactory in treating domestic work as being outside the economy.

8   The cost of caring

Heather Joshi[1]

Unpaid work caring for other people competes for the time and energy a person might otherwise devote to earning their own cash in paid work. Caring responsibilities are seldom undertaken at the expense of employment by men, except occasionally in the absence of any available female. In contrast there are few women who do not, at some stage of their lives, take on a caring responsibility sufficiently demanding to have some impact on their capacity to earn cash. This chapter examines the earnings that women forgo as a result of their role as carer of first and last resort. The notion of forgone earnings is an example of what is known as an 'opportunity cost'. This concept compares a course of action with the best possible alternative that it pre-empts; opportunity costs are the value of what has to be given up to achieve a particular goal. Although some carers sacrifice a lot more than their potential money earnings, the cash they forgo is a crucial component of the opportunity cost of their unpaid work and of women's mutually reinforcing disadvantages in the labour market.

The recipients of care are generally, though not necessarily, members of the woman's own family and the degree of care they receive varies enormously, from the round-the-clock attendance required by a newborn infant or a severely disabled invalid to the laundering of socks and shirts for otherwise not very helpless adult males. The degree to which caring work interferes with a woman's capacity to earn depends not only on the helplessness of those she cares for, but also on the extent to which their care is shared by other people, paid and unpaid; and on expenditures on commodities such as domestic machinery, pre-cooked food or children's summer camp which can make multiple roles easier to perform well. Some very heroic simplifying assumptions therefore have to be made in any attempt to generalise about the opportunity cost of caring.

The idea of comparing the cash that women actually receive with what they might have earned without their caring role is not to deny that such activity normally has its material and emotional compensations, and that its value to the giver and receiver is sometimes beyond price. Neither is it suggested that 'labours of love' could be remunerated by wages in exact compensation. However, they do need recognition, appreciation and above all support, rather than being taken for granted (Finch and Groves, 1983). The following description of how women's lives are affected financially by the current gender division of labour is intended to strengthen women's hands in the negotiations, private and public, which affect the allocation of work and income. An example of the application of the idea of opportunity costs to an issue of policy has been the success (in June 1986) of the campaign to extend eligibility for Invalid Care Allowance to married women. When this benefit was introduced to help compensate people for having to give up employment to care for the infirm the presumption was, as recently as 1975, that such costs were not incurred by married women.

An alternative approach to costing unpaid care is to value it at replacement; that is, what it would cost to pay somebody to do everything the unpaid carer does. This approach is particularly suited to the debate about policy on community care of the infirm and elderly (Henwood and Wicks, 1984) but it is not necessarily appropriate when considering the personal financial sacrifices which women make in the course of caring. In addition, estimating replacement costs raises some practical difficulties in observing the tasks performed and the time they take (or would take someone who did not also live in the home), and in putting a price on the hours required.

Piachaud (1985), for example, reported a survey of mothers' activities and concluded that the *extra* work involved in looking after a pre-school child amounted to 'round about 50 hours a week', before allowing for the time when the mother was 'on call' though not actually doing a specific tending task. Similarly, Nissel and Bonnerjea (1982) estimated from a time budget study that the time taken to perform the tasks needed by a handicapped elderly person ranged from 24 to 35 hours per week. They tentatively suggested valuing these tasks at the market rate for domestic work (£1.80 per hour in 1980). Henwood and Wicks (1984) suggest the official rate for local authority home helps (£2.90 in 1982–3). Either rate may be well below the market value of some of the nursing skills involved and, as Nissel and Bonnerjea show, well below what the carer might have been able to earn in her own occupation. They offer an annual valuation of caring tasks as replaced by paid workers of £2,500, and two estimates of opportunity costs: £4,500 for the earnings forgone by wives not in employment who would like to take up a job again (valued at the current rate for their previous occupation); and, for the earnings forgone by women working less than full-time, £1,900, a little less than the 'replacement' estimate. At the level of earnings prevailing in 1990, these annual opportunity costs would amount to around £11,600 and £5,000 respectively.

The equation of opportunity costs with forgone earnings is not the whole of the story because it makes no allowance for the free time which may be diverted into caring for others nor, on the other hand, for the social and psychological benefits of avoiding isolation in the home. However, it has the advantage that it is possible to identify and quantify the cash opportunity cost of caring, by observing what women do in the public domain of paid employment and comparing the amount of paid work that women with and without domestic responsibilities manage to do. This approach is followed here to examine how caring – for children, husbands or disabled relatives – affects first, women's labour market participation and their hours of paid work; and secondly, their pay both in the short term and the long term.

The effects of caring on participation and hours of paid work

The evidence used to quantify the effects of motherhood (and other caring activities) on employment participation was collected in the nationwide Women and Employment Survey (WES) conducted in Britain in 1980 (Martin and Roberts, 1984). Table 8.1 presents a regression analysis summarising and quantifying the most important identifiable determinants of a woman's chances of having any paid job and also of having a full-time paid job. The difference between the two formulae identifies the circumstances where women are likely to work part-time.

Multiple regression techniques control simultaneously for a number of possible influences on participation. The factors identified fall into three main groups: family responsibilities, potential pay and other sources of income. Thus at any given stage of the family life cycle and level of alternative resources, the women who are most likely to be in employment are those who would find it most financially rewarding.[2] Similarly, all else being equal, women with the greatest need for cash are more likely to be employed (particularly in part-time jobs) than women who have other resources to fall back on.

As these economic considerations tend to cancel each other out, it is possible to generalise about women without caring responsibilities for children or older dependants. They could normally expect to be in the labour force (employed or looking for work) most of the time. The average chance of their actually having a paid job is more than 80 per cent over most of the ages from 16 to 59, albeit on a part-time basis for many older married women.

Table 8.1 Regression analysis of participation in paid work and in full-time work, *Women and Employment Survey*, Great Britain, 1980

Dependent variable	Working		Full-time		Mean	S.D.
					0.651	0.477
					0.380	0.485
Independent variables	*b*	*t*	*b*	*t*		
Constant	0.805	18.56	0.754	32.34		
Family responsibilities						
Pregnant	−0.144	3.96	−0.099	2.89	0.032	0.175
Presence of child 0–15	−0.763	23.56	−0.663	21.71	0.495	0.500
Age of youngest if 0–4***	0.085	10.51	0.018	2.37	1.915	2.252
Age of youngest if 5–10**	0.041	6.77	0.036	6.33	1.285	2.256
Age of youngest if 11–15*	0.022	2.33	0.066	7.28	0.320	0.971
Number of other children 0–4	−0.071	2.50	−0.039	1.46	0.061	0.254
Any other child 11–15	0.041	1.87	0.069	3.33	0.137	0.344
Number of children 16+	−0.005	0.90	−0.016	2.86	0.834	1.365
Any other dependant	−0.088	4.87	−0.062	3.63	0.139	0.346
Potential earnings						
Imputed pay, top occupation	0.273	9.25	0.390	14.19	0.357	0.220
Local unemployment rate	−0.012	4.55	−0.003	1.27	6.594	2.788
Alternative resources						
Currently married	0.217	3.53	0.277	6.69	0.735	0.441
Non-labour income, married	−2.3E–03	11.57	−1.4E–03	7.66	66.264	52.807
Non-labour income, not married	−4.9E–03	7.57	−6.0E–03	10.23	4.150	12.486
Mortgage	0.059	4.25	0.042	3.21	0.426	0.495
Husband not working	−0.272	10.05	−0.128	5.06	0.065	0.247
Age (years) if married	1.9E–04	0.14	−0.012	13.88	28.041	19.302
Age (years) if not married	2.5E–03	1.64			8.403	15.721
Square age since 40, married	−8.0E–04	5.53			36.735	83.543
Square age since 40, not married	−6.2E–04	3.01	−9.3E–04	7.43	11.779	53.306
North of Mersey-Tees	0.066	3.88	0.043	2.70	0.280	0.449
Adjusted R squared	0.316		0.409			

Sample of 4,244 women aged 16–59, neither students nor permanently sick, no missing values on included variables. 140 cases paying cash for child care are excluded.

Notes: The *b* coefficients express the change in the participation rate associated with a unit change in any one of the independent variables when all others remain unchanged. For the categorical variables in the table a unit change reflects the change from a situation where the description does not apply to one where it does, and the mean value of the variable reported in the penultimate column gives the incidence of that state in the sample. For example, 42.6 per cent of the sample had a mortage and 49.5 per cent a child under 16.

The *t* statistics indicate the strength of each variable's explanatory power and the degree of certainty that can be attached to estimates of *b*. *t* values smaller than 2 indicate a margin of uncertainty at least as great as the size of the estimated *b*. Detailed definitions of variables are given in Joshi (1984). New transformations for the present analysis are as follows:

*s mark spline variables: all set to 0 when no child under 16. These variables, though measured in units of years, are based on data reported in months.
*** Set to youngest child's age, if that is 0–4; or 5 where it is 5–15.
** Set to age of youngest: minus 5 where youngest aged 5–10; 5 when youngest aged 11–15, or 0 when youngest aged 0–4.
*   Set to age of youngest: minus 10 when youngest 11–15 or 0 when youngest aged 0–10.
Potential pay is the value of log pay imputed by formula used in Joshi (1986a) but with employment experience set to zero.
Non-labour income excludes respondent's net earnings and any benefit income received by virtue of her unemployment or retirement, includes net earnings of husband, if married.
E Notation indicates the number of places the decimal point should be advanced.

Effects of motherhood

Responsibility for child-rearing is the major correlate of female labour force participation. It matters not so much how many children a woman has to care for, but how young is her youngest charge. The mother of an infant is very unlikely to have paid work, however many other children she has. The model fitted in Table 8.1 implies that if her other characteristics give her a 76 per cent chance of employment before child-bearing, it is certain that she would not work immediately after the birth. As the child gets older the chances of her having a job rise by nine percentage points per year until the child's fifth birthday, by which time the women in this example would have a work participation rate of 43 per cent. The chances of a mother being employed continue to rise, somewhat less steeply, as the youngest child passes through the ages of compulsory schooling. Mothers of teenagers are approximately as likely as women with no children to be employed – possibly slightly more so if they have more than one child in the age group. Mothers with more than one pre-school child have a somewhat smaller chance of being employed than those with just one, but this difference is minor compared to the contrast between families without any young children and those with at least one. The dampening effect of children on the chances of full-time employment is stronger than the effect on having some sort of job at all; women with children under 15 are more likely to work part-time than full-time. After a child reaches school-leaving age there are some minor effects, which continue to raise the chances of part-time rather than full-time employment. These are probably attributable to the long-term loss of labour market leverage (discussed further below) consequent upon the interruption in employment that most mothers have sustained.

The estimated effects of various patterns of child-bearing on subsequent employment histories can be summarised in an implied average difference in lifetime workforce membership between hypothetical groups of women with and without children (but, on all other counts, identical and average). As shown in Table 8.2, the time lost from full-time employment varies with the number of children but not proportionately, ranging from seven years for one child to twelve years for four, and is also sensitive to the spacing of births. There is an extra propensity to work part-time which is almost invariant with the number of children (roughly three more years than would be the case without children). The net effect on the average employment record of having one child rather than none is equivalent to 4.3 years of workforce membership. The net effect of a family of four, provided the births are closely spaced, is only double.[3]

Effects of marriage

After dependent children, the next most common candidate requiring a woman's time to be diverted (or freed) from paid work is the husband. Married women are no less likely to have a job than those living with no partner, but their jobs are

Table 8.2 Impact on average lifetime workforce membership of different numbers of children

Number of births	Ages at births	Fewer years of full-time employment	Extra years part-time	Net effect on time in paid work (years)
1	25	− 7.16	+2.83	−4.32
2	25, 28	− 9.05	+2.80	−6.25
3	25, 27, 29	−10.44	+3.10	−7.34
3	25, 28, 31	−11.04	+2.80	−8.24
4	25, 27, 29, 31	−11.77	+2.98	−8.79

more likely to be part-time. To some extent this must be because of the greater need for cash by those (especially lone mothers) who cannot share in income earned by a partner, but as I have argued elsewhere (Joshi, 1986a), the lower propensity of married women to take full-time jobs even when they have no young children must also partly arise from the extra demands on their time of looking after husband, home and social network.

Ironically, there is stronger evidence of this aspect of a wife's role in the low work participation of wives whose husbands are not currently earning. The timing of a husband's retirement often dictates that of his wife. Among a number of explanations for this phenomenon are: the desire to enjoy leisure activities together; the need for special care if the husband is in poor health or to cook his midday meal even if he is well; and the threat to the husband's status as chief breadwinner. Some similar considerations may also help account for the low rate of employment, other things being equal, of the wives of unemployed men, although there are also considerations connected with a benefit 'trap' and the likelihood that individuals at high risk of unemployment might have married one another. In any case, women in zero earner couples are at high risk of poverty.

Marriage, even to a healthy husband, impedes employment participation to some extent (and can also affect a woman's pay and prospects if it restricts her freedom to move, stay or travel), but such sacrifices of earnings may in fact be 'good value for money'. It is very difficult to say how far they might be outweighed by the benefits of the pooling and transfer of resources that normally take place between spouses. Some wives do very well out of the 'domestic bargain', but all too many do not.

Care for the physically dependent

Responsibility for handicapped, sick or disabled people potentially presents the most exacting and thankless claims on a woman's unpaid time. 'Community care' of the aged is typically undertaken by daughters or daughters-in-law, which in some ways complements the story of motherhood sketched above. The most difficult caring situations are relatively uncommon among women under 60. Only 14 per cent of the women in the Women and Employment Survey reported that they had responsibility for someone needing care. Of these a quarter were actually providing constant attention. Among those cared for were handicapped children and invalid husbands; some of the others, mainly elderly people, were living in separate households. The existence of these varied caring responsibilities on average lowered the employment rate, all else being equal, by nine percentage points, which is about the same order of magnitude as the effect of the average dependent child. Caring responsibilities for the disabled are often, like maternal responsibilities, combined with some employment. Detailed studies of their situation stress the emotional as well as the financial benefits of the carer having another role outside the home (Parker, 1990b). When the handicapped person is a child, the WES-based model predicts about the same reduction of employment rates as found by Baldwin and Glendinning (1983) in a study comparing families with disabled children with a control group. As the physical dependency of a disabled child is prolonged, mothers with handicapped children are less likely to manage the part-time employment that typifies mothers of healthy school children.

Effects of family responsibilities on the rate of women's pay

If current and past caring responsibilities affect the rate of remuneration while a woman is in work, this too should enter the calculation of the opportunity cost of caring.

Current effects

Through a variety of mechanisms, current domestic ties can lower the rate of pay a woman receives relative to what she might get if she were a free agent. Some women take jobs for which they are over-qualified in order to fit in with the demands of their dual role. Among mothers in the Women and Employment Survey who had made a return to work after their first birth, 37 per cent had returned to a lower level of occupation than their previous job (Martin and Roberts, 1984; see also Joshi and Newell, 1987). In other cases the woman's need for her job to have convenient hours and location permits employers to pay her less than they would have to pay to get the work done by someone else. Low pay for those with family responsibilities is doubtless also reinforced by their lack of time and opportunity to organise collectively. The poverty wages received by homeworkers are an extreme example of this process, but it also occurs in other circumstances. Freeman (1982) argues that the employed mothers she studied were primarily concerned to preserve employer tolerance of flexibility in their working arrangements rather than raise their rate of pay. Craig *et al.* (1985) cite among other examples employers near outer city housing estates taking advantage of the local women's inability to travel further afield to maintain low levels of pay. These mechanisms are particularly prevalent in part-time jobs, where employees are virtually all women (Robinson and Wallace, 1984b).

Postponed effects – care now, pay later

The effects of caring responsibilities in the past also have an impact on a woman's current rate of pay, even after she becomes more of a free agent in the labour market, for the market rewards accumulated employment experience just as it penalises workers with interrupted employment records. Employees with uninterrupted careers gain experience which may enhance their value to the employer, if only because they have had a chance to learn by making mistakes or to acquire, formally or informally, training on the job. Continuous service in large organisations also affords opportunities for earning increments and promotion within and between occupational grades. These pay-augmenting effects of employment experience are particularly strong in early adulthood (when people are most likely to be starting families) and in the knowledge-using non-manual occupations where the majority of women are now employed.[4]

Quantifying the effects

In an analysis of employees in the Medical Research Council's National Survey of Health and Development of a cohort born in 1946, Joshi and Newell (1989) compared the hourly pay of mothers who had returned to work by the ages of 26 and 32 respectively with that of their female contemporaries who had no children. The average mother employed at age 26 received 29 per cent less per hour than her childless colleagues. The regression analysis, controlling for other relevant differences, suggests that a differential of at least 14 per cent was attributable to maternal responsibilities. This 14 per cent is a product of a loss of 8 per cent on the rate of pay from lost employment experience (2.3 years on average); 4 per cent from the mother's higher chance of being in a part-time job; and 2.5 per cent from downward mobility into manual and sales jobs.[5] Among mothers employed at age 32 the corresponding estimates of effects of motherhood on pay are: 4.5 per cent less due to an average loss of employment experience since age 26 of 1.8 years; 5 per cent less due to the higher incidence of part-time employment and again about 2.5 per cent attributable to downward mobility – a total differential of 12 per cent attributable to motherhood out of an average shortfall of 26 per cent below the pay of childless women. The relative importance of lost employment experience among mothers returning to paid work at later stages could be expected to increase, because they would tend to have had longer gaps in their records. However, there are other indications that once a woman has returned after a given length of break, the penalty she sustains for having had an interruption in the past diminishes over time; as the break recedes into the past, some 'catching up' is possible.

Table 8.3 Regression analysis of pay differentials, *Women and Employment Survey*, Great Britain, 1980

	b	t	Mean	S.D.
Dependent variable				
Natural logarithm of				
hourly pay			0.518	0.389
Explanatory variables				
Years of post-compulsory				
education	0.068	15.3	1.332	1.967
Highest qualification				
attained:				
A level or above	0.179	7.4	0.183	0.387
O level or equivalent	0.050	2.9	0.203	0.402
CSE, etc.	0.036	2.0	0.156	0.363
(Age (years) − 40)^2 ′ 100	−0.041	6.5	1.54	1.51
Years worked full-time	0.017	5.8	11.043	8.770
Years worked part-time	0.013	4.5	4.275	5.854
(Years worked)^2 ′ 100	−0.031	4.4	3.061	3.856
Proportion of time since				
leaving education in				
employment	0.226	7.2	0.743	0.217
Years in current job	0.006	3.8	4.381	4.831
Current job part-time	−0.101	6.7	4.39	0.496
Constant	0.147	3.9		

Adjusted R squared 0.369	Degrees of freedom	11
Residual sum of squares 276.16		2893

Note: The b coefficients express the expected change in the log of hourly pay associated with a unit change in each explanatory variable. They are the logarithms of the proportional differentials in pay which are associated with each variable when the other variables are held constant. The t statistics indicate the strength of each variable's explanatory power and the degree of certainty that can be attached to the estimates of b.

Main's exhaustive analysis of the pay of a cross-section of women workers of all ages who reported their pay in the 1980 Women and Employment Survey found that broken employment histories dominate occupational and industrial mobility as factors which explain statistically the variations in women's pay (Main, 1988).

A somewhat simpler analysis of the same data is presented in Table 8.3. Differentials in pay per hour are statistically explained by a set of variables which record the woman's education, employment experience and whether or not her current job is part-time.

The coefficient of −0.101 in the penultimate row of Table 8.3 estimates a 10 per cent reduction in pay per hour of otherwise identical employees having part-time rather than full-time work. This is very close to Main's estimate of the same phenomenon and also very similar to the 9 per cent estimated by Joshi and Newell (1989) in two snapshots of young female workers in the 1970s. Our interpretation of this consistent finding is that it reflects the low grading of most part-time jobs, which in turn reflects the influence of domestic constraints.

The model used to analyse the WES pay data does not explicitly allow for domestic commitments having a direct negative effect on the pay of any full-time workers, though such effects probably apply with at least the same force to those whose lack of alternative income impels them to work full-time (such as many of the lone mothers not reliant on income support). There were insufficient cases in this general sample to provide this type of statistical evidence for a phenomenon which is well documented in case studies, such as those reported by Craig *et al.* (1985).

Though women workers on average would appear to gain financially from clocking up and maintaining an employment record, these returns diminish as the total amount of accumulated experience rises. They are also affected by whether the experience gained is with the same employer and by whether or not it is full-time. A curve describing the formula rises gradually less and less steeply over a hypothetical life cycle even for someone with continuous employment, and then turns down at high hypothetical values of experience. It seems unrealistic to assume that the profile of hourly pay for an individual living through a hypothetical life cycle would actually turn down if she worked continuously. This pattern probably reflects the fact that the data are actually comparing a cross-section of women of successively earlier generations who have other unmeasured differences in attitudes and aptitudes. Accordingly, the curves plotted in Figure 8.1 on the basis of the formula in Table 8.3 describe the upward sloping segment of the fitted curve, but have been arbitrarily fixed to level off once they reach the late career peak. The scale on the vertical axis of Figure 8.1 has been arbitrarily chosen to fit the case of someone who at the age of 24 would be paid an annual salary of £9,000 – in 1990 the sort of level available to fairly junior secretaries. Inflation is assumed away, the value of money in 1990 is assumed to apply over the whole of the hypothetical lifetime. Using these assumptions, Figure 8.1 shows what would happen to the pay of such a woman if her continuous full-time employment were interrupted. The continuous line illustrates a full-time career with a single employer, interrupted at the age of 25 for the birth of a first child and followed by a complete gap of eight years. This could happen if, say, a second child were born when the woman was 28 and she stayed away from employment until this second child was five (which means she never enters employment as a mother when the school system is not offering partial day-care). In our example she returns initially to part-time work for ten years and resumes full-time employment when she is 43 and her younger child 15. She reverts to part-time employment after another nine years, as other life cycle factors reduce her chance of working full-time. In the scenario where she never has children she is assumed to switch out of full-time into part-time employment at the age of 54, and to sustain the drop in pay per hour illustrated in the top line of Figure

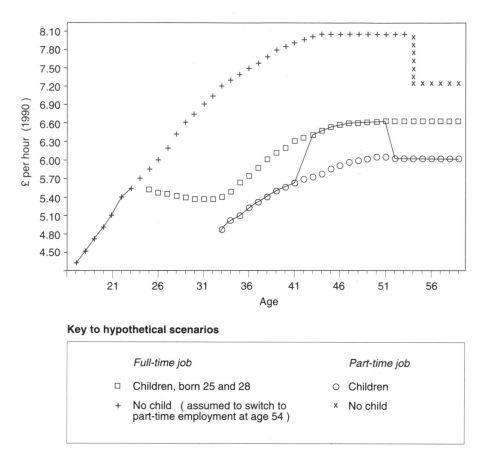

Key to hypothetical scenarios

	Full-time job		*Part-time job*
□	Children, born 25 and 28	○	Children
+	No child (assumed to switch to part-time employment at age 54)	×	No child

Note: Continuous line illustrates example discussed in text

Figure 8.1 Pay per hour over the life cycle: illustration of eight-year break in employment

8.1. These hypothetical scenarios are fairly arbitrary, but they have been informed by the participation analysis discussed above.[6] During the 1980s the minority of British mothers taking paid work before their children reach school age has been growing, but for most women this sort of scenario still applies. That long gaps in employment around child-bearing are not inevitable is also apparent in the employment patterns of mothers in other European countries (Davies and Joshi, 1990).

The lower lines in Figure 8.1 tell us what the woman's rate of pay per hour would be, given her employment record to date, if she started a full-time job and also, once she had made her return to employment as a mother, what it would be at the part-time rate. The rates that she would actually receive are joined by a continuous line. While she is out of employment her hypothetical rate of pay in full-time work falls because of lost seniority within her original firm and because of the estimated effect of time spent out of employment during her adult life. Thus when she eventually returns to work after an eight-year gap, her pay per hour is 83p per hour lower than what she last earned – 53p because she is now working part-time rather than full-time, and 30p through loss of seniority and reduction of the proportion of her working life spent in employment. On the other hand, if she had stayed in her original job her pay would have gone up by 144p over those eight years (even in the absence of inflation). The total gap of 227p between actual pay and what might have been is equivalent to 32 per cent of what she would have earned had she maintained continuous service with the same employer. The difference between the mother's actual rate of pay and what she might have earned does however eventually decrease – on these assumptions, in the long term, the differential levels out after age 50 to 17 per cent of what it might have been.[7]

Effects on total income

Figure 8.2 reports the story of Figure 8.1 in terms of total income, year by year. Annual hours of work are assumed to be 1,650 when employed full-time and exactly half that whenever the job is part-time. If the woman has no children, her total earnings over the ages of 17 to 59 are £439,500. On the assumption that child-bearing entails an eight-year break followed by twelve extra years of part-time employment (compared with those of her childless counterpart), the grand total falls to £237,000. The £202,500 forgone (more than twentyfold her annual salary when she dropped out) can be accounted for as follows:

Earnings forgone while out of employment	£81,000
Earnings forgone while working shorter hours	£73,500
Earnings forgone because of lower rates of pay	£48,000

These headings account for 40 per cent, 36 per cent and 25 per cent respectively of the total forgone. The 25 per cent effect on lower rates of pay consists of £7,050 attributable to current domestic constraints and £41,400 from loss of previous work experience. The total effect is more than double the immediate and most apparent absence of earnings while the woman is not working at all.

The size and composition of the forgone earnings depend on the assumptions adopted. Earlier child-bearing for example has a relatively minor effect on the eventual difference in hourly rates, but it exposes women to their effects for longer. A history with a shorter break would suffer less from years of absence and show a smaller drop in pay on return to work, but would also involve exposure to reduced rates of pay for longer. The costs would however be smaller

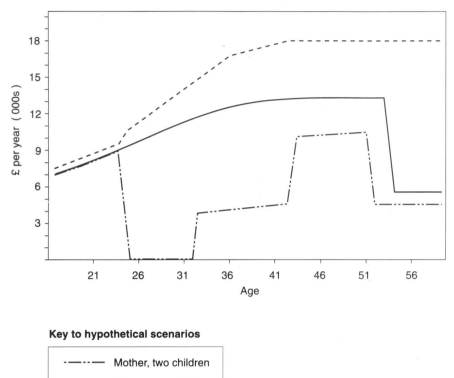

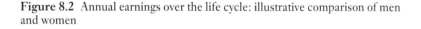

Figure 8.2 Annual earnings over the life cycle: illustrative comparison of men and women

if the woman's employment would anyway be less than continuous (or even if she occasionally changed employer).

Women whose caring responsibilities take them away from employment at later stages of the life cycle clearly incur the opportunity costs of the constraints on their employment while they are caring. Nissel and Bonnerjea (1982) estimated opportunity costs of £12,000 (uprated to 1990 levels), if full-time employment is given up entirely to care. Similarly, in our example, a childless woman would forgo £12,750 and a mother up to £10,500 per year if she gave up full-time employment at the later stage of the employment cycle. If and when carers manage to return to employment unconstrained by these responsibilities, the formula adopted here suggests that subsequent pay might be reduced through loss of seniority, though other effects of losing work experience are probably more severe at younger ages.

The lost earnings are expressed in gross terms. After allowing for tax and National Insurance contributions the net amount forgone would be moderated, but there would still be effects on pension entitlement to take into account. The effects of motherhood on state basic pension are neutralized by Home Responsibility Credits. Under the Fowler versions of SERPS, Home Responsibility protection also limits the amount of State Earnings Related Pension forgone. Private pensions, from occupational or personal schemes, which would tend to be worth more than SERPS, would show substantial differences between the pensions accrued by a childless woman and by a mother (see Owen and Joshi, 1990; Joshi and Davies, 1991). The precise extent to which the cash penalties of motherhood are carried into retirement depends on the particular pension scheme involved, and whether a woman qualifies for any pension rights at all while working part-time. Nevertheless, the proportional loss of occupational pension rights could easily be at least as high as the 46 per cent loss of lifetime earnings.

The cost of being female

Forgoing earnings as a result of parenthood is a price of this pleasure and privilege which is paid by women but not by men. Yet it is not the only penalty of being female in the labour market. Despite improvements attributable to equal opportunities legislation (see Zabalza and Tzannotos, 1985; and the chapter by Susan Lonsdale in this volume), women with no actual caring responsibilities and uninterrupted employment records still tend to be paid less well than the equivalent man. Our analysis of employees born in 1946 attempted to quantify this 'price of being female'. Although it varies between people of different social backgrounds, the gap between men's and women's pay tends to open up during their late twenties. The top line in Figure 8.2, based loosely on estimates from 1977 data (Joshi and Newell, 1989) puts the advantage of being male at 17 per cent of female pay at age 26, 32 per cent at age 32 and fixes it, somewhat arbitrarily, at 40 per cent by age 36. The man's curve is boosted by 8 per cent at age 25 on the basis of the enhancement of pay associated with men (but not with women) getting married. We would suggest that the caring work of a wife may also help to raise the amount that men are paid.

The extra income that the person in Figure 8.2 would have earned between the ages of 17 and 59 had they been male rather than female is represented by the area between the two top lines. It amounts, on these assumptions, to about the same as the earnings a woman typically gives up by becoming a mother. If this general disadvantage, to which all women are exposed, is itself an indirect outcome of the social expectations about the female caring role, the costs of caring are compounded – in this case, roughly doubled. Whatever its fundamental source, unequal treatment in the labour market helps to perpetuate gender inequalities in the home, for the opportunity costs of men taking on caring would generally be higher than letting them devolve upon women (see Ungerson, 1983).

The price a man pays for parenthood is generally being expected to support his children and their mother. The price a woman pays is that of continuing economic handicap and an increased risk of poverty. One of the many advantages of being male is that it is easier to opt out of the obligation to care. Perhaps that is why people prefer not to count the cost of caring but to think positively about its rewards. However, positive thinking should go further than just urging women to keep smiling. The challenge is to devise changes which will break women out of the double bind of the double burden (Joshi, 1986b). This requires simultaneous action to improve women's status outside the home and to encourage the sharing of caring work by men; to improve the support available for community care; and to enhance the opportunities to combine employment, other than at the lowest levels, with unpaid activities.

Notes

1. Research by the author on which this chapter draws was supported by ESRC funding. Bianca De Stavola, John Ermisch, Marie-Louise Newell and Susan Owen are thanked for their help.
2. Potential pay is inferred for all women, whether or not they are currently working, on the basis of the best paying occupational level they have so far attained. Unlike the imputed wage used in Joshi (1984 and 1986a), the length of previous employment experience is not brought into the formula used in Table 8.1.
3. These figures are virtually unaffected by different assumptions about age at first birth. Note also that they are averages of differences over a number of years (up to age 60), and not estimates of the length of the break around child-bearing that is typical of most mothers' employment (see Joshi, 1990). (Elias and Main (1982) report that women aged 35–44 in 1975 who had returned to employment after a single break had interruptions in their employment records of around nine years; among women then aged 45–54 the break averaged fourteen years. For evidence of a similar trend from the WES see Martin and Roberts, 1984, Chapter 9; Dex, 1984, Appendix A; and Martin, 1986.) Of course, some mothers manage shorter breaks than the average or no breaks at all.
4. When the WES pay regression sample was split into roughly equal sub-samples, of cases in manual and sales occupations on the one hand and other non-manual employees on the other, the work experience effects estimated

were stronger in the latter sub-sample, though not totally absent in the lower paying types of jobs. Since 1980 the proportion of women in non-manual, non-sales jobs has gone up. At the 1981 Census these jobs accounted for 55 per cent of females in civilian employment in Great Britain.

5. An extension of this line of analysis is reported in Joshi (1991).

6. The difference between the employment record with and without child-bearing is greater than the *average* gap estimated above because these histories attempt to say what would happen to a *typical* individual, as discussed in Joshi (1990). This typical individual does actually stay in work whenever the group rate of participation is over 50 per cent and never works if the aggregate rate falls below 50 per cent, giving her an even chance of employment. One reason to concentrate on an illustrative individual rather than averages in attempting to quantify the impact of an interrupted work history on pay is that women who return to work when their children are very young are likely to be incurring direct expenses on child care which ought therefore to be brought into the account; but these can be assumed to be fairly minimal (except perhaps in school holidays).

7. The differentials are roughly halved, 15 per cent diminishing to 8 per cent, on the rather radically different assumption of no gain from seniority with any employer on either scenario and an interruption as short as two years.

PART 4

Women, welfare and poverty

9 *Redundancy, unemployment and poverty*

Claire Callender

The purpose of this chapter is to demonstrate the inadequacy of redundancy payments provisions and social security benefits in alleviating the impact of unemployment and poverty upon women. The appropriateness of existing policy provision is assessed by exploring some of the financial consequences and other implications of job loss for a group of redundant women.

Unemployment is not equally distributed among all groups in society but is concentrated among some of the poorest and least powerful in the labour force and in society as a whole. One such vulnerable group is women. However, little is known about either the scope or nature of women's unemployment.

Many women workers exhibit labour market characteristics traditionally associated with vulnerability to unemployment. They frequently work within structures of insecurity – their jobs are unskilled, poorly paid and often part-time; they have few fringe benefits; and they may work unsocial hours in poor working conditions, lacking the security of trade unions or protective legislation (see Susan Lonsdale's chapter in this volume).

There is considerable debate, however, on the extent to which women or certain categories of women workers are particularly susceptible to unemployment in comparison with men (Callender, 1985). Official monthly statistics, based upon those claiming social security benefits, suggest that women's unemployment has at times risen at a much faster rate than men's, although the absolute and percentage numbers for men remain higher. For instance, when

Table 9.1 Unemployment: LFS and claimant count compared, 1990

	Numbers (000s) Women	Men	Percentage Women %	Men %	All %
Claimant count:	423	1,194	26	74	100
LFS: (a) unemployed by ILO/OECD definition*	802	1,147	41	59	100
(b) wanted work, available, but not looked in 4 weeks (or not stated)	694	330	68	32	100
(a) + (b)	1,496	1,447	50	50	100

* i.e.: no paid work, actively seeking work in past week and available to start within fortnight.

Source: *Employment Gazette* and 1990 *Labour Force Survey*.

unemployment was rising between 1979 and 1986, male unemployment rose by 146 per cent while female unemployment increased by 276 per cent. However, when unemployment declined between 1987 and 1990, the decline was greater for women than men. By 1991, as the recession deepened and unemployment rose, male unemployment grew by 13 per cent and female unemployment by 11 per cent in the first six months (*Employment Gazette*, Table 2.1, various volumes 1986–91).

These statistics and other measures of unemployment, all of which are socially constructed and based on certain assumptions, need to be treated with caution. For instance, the computation of the monthly statistics has changed over thirty times in the past decade. These statistics underestimate the levels of unemployment and are incomplete and biased (Unemployment Unit, 1991). However, they particularly misrepresent the numbers of women who do not have paid work and want employment or who are underemployed (Callender, 1985). Thus it has been estimated that one in four women who lose their jobs do not appear in the monthly claimant count. The variation in the definitions of unemployment used in statistics creates differing estimates. For example, the spring 1990 Labour Force Survey (LFS), which enumerates women who would like a job and are available for work, includes almost three-and-a-half times as many women as the monthly claimant count and puts the figure of female unemployment at about 1 million higher than the claimant count. By contrast, the LFS estimates lower numbers of unemployed men compared with the claimant count (Table 9.1).

Non-working women do not comply with our male-dominated conceptual framework for defining who is unemployed. If a man is healthy, of working age and not working, then he is unemployed. However, women in a similar position are not necessarily ascribed that status. Hence women may not 'fit' the classifications and categories used in statistics (Roberts, 1981). They may also be excluded because they are not entitled to benefits, do not register for work, or do not define themselves as unemployed. In other words, women's invisibility in the official statistics reflects both social security arrangements and differences between men and women's experiences of unemployment. Unemployed women are often defined out of the labour market by structures and ideologies which regulate that market. These forces not only exclude women from unemployment statistics but also from 'legitimate' experiences of unemployment. Women's experiences are marginalised so that their unemployment is not considered a problem or worthy of comprehensive social policy responses. One such experience which is peripheralised and rendered invisible is the poverty associated with unemployment, as Townsend (1979) has shown. We shall examine some of the social policies and structures which shape women's experience of unemployment and poverty before exploring some of those experiences.

Access to redundancy payments

One policy which influences women's experience of unemployment is the redundancy payments legislation. Since the legislation was introduced in 1965 it has been revised, more recently in recognition of its discriminatory nature. However, overall it remains deeply rooted in notions of a 'traditional' job and the 'standard' worker, namely, a full-time employee with a history of continuous employment who is typically male.

The concern here is with statutory redundancy payments, not *ex gratia* payments which are privately and separately negotiated either with individuals or in collective agreements. These *ex gratia* payments have attracted media attention which has contributed to the development of many myths about redundancy payments generally (Levie *et al.*, 1984). But *ex gratia* payments, like other occupational fringe benefits, are unequally distributed (Sinfield, 1978). Women do not have equal access to them because of their location in the labour market and consequently are more dependent than men on the less generous statutory minimum payments.

The economic rationale behind the redundancy payment legislation was to facilitate labour mobility so that industry could adapt to changing economic and technological requirements. The payments were part of a package of benefits which were to act as a carrot to persuade workers to accept being made unemployed. Today, the redundancy legislation is used to reduce the labour force because of economic decline. However, the ultimate aim of the legislation – to shed labour and alter workers' consciousness so that they accept being sacked – remains the same.

The Wages Act 1986 and the Employment Act 1989 radically altered the financing of redundancy payments by abolishing the government's subsidy of employers' redundancy costs.[1] These changes, which herald another shift in the purpose of the legislation, bring into question the role of redundancy payments and their relationship with the social security system, but above all they put a higher premium on dismissing the cheapest workers.

The Employment Protection (Consolidation) Act 1978 (amended in 1984, 1985, 1986 and 1989) secures the rights of redundant workers to financial remuneration. Eligibility for payments is now restricted to workers under the age of 65 who have a minimum of two years' full-time service since the age of 18. Payments are calculated on the basis of the worker's age, length of continuous service, and pay. These three criteria are discussed in turn below.

Redundancy payments are calculated on a sliding-scale according to age, so the cheapest workers to dismiss are the youngest workers and/or those with the shortest service. In practice, workers under the age of 20 do not receive payments and this especially affects women because girls have tended to leave full-time education earlier than boys.

Until the legislation was changed in 1990 by the 1989 Employment Act, women were also penalised because service after their statutory retirement age (60 years) was ignored in the calculation of payments. Yet women are less likely than men to leave paid employment at the statutory retirement age; it is estimated that in 1990 22.7 per cent of women between the ages of 60 and 64 were economically active, compared with 14.4 per cent of men aged 65–9 (Tinder, 1991). In addition, women received proportionately smaller payments on their sixtieth birthday because the number of years included in reckonable service was less for women. Finally, women could *never* receive the maximum compensation because of differential retirement ages, payments based on age, and the ceiling of twenty years' maximum that counted towards payments. These provisions were deemed discriminatory under the EC Equal Treatment Directive and consequently the 1989 Employment Act raised the age limit to 65 years for women.

The value of redundancy payments increases with a worker's length of service and any break deprives workers of their rights to payments. An employee must work a minimum of sixteen hours for two years continuously with the same employer to be eligible for payment. This clearly affects women adversely because it overlooks their discontinuous patterns of employment (Martin and Roberts, 1984). Moreover, part-time workers, the majority of whom are women, are doubly disadvantaged. If they work between eight and sixteen hours a week they need five years' continuous employment before they qualify for payment, while those who work less than eight hours a week have no entitlement to redundancy payments.[2]

The final component in calculating compensation is weekly pay levels. This also disadvantages women because, despite equal pay legislation, men and women's pay remains unequal. Moreover, these disparities in earnings increase with age over the lifetime, varying according to occupation (see Heather Joshi's chapter here). Consequently, proportionately fewer women receive payments based on their peak earnings.

The cumulative impact of these three determinants of redundancy payments is that women are discriminated against both directly and indirectly by the legislation. The 1980 Women and Employment Survey showed that 36 per cent of employed women were not eligible for redundancy payments, primarily because they had insufficient lengths of service (Martin and Roberts, 1984, p. 35). Anderson (1981) also found that a higher proportion of redundant women were not entitled to any payments compared with men. Furthermore, eligibility for statutory payments declined down the occupational ladder and those eligible for payment earned more than those ineligible – findings particularly significant for women. Thus, those who benefit most from this gender-blind legislation are non-manual male workers.

Women's disadvantaged position is confirmed by unpublished figures from the Department of Employment (based on a sample of people receiving payments direct from their employers) which show that in 1986 only about a third of all payments went to women. The median payment for men in 1986 was £1,780, for women it was only £697; while the mean was £2,028 and £1,016 respectively. The distribution of the payments likewise shows considerable differences between the sexes. Over half (53 per cent) of women's payments were under £750 and three-quarters under £1,500. By contrast, a quarter of the men received under £750 and 45 per cent under £1,500. Only 5 per cent of all women received payments between £3,251 and £4,750 (maximum payment for 1986) while the respective figure for men was 25 per cent. More recent payments made only to employees whose employers were insolvent show similar trends (Figure 9.1).

These figures highlight the low level of statutory minimum redundancy payments for both men and women. However, women receive lower redundancy payments than men and a larger proportion of them are ineligible for payments altogether. This makes women cheaper to dismiss and makes them more vulnerable to redundancy. The legislation therefore perpetuates women's disadvantaged position in the labour market and reinforces their economic dependency out of employment, as will be shown shortly. Nevertheless, redundancy payments play a special role for women because they may be the *sole* source of financial compensation for job loss. This is due to the nature of social security provision to which we now turn.

Access to social security payments[3]

Men's and women's claims to social security income maintenance have been subject to different assumptions. Assumptions about the economic relationship between men and women in the family and the sexual divisions of labour in the

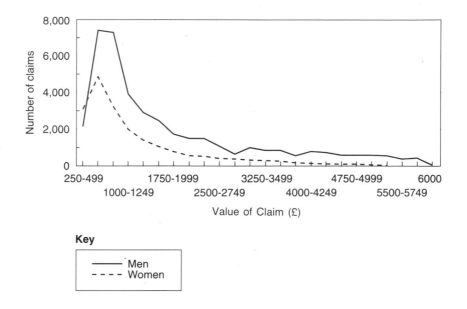

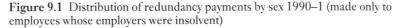

Figure 9.1 Distribution of redundancy payments by sex 1990–1 (made only to employees whose employers were insolvent)

(Source: Department of Employment unpublished statistics)

home and workplace underpin social security provision. These assumptions are very apparent in relation to unemployment benefit.

Unemployment benefit

Until the Social Security Pensions Act 1975 married women were either ineligible for full unemployment benefit or, by opting for reduced National Insurance contributions, were excluded altogether. Since the implementation of this legislation in 1978, only married women and widows already paying reduced contributions could continue to do so, provided they did not leave the labour market for more than two years. Married women, like single women and men, therefore became eligible for unemployment benefit (if they had paid full National Insurance contributions). However, in 1989, 20 per cent of married women were still paying reduced National Insurance contributions compared with 34 per cent in 1984 and 64 per cent in 1978 (unpublished statistics, DHSS, 1986; DSS, 1991).

There are other reasons why women are unable to build up sufficient National Insurance contributions and are thereby denied access to unemployment benefit. Indeed, a recent survey showed that more women than men did not receive unemployment benefit because of inadequate contributions (Erens and Hedges, 1990). Changes in contribution conditions mean that higher paid people qualify for benefits faster than lower paid people and this especially affects women who make up the majority of low-paid workers. The 1988 Social Security Act also tightened the contribution tests, making receipt of benefit conditional on two years' consecutive employment immediately prior to claiming. In the same year, it became harder to re-qualify for unemployment benefit once entitlement had been exhausted. All these changes in contribution conditions strengthened the link between recent employment and unemployment benefit, whereby claimants have to 'earn' their right to benefit. Paradoxically, they also encourage a greater reliance on means-tested benefits, which are divorced from employment records. However, they particularly affect women with their discontinuous employment patterns and temporary jobs. Most important of all, their impact falls in particular on those groups of women who have the least recourse to income support (see below).

Other recent changes have generally restricted access to unemployment benefit (Atkinson and Micklewright, 1989) and, in particular, they have denied benefit to women who had been eligible to at least some benefit in their own right. Two examples will suffice. First, the Social Security Act 1986, which abolished the reduced rate of unemployment and other National Insurance benefits where contributions were not fully satisfied, especially affected the low paid and those with discontinuous employment patterns. In 1985, 21,838 women received reduced rates of benefits, of whom an estimated 78 per cent would have been unlikely to have had any independent entitlement to any other benefit, thus rendering them economically dependent upon their partners (unpublished statistics, DHSS, 1986).

Secondly, unemployed people with temporary part-time jobs, who earn above the lower earnings limit, can no longer claim unemployment benefit. Since 1989 benefits have been calculated on a daily basis rather than a weekly basis. If a part-timer earns above the limit (£52 per week for 1991/2) on any one day, s/he receives no benefit at all for the rest of the week. Previously they would have lost benefit solely for the one day on which they earned above the limit. Women are most affected by this change as they are much more likely than men to receive money from a part-time job while unemployed (Erens and Hedges, 1990). The net result is to deter part-time employment among unemployed people and to increase women's economic reliance on their partners.

People who normally work part-time and earn below the National Insurance earnings threshold pay no contributions and receive no contributory benefits. Data on the numbers of people affected, and women in particular, are not readily available and are difficult to calculate (Hakim, 1989). In 1984 it was estimated that three-fifths of part-time workers – some 2.75 million employees, mostly women – were earning below the National Insurance threshold (*Employment Gazette*, 1984) and, given the rise in female part-time employment, the figure would be much higher today.[4] Indeed Hakim (1989) suggests that during the late 1980s there was a gradual increase in both the absolute numbers and the proportion of the workforce outside the National Insurance net. She estimates that for 1987/8 about 2.2 million people in employment fell outside this net. Of these, four-fifths were women and over four-fifths were part-time workers. Overall, about 18 per cent of all working women, but only 3 per cent of men, had earnings below the National Insurance threshold and so women were seven times more likely than men to be outside the National Insurance net (Hakim, 1989, p. 480).

Even where part-time (and full-time) workers earn above the limit, they still may be disqualified from unemployment benefit unless they can satisfy the DSS that they can make adequate care arrangements for children or an elderly/sick person within twenty-four hours of finding a job. Thus the presence of dependants is used as a means of excluding women from benefits.

The 1989 Social Security Act, which strengthened the tests of availability for work and actively seeking work, penalises women with domestic commitments yet further. Now claimants have to be both available and be prepared to accept *full-time* employment. After a maximum 'permitted period' of thirteen weeks, claimants can neither impose restrictions on the nature, hours, rate of pay or location of work for which they are available, nor refuse a job handled by the Employment Service for those reasons. Hence the many women who, for domestic reasons, only want a part-time local job may have their unemployment benefit and income support reduced or withdrawn.

Claimants also have to show that they are taking 'reasonable steps' to actively find work each week. They are expected to use a diversity of job search methods and to keep records of their job-seeking activities which they have to show when interviewed by an Employment Service counsellor. These regulations put a premium on formal job search methods which can be recorded, such as Jobcentres and newspapers, rather than informal methods of seeking employment, such as unsolicited visits or letters to employers. Not surprisingly, employers have reported an increase in formal methods, especially Jobcentres, and unsolicited written applications from the unemployed since the regulations came into force (Callender and Metcalf, 1991). However, other research shows that these methods are not the best for actually securing a job, especially for women (Callender, 1988). Women are *most* likely to get a job, and particularly part-time work, via informal social networks and the importance of this successful method increases with duration of unemployment (Erens and Hedges, 1990). Hence, these regulations penalise those unemployed who use successful, but the least observable, job search strategies and may discourage them from using those strategies. It is paradoxical that the single most successful job strategy is the least active and the most difficult to prove (Callender, 1989).

Other recent regulations concern the suspension of unemployment benefit or a reduction of income support for people who left their job voluntarily without good cause. The 1986 Social Security Act extended the disqualification period from six to thirteen weeks and in April 1988 it was increased again to twenty-six weeks. The distinction between voluntary and involuntary unemployment is blurred and may affect women disproportionately. For instance, women may be forced to leave their job for domestic reasons or to follow their partner to a new job. Indeed, research suggests that being classified as 'voluntary' unemployed is one of the most important reasons why women in particular are denied benefit (Erens and Hedges, 1990).

In addition, both unemployment benefit and income support, under certain circumstances, can be withdrawn or suspended if claimants fail to comply with the range of new procedures aimed at policing their behaviour; for instance, if they fail to attend counselling or Restart (introduced in 1986) interviews with Employment Service Officers or turn down 'positive offers' of help from the Restart menu, such as employment or a training programme. However, figures disaggregated by sex on the numbers of claimants who have had their benefit withdrawn for such reasons are not readily available.

Income support

Unemployed people, depending on their circumstances, may be eligible for means-tested income support in addition to unemployment benefit. Once their entitlement to unemployment benefit expires (after twelve months), they are totally dependent on income support.

Until 1983, married and cohabiting women could never claim the means-tested benefit of the time – supplementary benefit. To comply with the EC Directive 79/7, complex rules were introduced allowing them to claim under very restrictive circumstances. However, when income support replaced supplementary benefit in 1988 under the 1986 Social Security Act, either partner was freely allowed to claim income support when both were unemployed. However, a couple's income continued to be aggregated and any progress towards the effective (rather than formal) equal treatment of men and women was undermined by the introduction of the 'full-time exclusion clause'. If one partner is in full-time employment (redefined as twenty-four hours or more per week and from April 1992 as sixteen hours per week), the other no longer has the right to claim income support. As a result, the number of women eligible for income support has been radically reduced. In addition, the clause is likely to deter both employed women from continuing with low-paid jobs and women returners from entering such employment when their partners are unemployed. If the partner continues working, the couple may have to survive on an income below the statutory safety net. As the Social Security Advisory Committee has commented:

Table 9.2 Benefit position of unemployed claimants in Great Britain by sex and marital status – February 1991 (percentages)

	Men	Married women	Other women	Total	Women as % of each recipient group
	%	%	%	%	
Unemployment benefit only	18.8	45.1	17.3	20.6	30.7
Unemployment benefit + income support	5.4	1.0	1.8	4.4	8.3*
Income support only	61.8	19.9	66.2	59.2	20.5*
Not in receipt of benefit	13.8	33.8	14.5	15.5	32.0
Total	100	100	100	100	

* The majority of these are 'other women' rather than 'married women'.

Source: Department of Social Security, 1991, *Unemployment Benefit Statistics: Quarterly analysis of unemployed claimants* (UB2), February.

> There is already substantial evidence to show that the wives of unemployed claimants are less likely to work and more likely to stop working once their husbands are unemployed, than other women. This tendency should not be encouraged by the benefit system. (SSAC, 1985, p. 83)

One of the main thrusts of the social security reforms of the 1980s was to improve labour market discipline and, in particular, increase work incentives and reduce reliance on state benefits. However, the concern was gender-specific, focusing on men and appearing unnecessary or irrelevant for women. As Lister (1987, p. 15) has commented, 'The concept of financial and economic independence for women does not get a look in.' Overall, women's claims to maintenance from the state both determine and are determined by their relationship to their families and the formal labour market.

Together, these factors contribute to the low percentage of unemployed women claiming unemployment benefit and income support and to the stark gender differences in patterns of income maintenance among unemployed people (Table 9.2). Moreover, as suggested earlier, these figures under-represent the number of unemployed women, rendering their unemployment invisible.

In these social security provisions we see a set of values and institutional arrangements which condition the position and experience of those out of work, and which is both premised upon and reinforces a male-dominated notion of unemployment. It is to these experiences of unemployment and social security that we now turn.

Women's experiences of unemployment and social security

There is debate on the extent to which women's varying experiences of social security and unemployment are different from those of men. Coyle (1984) stresses the differences, while Dex (1985) emphasises the similarities, although she acknowledges the lack of research in this area. More recent research (Erens and Hedges, 1990) shows both important similarities and differences. Several factors point to the differences in the experience of unemployment: women's position in the labour market and access to occupational benefits; their domestic roles and the dominant familial ideology; their lack of control over household resources; their problematic identification with the 'unemployed status'; and their treatment by the DSS, Jobcentres, the Benefits Agency, Training and Enterprise Councils and the Training, Enterprise and Employment Directorate of the Department of Employment.

Ironically, these qualitative differences between men and women have actually been used to explain away and neglect women's unemployment; their unemployment is not perceived as a problem because it is not the same as men's. The 'real' problems, which are associated in politics, policy and academe with persistent high unemployment, are those of men.

The following empirical evidence suggests that despite the existence of some differences in the experience of unemployment, women's unemployment is a significant issue, although the nature of women's problems and concerns do differ from those of men. However, significant similarities do exist, too. These similarities belie the assumptions (based on the declared differences) that women's unemployment does not matter. The point is that the differences and similarities are not necessarily mutually exclusive; rather, they both raise gender-specific issues.

Some of these issues will now be illustrated by the experiences of a group of married women made redundant following the partial closure of a clothing factory in South Wales. The clothing factory, which was opened in 1939, is part of a multinational company and until recently the major employer of female labour in the area. The factory is located in a sub-region where both male and female unemployment rates are well above the national average. The redundancies took place in stages from 1979 to 1981, reducing the workforce from more than 1,500 to 500. However, certain types of women were 'selected out' by the redundancy process; they tended to be disadvantaged in human capital terms, which made them vulnerable to poverty (Callender, 1986b).

All the women in the study were or had been married and were aged between 20 and 59. They had been made redundant involuntarily and had worked full-time in the factory in low-paid, unskilled manual jobs on the shopfloor. When the women were made redundant in 1981, their weekly take-home pay averaged

£55 and for half of the women it was the only wage in the household. The majority of the interviews took place between nine and twelve months after the women's redundancy.

The women's financial situation on becoming unemployed depended on their eligibility for redundancy payments and unemployment benefit. Redundancy payments, ranging from £50 to £598, were received by most of the women. The majority of payments were too small to replace the income lost from earnings and, therefore, were used to supplement other income, to buy goods for the home or saved for emergencies. The women recognised the inadequacy of their compensation:

> If Brian [husband] was working . . . maybe I could have put the money away for a rainy day, but in our place . . . you more or less need it. What is £300? It's nothing, is it? Nothing compared with when you've got a wage of £60 a week, is it?

Claiming unemployment benefit and registering for work

Once unemployed, redundancy payments were the only monies received by half the women interviewed, because they were ineligible for unemployment benefit. Older women were least likely to be eligible because they had started working at the factory when the married women's option (i.e. to pay reduced NI contributions) was in full operation and the majority had not considered it financially worthwhile to pay full contributions. They had entered into complex calculations, weighing up the potential loss of both short- and long-term benefits against the extra cash in their pay packets and had decided to maximise their already low pay at the time they most needed it. Other women had thought their employment would only be temporary and so believed they would not be in the labour market long enough to build up sufficient contributions. Yet others had correctly calculated that they were too old or their employment patterns too discontinuous to be eligible for pensions. Although not all women were aware of the consequences of having paid reduced contributions, none of them had anticipated being made redundant.

All the women who had paid full National Insurance contributions had sufficient contributions to be eligible for unemployment benefit. Most of these women had negative experiences of claiming benefit. Like men in similar situations, the women stressed the feelings of stigma, shame and humiliation in claiming benefit. Encountering unsympathetic staff in a physically depressing environment ('It's a depressing place, cold, the clocks don't work'), many women found the experience alienating and impersonal: 'I just sign my name, feel like a convict, lining up and all that.' Another woman observed: 'You are nothing. You go in a line like everybody else, you feel the same as everybody else . . . You are just one of a million.' It was an experience which could not be divorced from the notion of scrounging. Indeed, a recurrent theme among these women was that they felt they had no right to benefit, that they were getting something for nothing, in marked contrast to a wage. As one woman said:

> It's the thought of having to be there . . . You feel you're going begging – oh, give me a job, give me a job, sort of thing. You feel you're begging for something that isn't there. You feel you're begging for money . . . Probably it's money that's coming to me because I have paid insurance. But it's not the same as having a wage, it's not the same as having a pay-packet. You sign this piece of paper, you feel as if you're scrounging, you're getting something for nothing.

The 'street-level bureaucracy' (Lipsky, 1981) which the women faced added to their sense of powerlessness, alienation and distrust of officialdom. Only a small minority had claimed unemployment benefit before and so they found the complex procedures bewildering and confusing. As one woman said, 'It all made me feel uncomfortable. What questions are they going to ask now, and have I got the right answers. Oh I don't like signing on the dole.'

Women's receipt of unemployment benefit automatically meant they had registered for work.[5] However, several women who received no benefits also registered, although the majority in this position did not, because they desired to be self-sufficient and free from official agencies. They preferred to avoid contact with what they considered an alienating agent of the state's authority. This feeling was compounded by confusion over the respective roles and functions of the Department of Employment, the Department of Health and Social Security, the Manpower Services Commission, the 'dole', unemployment benefit offices, employment offices and Jobcentres. Not surprisingly, there was a widespread uncertainty about what registration entailed, about whether they were eligible to register, and about whether it was relevant to their needs, as Cragg and Dawson (1984) also discovered.

Some women did not perceive themselves as unemployed and so felt it was not legitimate to register. This rejection of the 'unemployed' label is probably associated with the blurring of the boundaries for women between employment and economic inactivity and between unemployment and economic activity which renders their classification in the labour market problematic (Callender, 1985). Other women did not want to adopt the 'unemployed' label associated with registering for work or did not want confirmation of their unemployed status. Some women did not register because they were discouraged from looking for paid work because of the poor state of the economy. Finally, the attitudes of some women illustrated the 'queuing principle' (Martin and Wallace, 1984), namely, that in times of high unemployment, certain social groups are felt to have greater claims to paid employment. In other words, some women defined themselves out of the labour market because they felt that they were unlikely to get paid work or because they believed that they had no right to paid work. However, it must be emphasised that all the women who chose not to register for work actually did want paid employment and took up any employment opportunities which arose (Callender, 1986a). Moreover, as Cragg and Dawson (1984, p. 43) found, there was no significant correlation between registration and success in finding employment.

The financial impact of unemployment

Townsend's (1979) work has firmly established the links between unemployment and poverty. His notion of relative deprivation, with its focus on social well-being, activities and the social construction of need, highlights the importance of employment as a major source of participation within society. However, his analysis fails to consider fully how experiences of unemployment and thus poverty associated with unemployment are gender-specific (Callender, 1988). The following analysis therefore incorporates Townsend's emphasis on the non-material aspects of poverty but, in addition, exposes the gender-specific dynamics of poverty.

A common assumption made about female unemployment is that it does not cause financial hardship in the same way it does for men. Such assumptions have been used as a partial justification for women's ineligibility for social security benefits. However, the loss of income of the women studied did have a considerable impact upon them and their families.

The extent of financial hardship varied among the women depending upon the size of their redundancy payment, whether they received unemployment and/or supplementary benefit, their earning status in the household, the employment status of their partner, whether there were other sources of income and how the family managed its income. Inevitably, the financial consequences were most immediate and dramatic for those women who were not in receipt of benefit or who were the sole wage earners. In fact, about a third of the women were both the sole earners *and* were ineligible for unemployment benefit. However, without exception, all the women had to make some economies because their wages had been an essential part of the household economy and their benefits were too low to compensate for their lost earnings. Interestingly, it was only with this loss that many husbands realised the importance of their spouse's wage to the family.

There were large variations in the systems (Pahl, 1989) used by the households both to manage and control their income (see Gillian Parker's chapter here). Nevertheless, in the majority of cases it was the women who managed the money by taking responsibility for day-to-day budgeting arrangements, paying the bills and organising the family finances. Consequently, they had the worry of juggling finances and trying to make ends meet. However, they did not always have control over the money or make the key decisions over how it was spent and distributed.

In general, the women in the study had spent their wages on food, items for the children or had saved some money while their husband's wages were spent on larger bills. Usually the women kept some money 'for their own' to buy themselves make-up, tights or clothes, and pay for the occasional trip or night out (see Pahl, 1989). Once unemployed, this small sum was the first economy all the women made. Even if they received unemployment benefit it was usually spent entirely on food. In other words, they cut first and most their personal consumption rather than collective consumption. With the loss of their pay-packet and 'their' money they lost a sense of independence and freedom – vital ingredients to women's social well-being. They lost their 'little treats' and 'extras' which were an important bonus of paid employment. By contrast, the husbands, irrespective of their employment status, nearly always had some 'pocket money' (although the sum may have been reduced) which reflected their control over the family finances.

The economies made on collective consumption and their effects on the family ranged from cutbacks on savings, which had little immediate impact but rocked their sense of security, to cutbacks on essentials like food, which signalled hard-hitting poverty. Most women were more cautious and conscious about how they spent the household's money but about half were just 'living from week to week', struggling to meet their financial commitments with every penny of the weekly budget accounted for. They curtailed their social activities, they abandoned trying to save, they dispensed with their holiday plans, home improvements and repairs, their cars, telephones and televisions. As one woman who had a disabled unemployed husband commented:

> The telephone bill came, it was only £24. Well it was either that or stuff for the kids. You can't see the kids without so he [husband] let it be cut off. Of course to have it put back on would cost another £9 extra. With his leg and one thing and another it does make a difference having a 'phone . . . Now it's like robbing Peter to pay Paul, you're not living, you're just existing. Now you've got to think twice before you can breath tidy.

The women cashed in insurance policies and used up their savings and redundancy money. They cut down on cigarettes, food, heating and lighting, and stopped buying clothes and presents. Little or no monies were allocated to maintaining their worker status – they could not afford special trips to the Jobcentre or to visit factories, a finding echoed in more recent research (Erens and Hedges, 1990). All these economies were necessary not because the women's husbands were unwilling to share the money but usually because none was available.

It was the women who had to make hard decisions and choices as to what expenditure to cut or what bill could be postponed for yet another week. They dreaded the unanticipated bill or unforeseen expenditure. It was primarily up to the women to devise strategies for saving money, especially within spheres of expenditure that they both managed and controlled. They shopped around for bargains and cheaper food; were more selective as to what food was bought; and cooked cheaper but filling meals which often took longer to prepare. As one woman remarked: 'I used to buy a lot of biscuits and things. Well, cake, we don't even know what it looks like now, a piece of cake. It's a luxury isn't it? Meat, you just can't run to it.' Shopping was a skilled but painful exercise, as one woman observed:

> Shopping in the supermarket, you're going around and looking and you know you can't have it, you have to leave it. That's the hardest thing . . . You can't just go in and pick up everything you need, you've got to stop and you've got to think. And you'll have one thing one week and something else another.

Other strategies to 'save' money included joining clubs to purchase essentials which they could not afford to pay for in a lump sum, although being aware of the extra costs of the high interest on such purchases; having slot meters installed to control electricity consumption; and delaying lighting the fire until later in the day to conserve coal:

> In the morning some get up and light the fire straight away, I can't afford to. When the children go to school I leave Brian [unemployed husband] and Kim [unemployed daughter] to stop in bed. Well, perhaps I won't light the fire until half past eleven or something to try and make it go that bit further.

It was the women who had to face their children's disappointment at their unmet wants and it was the women who constantly had to say no:

> You tell the kids they can't have this and they can't have that. And they want to know why . . . 'cos the other children have got them and why can't they have this and why can't they do this . . . it's hard, it's really hard on them. The children would come in, perhaps their friends are going to the pictures, and sometimes I'd cry because I know mine can't go. Whereas before, when I was working, I could give it to them. But not now and they don't understand.

And often it was the women who sacrificed their own needs to satisfy those of the rest of the family. It was a draining and depressing experience, as one woman commented:

> You do get a lot of tension trying to make ends meet . . . And the worst part of being unemployed is having to be always broke . . . thinking over where's the next money going to come from.

The social effects of unemployment

The material deprivation many women and their families experienced was only one aspect of their poverty. A major economy all the women faced was a reduction in their social lives. They could no longer afford to go to the pubs, clubs or bingo, nor the occasional day out or trip. These activities had to be either totally abandoned or curtailed. Fun was an expensive commodity that many of the women could no longer afford. With this reduction of social activities came a sense of social exclusion. Even prior to redundancy, many of the women did not have a particularly extensive social life because of the constraints of their working and domestic lives. They had had little time to socialise and some had lost contacts with friends and neighbours as a direct result of being in full-time employment. Most socialising had been concentrated within the private domestic sphere with their female kin and children. Unemployment exacerbated and accentuated the already privatised nature of their lives. With the loss of their paid employment outside the home, both their social contacts and horizons were radically curtailed. Their world became even more confined and focused on the home. They thus became excluded from the social networks of employed people which are vital for job-acquisition (Callender, 1986a). With this constrained lifestyle came boredom and loneliness. In this respect, unemployed married women probably find their circumstances significantly different from those of unemployed men, many of whom are likely to have their wives at home to provide company (Martin and Wallace, 1984).

Two of the things the women had valued most when they were in employment were the social interaction and companionship of their friendly workmates. It was this company they sorely missed once unemployed. For most of the women, paid work had been a route out of the family and domestic and financial dependence. As one woman commented:

> I have missed working. I've missed the company as much as the money. Before, I loved being at home but I loved being in work too and I do miss it, the girls and all. I still haven't really settled to it because my nerves have gone all wonky being in the house. It's all right when the children are here but when everybody goes I am back on my own all day.

With the loss of their jobs they not only lost a sense of financial security, they also lost a sense of personal security. Being in employment had given these women personal confidence, a sense of independence, autonomy and pride. As one woman said:

> I think you feel more of a person because you're independent. I loved that. You are more independent, you're contributing, not only helping and doing in the home but you're bringing in some money as well. You're not entirely dependent on your husband. And I think you have much more confidence, you're bound to, mixing with people. As I say, you feel more of a person.

Time and again the women stressed their loss of independence and with that loss came frustration, insecurity and a sense of worthlessness 'commensurate with that which men experience over the loss of their breadwinner status' (Coyle, 1984, p. 107).

It should be stressed that the women did not question their roles as housewives and mothers. Rather, it was the financing of that role that led to the feelings of dependency. Moreover, housework was a highly privatised activity which was not as well regarded and was much less interesting than paid employment. Nor could these married women return easily to their previous domestic roles if, in the course of their employment, their children had grown up.

In short, the expectations and attitudes of these women had changed as a result of their experiences of paid work. Going out to work had become the normal pattern of their lives, not a deviant one. The loss of paid work did not mean, therefore, a return to a 'normal' way of life, but a change to a new, more restricted and less rewarding one. As Martin (1983, p. 22) suggests: 'When full-time working women become unemployed they do not move from one role to another, they simply lose one – like men.' Nevertheless, the family did cushion the blow of job loss for some women and their domestic role did offer a way of making sense of their experience. Indeed, a few women embraced domesticity and the family and tried to become more involved in, for example, their extended family. One woman 'decided to have a baby so I wouldn't be lonely in the house on my own and there was not much chance of me getting a job'. What is evident from the women studied is that they wanted and needed paid work for economic, social, psychological and personal reasons. These wider, non-material aspects of unemployment and poverty remain untouched by any legislative provision.

For a third of the women these hardships were temporarily alleviated when they obtained new paid employment. However, with one exception, none of these new jobs were permanent; some were part-time, and all were low-paid. Yet again, these women continued to be excluded from both redundancy and social security provisions but this time in rather different ways. None of their jobs lasted long enough for them to be eligible for redundancy pay and they remained unprotected by employment protection legislation. Some jobs were too short-lived for them to build up sufficient contributions to acquire eligibility for unemployment benefit. Several jobs were paid below the National Insurance contribution threshold (Hakim, 1989), while other women did jobs like running catalogues which were not recognised as 'work'.

These women's experiences reflect the disenfranchisement and casualisation of many women's work. They highlight the false assumptions which underpin much social security provision. Women's role in the labour market was not secondary to their domestic responsibilities. For many of the women, paid employment was part of being a 'good' mother and providing for their children – providing not extras but vital necessities. These women did not work for 'pin money' – their contribution to the family economy was paramount. Part-time employment was often the only paid employment they could find, while others had little choice but to work part-time if they were to fulfil their changing domestic commitments. Discontinuous employment was an integral part of these women's working lives.

Conclusion

Poverty not only exists as a consumption experience but it is also related to labour market experience. We have seen how the redundancy payments scheme disadvantages women in comparison with men. Its effects are to make women more vulnerable to job loss, to exclude or only inequitably compensate them, and to perpetuate poverty through insufficient payments. Once women are unemployed, social security benefits are also unlikely to provide an adequate (if any) replacement income for their lost wages. Both redundancy payments and social security benefits are totally inappropriate for dealing with today's long-term structural unemployment and play no role in compensating for recurrent unemployment or the casualisation of work. Their shortcomings help swell the growing numbers of the 'new' unemployed and the 'new' poor; women whose unemployment and poverty remain hidden. Neither redundancy payments nor social security benefits are rooted in the reality of women's working lives. Rather, they are based on misplaced assumptions and upon male-dominated notions of employment. They therefore fail to consider the position of women in the labour market. But that market, by its very nature, leads to gender inequalities and poverty, too, as the unemployed women's replacement jobs illustrate.

These women's experiences of poverty demonstrate its different facets. Being unemployed has all the social, psychological and moral effects characteristic of men but with additional gender-specific dynamics. The women in this study may not have identified with the 'unemployed' status, but employment remained a central organising principle of their lives. They acutely felt its loss; the loss of their independence in both the public and private spheres; the constant financial pressures; and the frustrations of having 'to live every day at home in poverty'.

Notes

1. All employers used to receive a rebate of 35 per cent of their redundancy bill from the Redundancy Fund. From 1986, only employers with less than ten employees were eligible, but this exemption was subsequently abolished in 1990. It is estimated that nearly £200 million in 1987–8 would be saved by the government (Department of Employment, 1986). As a result of this change, no statistics are now available on the size of redundancy payments made directly by employers. The only data currently available are on payments to employees whose employers were insolvent.
2. In October 1991, the Equal Opportunities Commission unsuccessfully challenged these hours thresholds in the High Court under a Judicial Review. The EOC claimed that the thresholds contravened the European Directive on Equal Treatment by discriminating against part-time women workers. The Court decided that although the hours thresholds did amount to indirect

discrimination, they were not contrary to European Community law since they could be 'objectively justified' on policy grounds.

3. The following review is selective and concentrates on the way unemployment benefit impacts on women. For a fuller review of social security provision for the unemployed and the detailed regulations, see Morris and Llewellyn, 1991; CPAG, 1991.

4. Unfortunately, the Department of Employment was unable to provide more recent statistics on the grounds that they would be too costly to collate.

5. At the time the fieldwork was conducted and until the Social Security Housing Benefit Act 1982, it was compulsory for all those claiming unemployment benefit to register for work at a Jobcentre. Registration is now voluntary at Jobcentres.

10 *Lone mothers and poverty*

Jane Millar

Currently there are over 1 million lone mothers in Great Britain, of whom about two-thirds are living in poverty. Lone mothers are perhaps the most 'visible' of all poor women. One of the themes of this book is that measures of poverty which are based on the family or the household as the unit of measurement cannot accurately reflect the true extent of poverty among women because they take no account of what happens inside the family. However, because they are 'heads of households', lone mothers do show up more readily in the statistics (that is, when they are not partially hidden in the category of 'lone parent'). Thus we know much more about the extent of poverty among lone mothers than among other women.

However, this does not mean that the causes of poverty are different for lone mothers. On the contrary, it is precisely because lone mothers are women that they have a very high risk of poverty. The situation of lone mothers – their position in the labour market and their treatment in the social security system – reflects particular assumptions about women and their roles. Analysing the economic position of lone mothers in the context of the economic position of women in general is therefore the only way to understand the causes of their poverty. Conversely, examining the situation of lone mothers, where the consequences of the economic inequalities between men and women are so clearly seen, also casts light upon the nature and causes of these inequalities.

Since the first edition of this book was published in 1987 the financial situation of lone mothers has deteriorated – the gap between the incomes of lone mothers and other families with children has widened and the risk of poverty has significantly increased. In October 1990 the government published a White Paper *Children Come First* (DSS, 1990a) which proposed substantial changes to the arrangements for child maintenance when parents separate. In effect these proposals, due to be enacted in 1992 and 1993, set out to replace state financial support for lone mothers with private financial support from former partners. The second part of the chapter looks at these new arrangements and the issues they raise in more detail. The first part sets the scene by examining the extent of poverty among lone mothers in the 1980s and the impact this poverty has on the lives of lone mothers and their children.

The extent of poverty among lone mothers

As discussed in Chapter 1 government statistics obscure almost as much as they reveal the extent of poverty among women. Nevertheless the official statistics show that, in the 1980s, lone parents have come to be more and more concentrated at the bottom of the income distribution (House of Commons Social Security Committee, 1991). In 1979 29 per cent of lone parents had incomes of less than half of the average (income here is measured net of tax and National Insurance, after housing costs, and taking into account family size). In 1988 59 per cent of lone parents had incomes below this level, amounting to 1.6 million adults and children. Couples with children also fared badly during the 1980s, but their risk of poverty still remains much lower than that of lone parents (18 per cent in 1988, up from 9 per cent in 1979).

Family Expenditure Survey data also show the widening gap between the incomes of lone parents and the incomes of couples with children. In 1979 the average disposable income (after tax and National Insurance contributions) of households consisting of a lone parent and children was £70.46 compared with £123.30 for a couple with two children (DE, 1980). Thus the incomes of the lone parents were equivalent to about 57 per cent of those of the couples. In 1989 the average income for lone parents was £134.61 compared with £339.71 for the couples with two children, equivalent by then to only 40 per cent (DE, 1990c). In real terms the average incomes of lone parents have fallen – if their incomes had gone up in line with the Retail Price Index then they would have been about £12 per week higher in 1989. By contrast the incomes of couples with children have risen significantly above the rate of inflation. Thus lone parents were both relatively and absolutely worse off by the end of the 1980s than they had been at the start of the decade (see also Roll, 1988a, 1988b). All these statistics relate to lone parents as a whole and not separately to lone mothers and lone fathers. However, other evidence shows that lone mothers are in general worse off than lone fathers (Knight, 1981; Millar, 1989; Bradshaw and Millar, 1991).

There are two main, and related, reasons why lone mothers have become so much worse off financially during the 1980s. The first is that they have become much more reliant upon state benefits: first supplementary benefit and latterly income support (which replaced supplementary benefit in 1988). In 1979 there were 309,000 lone mothers receiving supplementary benefit, by 1989 this had risen to 737,000 lone mothers receiving income support (DSS, 1991). To put it another way, in the late 1970s about 45 per cent of all lone mothers were receiving supplementary benefit, by the late 1980s over 70 per cent of all lone mothers were receiving income support. Of all children in families on income support, 62 per cent are in lone-parent families.

The second reason for rising poverty – and the flip-side of increased receipt of state benefits – has been falling employment rates, especially the rates of full-time employment. In 1977/9 about 47 per cent of lone mothers were employed, 22 per cent full-time and 24 per cent part-time. In 1986/8 only 39 per cent of lone mothers were employed, 17 per cent full-time and 22 per cent part-time (OPCS, 1990). However, employment is not a guarantee against poverty, even for those who have full-time jobs. A national survey of lone parents carried out in 1989 found that 65 per cent of lone mothers working twenty-four or more hours per week were low paid, defined as earning less than two-thirds of median male hourly earnings (Bradshaw and Millar, 1991). So both lack of employment and low pay for those who are employed have contributed to the higher poverty rates.

While the employment rates of lone mothers have been falling those of married mothers have been rising. In 1986/8 56 per cent of married mothers were employed, 18 per cent full-time and 38 per cent part-time (OPCS, 1990). Many of these married women are also low paid, especially those in part-time jobs, and this means they too have a high risk of being poor (Millar, 1991a; Susan Lonsdale's chapter here). But in terms of family income the growth in the number of two-earner couples means that the gap in the incomes and living standards between lone mothers and other families with children has become wider.

Looking back

However, neither the fact that lone mothers have a very high risk of poverty nor the fact that they are very likely to be dependent on state income support are particularly new. For example, in York at the turn of the century Rowntree found that the second most common cause of poverty after low wages was the 'death of the chief wage-earner', accounting for 28 per cent of all poor households and 16 per cent of all poor persons (Rowntree, 1902, p. 120). Most of these women were widows, although a small number (3 per cent) were 'deserted or separated' wives. Not all of these widows would have had dependent children of course, but a significant proportion must have done as there were 460 children under 14 in the 403 households in this group.

Rowntree's later study in York (Rowntree, 1941) suggested that the introduction of widow's benefits had led to a substantial decrease in the extent of poverty among lone mothers. But of course these benefits did nothing for the increasing number of lone mothers who were not widows but who were unmarried or, more commonly, divorced or separated. Thus in the early 1950s – after the post-war welfare reforms – lone mothers were again heavily over-represented among the poor. In 1953/4 19 per cent of all poor families with dependent children were 'headed' by a lone mother compared with only 5 per cent of all families with dependent children (Abel-Smith and Townsend, 1965, p. 33). This over-representation of lone mothers among poor families has been found over and over again (e.g. Finer, 1974; Fiegehen *et al.*, 1977; Layard *et al.*, 1978; Townsend, 1979; Mack and Lansley, 1985).

Similarly, there is a long tradition of receipt of state benefits. Snell and Millar (1987) have estimated that about 30 per cent of all families receiving parish relief under the old Poor Law (prior to 1834) were lone mothers; and Thane (1978) has pointed out that, throughout the period of the operation of the new Poor Law, women (often widows or deserted or separated mothers) made up the majority of adult recipients of relief.

Thus although poverty among lone mothers has increased in the 1980s, as a group they have long been vulnerable to poverty. This poverty has become much more visible in recent years because the number of lone-parent families has increased so dramatically. In 1971 there were about 570,000 lone parents in Great Britain, in 1976 about 750,000, in 1986 about 1,010,000 and in 1989 about 1,150,000 (Haskey, 1991). About 17 per cent of all families with children are now headed by a lone parent, nine in ten of whom are lone mothers. However, even this situation is not 'new' if looked at over the longer term. As Anderson (1983) has pointed out, marital breakdown rates in the nineteenth century were probably not very different from those found today, the difference being that divorce rather than death is now the main cause of lone parenthood. Similarly, estimates based on parish records suggest that in the late eighteenth and early nineteenth centuries on average about 19 per cent of all families with children were lone-parent families (Snell and Millar, 1987).

The experience of poverty

The 'typical' lone mother is hard to find because the phrase covers so many people with so many diverse experiences. Table 10.1 shows some of the family characteristics of lone mothers, lone fathers and couples. Just over half of lone mothers have only one dependent child, two-fifths have a youngest child of under school age, the average age of the women is 32 years but a fifth (mainly

Table 10.1 Family characteristics of lone parents and married couples, 1987/8

	Lone mothers	Lone fathers	Couples with children
	%	%	%
Number of children			
One	56	65	40
Two	28	27	43
Three or more	15	8	17
Age of youngest child			
Under 5	42	9	42
5–9	27	21	25
10 plus	32	71	33
Age of parent*			
Under 25	21	1	4
25–34	39	13	31
35 plus	40	84	66
Mean age	32	40	38
Base (= 100%)	(886)	(82)	(5,602)

* Age of father in couples.

Source: OPCS (1990), *General Household Survey 1988*, Tables 2.20, 2.21, 2.39.

single women) are aged under 25. Lone fathers are older and usually have only one, often teenage, child. Couples are also older than lone mothers, tend to have larger families, but about the same proportion have a youngest child of under school age.

Most lone parents – both men and women – have been married and are separated or divorced from their former partners. Among lone mothers 58 per cent are ex-married, 35 per cent are single and 7 per cent are widowed (Haskey, 1991). The numbers of single mothers have risen dramatically in the 1980s (from 130,000 in 1976 to 360,000 in 1989) but they nevertheless remain in the minority among lone mothers. Bradshaw and Millar (1991) found that about 17 per cent of the single mothers in their sample had lived with their former partners before becoming a lone parent. They also found that the ex-married women had been married for about eight years, on average, before becoming lone mothers. Sixty per cent of the single women and 47 per cent of the ex-married women no longer had any contact with their former partner.

About 18 per cent of Black families are headed by a lone parent compared with about 15 per cent of white families (Haskey, 1991). There are quite wide variations between the different ethnic groups in the proportion of lone-parent families. Among families of West Indian origin as many as 49 per cent are lone-parent families, as are 30 per cent of African families but only 6 per cent of Indian and 8 per cent of Pakistani families. For all these different groups, and for white families, the experience of being a lone mother will differ with differences in family and kinship networks, and in attitudes towards lone parenthood. For Black families racism and labour market disadvantage (see the chapter by Juliet Cook and Shantu Watt here) mean an increased risk of poverty.

Clearly therefore lone mothers are not all the same and what they experience as lone mothers will be affected by many factors including age, race, class, family relationships and so on. The interaction between these factors is complex. Phoenix (1991), for example, argues that for young teenage mothers it is their lack of resources, rather than their race, which most structures their lives. But whatever the differences between them, what is common to very many lone mothers is the importance of state social policy in determining their lives. In particular, lone mothers are likely to be dependent on the state for two very basic needs: housing and income.

About half (54 per cent) of all lone mothers are local authority tenants, compared with only 18 per cent of two-parent families (OPCS, 1990). With the policy of selling local authority properties it is increasingly the worst housing that remains and thus lone mothers are becoming concentrated in this poor housing. Only 34 per cent of lone parents live in a detached or semi-detached house compared with 61 per cent of other families; and 13 per cent of lone parents are over-crowded compared with 6 per cent of other families (OPCS, 1990). Marital breakdown often means that families must move – 58 per cent had done so in the Bradshaw and Millar survey. About 27 per cent of single mothers share accommodation, usually with their parents. Many lone mothers, especially Black women, live in inner-city areas, where housing conditions and amenities are often very poor.

Income support is the main source of state social security for non-employed lone mothers and most lone mothers will spend at least some time, and often lengthy periods, in receipt of income support. Bradshaw and Millar found that about 85 per cent of all lone mothers had spent some time on income support since becoming a lone parent with 72 per cent still in receipt at the time of the interview. Of those on benefit half had been in receipt for more than 2.6 years.

State benefits create contradictory and ambiguous responses among those who must rely upon them. On the one hand for many lone mothers benefits provide a relatively stable and secure source of income at a time when there may be no other alternative. Many lone mothers are excluded from employment by lack of jobs, lack of child care, and negative attitudes towards working mothers, and few lone mothers receive regular maintenance. Thus for many families there is no choice but to spend some time on income support. On the other hand, income support provides an income which is very low and this means many families struggle to make ends meet. Bradshaw and Millar found that only a quarter of lone mothers on income support said they were managing all right financially and 52 per cent said they 'almost always' worried about money. Berthoud (1989) also reports that many lone parents on benefit have debts and money problems. Furthermore, the majority of lone parents lost out financially as a result of the

1988 social security changes (Svenson and MacPherson, 1988; House of Commons, 1989).

Living on income support is for many a very negative experience – the intrusive questioning about income and about personal relationships; the difficulties of queuing with young children; the problems when benefits are delayed or lost; the lack of control over income as more and more direct deductions are made – all these and more contribute to the difficulties of bringing up children alone on a low income. Not surprisingly perhaps, lone mothers suffer consequences in terms of their health. Popay and Jones (1990), analysing General Household Survey data, found that lone parents report themselves to be in poorer health more than parents in couples; and that more lone mothers report poorer health than lone fathers (see also Hilary Graham's chapter here).

For lone mothers the experience of poverty and the consequences of poverty are in some respects similar to, and in others different from, those of married mothers. One of the key differences between the two relates to the impact of a male partner in the household. Men in general bring in higher wages than women so a family with a male partner will almost always have a higher family income than a family of a lone woman. On the other hand, a number of studies (Houghton, 1973; Evason, 1980; Pahl, 1985; Bradshaw and Millar, 1991) have found that some lone mothers, typically between a quarter and a third, say that they feel better-off as lone mothers than they did as married women because being alone means that they themselves have control over their (albeit limited) resources. This control extends into other areas of family life. Charles and Kerr (1986) found that food consumption differed significantly between lone-mother and two-parent families in a way that was related to the presence of male partner. The lone mothers in the Bradshaw and Millar study reported that the best thing about being a lone parent was 'independence' (while the worst was 'loneliness') and 47 per cent said they preferred to stay as lone parents in the near future, rather than re-marry (23 per cent) or live with a partner (13 per cent).

Recent policy developments

Up to and including the 1988 social security changes, the basic policy response to the growing numbers of lone-parent families has been to add to or modify the existing system of benefits rather than make any fundamental changes. The basic benefits available to lone parents (with the exception of widows) are the same as those available to other poor families with children: income support for the non-employed and family credit, and other means-tested benefits, for the low-paid workers. Lone parents do receive slightly more advantageous treatment than couples, with a lone-parent family premium in income support, a small weekly addition to child benefit in the form of one-parent benefit and an additional tax allowance.

However, the government has recently started to question policy in this area for a variety of reasons. First, the costs of providing benefits for lone parents have risen very rapidly as a consequence of the increased receipt of income support among lone parents. Between 1981/2 and 1988/9 real expenditure (taking inflation into account) on income-related benefits for lone parents rose from £1.4 billion to £3.2 billion (DSS, 1990a). Secondly, changes in the labour market and the increased participation of women in employment has raised questions about the extent to which lone mothers – like more and more married mothers – should be expected to take paid employment (Brown, 1989). Thirdly, concern about the supposed negative consequences of benefit 'dependency' in creating an 'underclass' of individuals and families who have no self-motivation has very much focused on lone-parent families (Field, 1989; Murray, 1990). Finally, and closely related, have been moral concerns about family breakdown and unmarried motherhood. Partly, these relate to fears that state policy (especially social security and housing policy) might be helping to create such families; and partly to disapproval of the way in which absent parents are able to evade their 'responsibilities' to provide for their families. These financial and moral concerns have given rise to a change in policy, which has led to the Child Support Act due to be implemented fully by April 1993.

Maintenance and child support

Bradshaw and Millar found that only 29 per cent of lone parents received maintenance from their former partners. Only 13 per cent of single mothers received any payments compared with 32 per cent of separated women and 40 per cent of divorced women. On average, maintenance made up only 7 per cent of total income, with the mean amount being about £26 per family, or £16 per child per week. Among those on income support only 22 per cent were receiving any maintenance, which represents a substantial fall since 1979, when half of lone parents on supplementary benefit were receiving some maintenance.

The Child Support Act sets out to increase the amount of maintenance paid by former partners, both in terms of the actual amounts paid by individuals and in terms of the number of people paying. There are two main elements to the new system – the use of a formula to determine payments and the establishment of a Child Support Agency to set, collect and enforce payments.

The formula sets an amount for maintenance (based upon income support rates), allows the absent parent an amount of money for his personal needs (again set by income support rates and also including reasonable housing costs), and then requires the absent parent to pay half of his remaining income in child support. (The scheme applies equally to women if they are the absent parent but the vast majority of absent parents are in fact men.) The White Paper sets out the details of the formula (DSS, 1990a; see also Millar and Whiteford, 1991 for further details and a comparison with the recently introduced Australian scheme). The DSS estimate that the average assessment will be about £40 per week (compared with £25 now) and that in about 25 per cent of cases the bill will be payable in full.

The Agency is to be established within the Department of Social Security and will take responsibility for all aspects of child support, leaving spouse support, property settlements and issues of custody and access within the jurisdiction of the courts. All lone parents who claim benefits will be required to use the Agency to establish child support liabilities while non-claimants may choose whether or not to do so. Both newly separating couples and already existing lone-parent families will be brought into the scheme, which means that existing maintenance orders will be re-assessed according to the formula. The Agency will have powers to trace absent parents through Inland Revenue records and to enforce payments through measures such as attachments of earnings.

These proposals clearly raise a number of very fundamental issues. The first, and probably most important, point on which to judge their value is their likely impact on poverty – to what extent will these changes reduce poverty among lone mothers? On the face of it, if such increased levels of maintenance can be collected from many more absent parents, then it looks as if lone mothers stand to gain quite substantially. However, the reality is that for very many lone mothers there will be no financial gain at all. This is because, for those on income support, any maintenance received will continue to be deducted from their benefit. Given that almost three-quarters of lone mothers are on income support this means that for the majority income will not change, regardless of how much maintenance is collected. Those very few who do receive enough child support to 'float' them off income support may nevertheless lose financially because of the consequent loss of passported benefits such as free school meals. Owner-occupiers will also lose help with mortgage payments. The government estimates that about 50,000 lone parents will come off income support as a result of the new scheme (DSS, 1990a, para. 5.35). At current rates of receipt this means that there will still be over 700,000 lone parents on income support with no financial gain from any maintenance collected.

The government has resisted introducing a 'disregard' of maintenance for those on income support partly because of fears that this might create a disincentive to work. It argues that if child support was received in addition to income support the resulting higher incomes would mean that more lone mothers would remain longer on benefit rather than looking for paid employment. In order to create such an incentive to work there will therefore be a £15 disregard of child support for family credit, housing benefit and community charge benefit. Maintenance will therefore add to the incomes of those in work, but the existence of different earnings disregards and tapers in the various in-work benefits mean that the impact will be difficult to work out, and could create substantial uncertainty in decision-making. For some lone mothers the level of maintenance received might actually fall (Bingley *et al.*, 1991).

Furthermore, some lone mothers on income support will have their benefit cut if they refuse to name the absent parent. This has been one of the most controversial clauses in the Act and was deleted in the House of Lords but reinstated by the government. It involves a 20 per cent reduction in the personal allowance of a lone parent who refuses to name the absent parent, unless she has 'good cause' not to do so, for example because of violence, incest or rape. For many women this will cause no problems but for some it might cause very substantial difficulties. Bradshaw and Millar found that 24 per cent of lone mothers who were or ever had been on income support said they had been, or would be, unwilling to give such information to the DSS.

There are many reasons why women might be unwilling to name the absent parent. For some it might be fear of violence (Bradshaw and Millar found that a fifth of the lone mothers in their study said violence was a factor in the marital breakdown). For others it might be that they wish to maintain the relationship between the father and the children and fear that ill-feeling will be created by a vigorous pursuit of maintenance. For others it might be that they want the relationship to end completely and do not want to be financially dependent on their former partners (Bradshaw and Millar found that a fifth of those not receiving maintenance said that they did not want any). For men being named as an absent parent will mean a much higher maintenance bill than in the past and thus some men may put pressure on the women to avoid this. The benefit penalty means that it will be the lone mothers – and their children – who will bear the cost of this.

Another reason why lone-parent families could gain very little from these new measures is simply that absent parents may not have incomes high enough to enable them to pay child support at the levels required. There are very little data available on the incomes and circumstances of absent parents but the data collected by the government as background to the White Paper suggest that such men tend to have lower than average earnings (DSS, 1990a, Vol. 2, para. 3.6). Forty per cent of lone parents estimate that their former partners cannot afford to pay (or pay more) maintenance (Bradshaw and Millar, 1991). In addition many divorced men re-marry and have second families. The formula 'protects' the incomes of second families by not allowing them to fall below income support levels plus £8 and 10 per cent of the difference. This puts the second family at only just above income support levels and there is therefore a danger that one of the main effects of these changes will be to impoverish second families without directly helping first families. Conversely, if the absent parent has a high income, the lone mother and the children will not share in this because, once the maintenance bill is met, the absent parent is liable for only 25 per cent more of any additional income. Men with high incomes will therefore pay proportionately less than men with low incomes.

The way in which child support is calculated means that the amount payable can vary according to a number of different factors. If the lone mother takes employment her earnings enter the calculation and reduce the maintenance bill for her former partner. If the former partner has a change in housing costs, or in earnings, or if he has more children, then his maintenance bill will be varied.

And if he does not pay, or does not pay the full amount, then payments will have to be enforced leaving the lone mother to cope in the meantime (although for those on income support maintenance can, as now, be signed over to the DSS). Child support will therefore not necessarily be any more reliable or regular in the future than it has been in the past. Thus the financial dependency of individual women on individual men is perpetuated in that at least part of her income will still depend on his actions and circumstances. In addition, the way in which the amount of child support is calculated includes an amount of money in respect of the lone mother. This is intended to reflect her costs as 'carer' of the child(ren) but it seems probable that many people will interpret it as being money for her maintenance. This is likely to be very unpopular and further reinforces individual dependency.

Furthermore, this focus on child support does nothing to compensate women for the real inequalities that marriage and child-rearing brings. The contribution that women make to families through their unpaid domestic labour, and the costs they incur in doing so in terms of lost current and future earnings, are inadequately recognised in the current financial arrangements following divorce. One very significant example concerns pension rights. Many women lose access to a pension through their partner because of divorce and there is no compensation for this (Joshi and Davies, 1991). These wider questions remain unaddressed.

The Child Support Act highlights the complexity of the issues surrounding financial relationships and obligations in a society where family structures are rapidly changing. On the one hand, setting and enforcing more adequate levels of child support goes some way to redressing the balance of the current situation where the costs of supporting children fall almost entirely on the mother. On the other hand, as the new scheme stands, it will make little impact on the poverty experienced by lone mothers; there is still no adequate compensation for women for the costs they bear as a consequence of inequalities in marriage and child-rearing; and the financial dependency of individual women on individual men is maintained. This approach to child support also gives priority to a particular type of family relationship – that based on biological parenthood. As Margaret Thatcher put it, when introducing these proposals: 'Parenthood is for life' (*The Independent*, 19.7.90). But biological parenthood is only one element in actual patterns of family structure and family life and its importance is not necessarily always paramount. Step-parents provide most of the economic and emotional care for some children. Some separated parents share care by having their children live sometimes with one parent and sometimes with the other. Some women choose to bring up children alone without a male partner. There are lesbian couples with children, and increasing numbers of children born as a result of artificial insemination. Clearly, not all children have two 'natural' parents, a mother and a father. Nevertheless the 'family' in this form is still explicitly and implicitly upheld and supported by social policy and the Child Support Act can be seen as another example of this.

Employment

The third change introduced in the Child Support Act – alongside the introduction of the Agency and the use of the formula – is the change to the benefit rules regarding hours of work. For all claimants, not just lone parents, income support will cease to be payable to those employed for more than sixteen hours per week, and family credit will become payable instead. (Under current rules the change-over occurs at twenty-four hours.) This is potentially a very radical change, bringing part-time work much more within the remit of social security benefits. For lone mothers the aim is to encourage more employment, with what are likely to be low earnings from part-time jobs supplemented by both means-tested benefits (especially family credit) and child support (as discussed above, with a £15 disregard).

These changes do reflect a recognition of the growing importance of part-time work (which is where most of the new jobs have been created in recent years) and a recognition that full-time work is difficult for many lone mothers to sustain, given their domestic responsibilities. However, there are likely to be a number of problems with this approach in practice. First, focusing again on poverty, this income 'package' of earnings, benefits and child support will create a strong poverty trap for lone mothers, making it very difficult for them to improve their incomes. An increase in earnings will lead to a reduction in both benefit and child support and so lone mothers will tend to be trapped at a low level of income. Unless lone mothers can be helped out of low-paid jobs they will still remain poor.

Secondly, the package is insecure. Living on a low income requires strict budgeting and control over expenditure. But this is very difficult to do if income fluctuates. So a week in which the former partner misses his child support payment is likely to cause substantial problems; likewise the period while benefits are being assessed or re-assessed. Earnings might vary because of piece-work, overtime or short-time working. Some lone mothers are therefore likely to take the view that their children can be more securely supported by remaining on income support.

Thirdly, the lack of adequate and affordable child care remains a significant barrier to employment, even part-time employment. The UK has one of the worst records in Europe in relation to the provision of child care (Moss, 1991). Bradshaw and Millar found that most employed lone mothers relied on their families to provide care, often unpaid; and that lack of child care was one of the main factors keeping lone mothers out of employment.

The issue of employment for mothers, and especially mothers of young children, is surrounded by some ambiguity both in policy and in popular attitudes (Brown, 1989; Brannen and Moss, 1991). On the one hand, more and more mothers are employed outside the home but on the other hand there is still a strong ideology supporting the view that mothers ought to stay at home to care for their children. The government remains reluctant actively to support or encourage women's employment despite the fact that women's employment is growing steadily.

For lone mothers employment – even though often low paid – does mean higher incomes and greater independence. Work also provides social contact and reduces the isolation experienced by those bringing up children alone. However, it also has to be remembered that employment is not a solution for all lone mothers. Bradshaw and Millar found that about two-thirds (62 per cent) of lone mothers on income support said that they did not want to work immediately although they would want to work in the future. The main reasons for not wanting immediate employment were to do with their children and their perceptions of their children's needs. Some had very young children and (like many mothers of young babies) felt they ought to stay at home and care for them. Some felt their children had been hurt by the family breakdown and that they needed additional care. Some felt that they needed to compensate their children for the 'loss' of the other parent, and so should devote more time to them. Some felt constrained by lack of alternative child care – as many as two-fifths said they would return to work sooner if they could get child care.

Thus there are many reasons why employment may not always be possible or desirable. However, there is clearly much untapped potential for paid employment among lone mothers. Bradshaw and Millar estimate that up to 70 per cent of lone mothers could be employed if all who said they wanted to could immediately get jobs and child care. But even if this were possible a substantial number of lone parents (about 300,000 on current figures) would continue to be reliant on the state for at least some period while caring for their children. Thus policy-makers need to consider not just how to open up employment for lone mothers, but also how best to support those who are not employed.

The 1980s have been bad years for lone mothers, as for so many others. In the long term it will be impossible to improve the financial situation and security of lone mothers without directly tackling the wider issue of gender inequalities in employment and in the family. Women face impossible difficulties in trying to combine the roles of mother, paid worker and unpaid domestic worker, and when marriage breaks down the consequences are obvious in terms of the vulnerability of lone mothers and their children to poverty.

11 'Community care': The financial consequences for women

Caroline Glendinning

This chapter considers the financial consequences of 'community care' policies for those women on whom such policies increasingly depend – the mothers, daughters, wives, sisters, neighbours and friends who are providing a substantial amount of help and support to a disabled or elderly person. It is important to bear in mind that these financial consequences have, until very recently, remained largely hidden. Indeed, one of the major arguments for the promotion of 'community care' over the past decades – its lower cost, compared with institutional and residential alternatives – has been sustainable precisely *because* the costs to carers and their families have been largely ignored. Only the public expenditure costs have been counted, not those which fall within the private, domestic domain (Rimmer, 1983; Parker, 1990a). However, 'community care' appears far less of a cheap option if the unwaged labour of women is included in the financial calculations (Finch, 1990). Apart from the important political issues surrounding the recognition (financial or otherwise) of women's domestic work (see Ungerson, 1990; Land, 1991), full acknowledgement of these private costs is also important if individual women are not to experience increased impoverishment, insecurity and dependency as the consequences of providing care.

'Community Care' Policies in the 1980s and 1990s

It has been suggested (Walker, 1982, p. 11) that the popularity of 'community care' owes much to its flexibility and adaptability – the term can be used to describe a wide range of institutions and services (and, critics would add, the lack of them too). This flexibility can be illustrated by the subtle shift in official notions of 'community care' which has been evident in policy documents of recent years. Original intentions to replace large-scale institutions with statutory services provided *in* the community have increasingly been modified, with a growing emphasis being placed instead on the role of families, friends and neighbours as the main providers of 'community care'. Thus care *in* the community has increasingly become care *by* the community (Parker, 1990b, p. 10). There has also been a corresponding shift in the role advocated for statutory social care agencies, from the direct provision of services for elderly and disabled people themselves, to supporting instead those relatives, friends and neighbours who are increasingly responsible for providing most of their care:

> the primary sources of support and care for elderly people are informal and voluntary. These spring from the personal ties of kinship, friendship and neighbourhood . . . It is the role of public authorities to sustain and, where necessary, develop – but never to displace – such support and care. (DHSS, 1981, para. 1.9)

Similar assumptions underpin the 1993 planned reorganisation of 'community care' services, with the role of statutory agencies as direct service providers reduced yet further. Instead they are destined to become 'enabling authorities', purchasing and managing the services provided by other statutory, voluntary and private sector agencies and supporting informal carers in *their* role as the primary care-givers:

> the great bulk of community care is provided by friends, family and neighbours . . . it is right that they should be able to play their part in looking after those close to them . . . service providers should make practical support for carers a high priority. (DHSS, 1989a, pp. 4–5)

Moreover, public expenditure restraints during the 1980s in particular have helped to turn the rhetoric of care *by* the community into *de facto* reality, as support services such as home helps and nursing auxiliaries have been reduced or withdrawn – a theme developed by Hilary Land in her chapter here on the demise of the social wage. There is extensive research evidence that disabled and elderly people who are living with someone else, particularly when this includes a non-elderly married female relative, are less likely to receive statutory services than are those living alone (Qureshi and Walker, 1986, 1989; Arber *et al.*, 1988; Arber and Gilbert, 1989; Parker, 1990b). The 1993 changes are likely to intensify yet further this shift from public to private provision. As Baldock and Ungerson point out, these changes can be characterised as the public case-management of a plurality of private and voluntary welfare services, which signifies and requires a substantial redefinition of the traditional relationship between these sectors. Whereas until now the doing of tasks was a public function (home help, care assistant, district nurse, meals on wheels) and their integration into an overall care plan was a private function, now the public sector proposes to do the co-ordinating and the private, voluntary and informal will do the actual caring work. (Baldock and Ungerson, 1991, p. 141)

What are the implications for women of this historical – and continuing – trend?

Community care – a women's issue?

It has long been argued by feminist critics that 'community care' is merely a euphemism for care by the family – which in turn means care by women. (For a summary of this argument see Finch, 1990, pp. 43–4.) Furthermore, anxieties about an increasing 'care gap' – the growing disparity between the numbers of elderly people likely to need care in the future and the contracting pool of potential informal carers – invariably arise from discussion of the demographic factors affecting the availability of *women* to care. Qureshi and Walker (1986) for example cite the effects of family breakdown on daughters (and daughters-in-law) and women's increased labour market participation as two major factors prompting concern about a shortfall in the supply of informal care. As will be discussed below, recent evidence on the demography of informal care suggests that some modification of these assumptions may be necessary, but in some very important respects the work of providing 'care' in the 'community' remains an issue of central importance to women.

The 1985 General Household Survey (GHS) and the OPCS surveys of disabled people, also conducted in 1985, provided for the first time national data on the numbers and characteristics of those involved in giving additional domestic or personal help to an infirm, sick or disabled person. Fourteen per cent of adults aged 16 and over – about 6 million altogether – were found to be looking after or providing regular help to someone who was sick, elderly or disabled. Around 1.7 million of these were looking after someone in the same household; 1.4 million were providing help or supervision for at least twenty hours a week; and 3.7 million were carrying the main responsibility for providing that help (Green, 1988).

Surprisingly, perhaps, the GHS figures showed little difference between the proportions of women and men who said they were caring (15 per cent and 12 per cent respectively). These proportions represent about 3.5 million female and 2.5 million male carers overall (Green, 1988, p. 6). However, the similarities between men and women carers, both in terms of their personal characteristics and in terms of the kinds of help and support they give, are more apparent than real. At all ages up to 75, a higher proportion of women are likely to face caring responsibilities than their male counterparts. The widest difference occurs in the 45–59 age group, where 24 per cent of women are carers compared with only 16 per cent of men (Green, 1988, p. 8). Only among the over-75s are men more likely to be caring than women (10 per cent compared with 6 per cent), mainly because of the care they are providing for a disabled spouse (Evandrou, 1990, pp. 6–7).

Women informal carers are also likely to be carrying heavier responsibilities than male carers. Sixty per cent carry the main responsibility for supporting the disabled or elderly person compared with only 46 per cent of male carers, while the latter are more likely to play a role which is ancilliary to another main carer – 42 per cent compared with 31 per cent of female carers (Evandron, 1990, p. 15). Although there is apparently little difference in the proportions of male and female carers who are providing twenty hours or more help and support each week, clear gender differences do emerge as care-giving becomes more intensive. Of the carers in the 1985 GHS who were living in the same household as the person receiving care, 51 per cent of women reported spending at least fifty hours a week giving help compared with only 39 per cent of men. A similar gender difference was apparent in the time spent helping someone who lived in a separate household; here 32 per cent of women but only 22 per cent of men spent ten hours or more each week on care-giving (Green, 1988, p. 21).

Differences are also apparent in the types of help and support which carers give, suggesting that women care-givers are likely to be involved in more intensive and intimate activities. As a whole, women (28 per cent) are more likely than men (19 per cent) to provide help with personal care. Among carers living in the same household as the person receiving care, this difference is even more apparent, with 62 per cent of women providing help with personal care and 53 per cent being responsible for giving medication, compared with 43 per cent and 37 per cent of men respectively. The only type of help in which, according to the 1985 GHS, men clearly outnumber women is in taking the disabled person out – 60 per cent of men compared with 49 per cent of women carers living in the same household as the person being given care (Green, 1988, p. 27).

An unexpected finding of the General Household Survey was the continuing high proportions of single women carers. As Lewis and Piachaud point out in their chapter here, unmarried women have traditionally played a significant role in the care of elderly parents and other relatives and the same appears to be true today. Twenty-nine per cent of unmarried women in the 45–64 age group were carers, according to the 1985 GHS, compared with 24 per cent of married women and only 16 per cent of men. Younger women who have previously been married may also be assuming this traditional role. Twenty per cent of widowed, divorced and separated women aged 30–44 were carers, compared with only 10 per cent of men of similar age and status. In addition, unmarried women carers are more likely than either married women or men to be carrying particularly heavy caring responsibilities. Again in the 45–60 age group, noticeably higher proportions of unmarried women were caring for someone in the same household, were the main carers of their disabled relatives and friends, and were caring for over twenty hours a week than were either their married or male counterparts (Green, 1988, pp. 9–10).

Whilst, overall, only slightly larger proportions of women than men may be likely to identify themselves as carers, the greater numbers of women in the adult population mean that in absolute terms more women are involved in care-giving than men. Moreover, among those who are involved in caring, women are more likely to be heavily involved and to undertake activities which are arguably more demanding and unremitting. Furthermore, some groups of women, particularly those in middle age, those who have never married, and those whose marriages have ended, are particularly likely to have heavy care-giving responsibilities.

Apart from these demographic characteristics of informal care-giving, in other important respects it remains an issue of central importance to women. First, it shares characteristics which are common to many of the activities typically undertaken by women, especially on an unpaid basis – routine, repetitive tasks which have few circumscribed limits of time or obligation. Moreover, the ambiguous meaning of 'caring', especially the unarticulated elision of 'caring for' with 'caring about', adds important emotional overtones to these tasks: 'the dominant cultural perception of caring sees it as involving essentially female qualities' (Baldwin and Twigg, 1991, p. 123).

Secondly, there are deeper connections between care-giving and the social construction of masculine and feminine identities, as Ungerson (1983) and Graham have explored: '"Caring" becomes the category through which one sex is differentiated from the other ... it becomes the defining characteristic of [women's] self-identity' (Graham, 1983, p. 18).

The personal meanings which are attached to caring, and their relationship to the wider sexual divisions of labour, therefore have especial significance for women. However, too heavy an emphasis on the affective dimensions of care-giving can obscure the sheer physical and emotional labour involved (as the current rhetoric of 'community care' indeed does). This leads to a third reason why caring is of special significance to women. It has a strategic significance in bridging the gap between women's unpaid and unacknowledged domestic work and that which is rewarded by (albeit low) wages. Indeed, because care-giving is so crucially important to current community care policies, it is increasingly difficult to keep it entirely confined within the private domestic domain. The recent development of 'paid volunteer' schemes, where small payments are made to untrained local people to provide regular help and support to disabled and elderly people in order to sustain their continued residence in 'the community', illustrates precisely this growing interface between private unpaid and public waged caring work (Leat and Gay, 1987; Qureshi, 1990; Baldock and Ungerson, 1991). Indeed, Baldock and Ungerson have argued that 'because most care-work is actually carried out for no payment at all ... these payments, however small, are an improvement on the usual position of informal carers' (Baldock and Ungerson, 1991, p. 147). Despite the potential for exploiting volunteers, Baldock and Ungerson argue that such schemes may provide the basis for a shift from unpaid to paid care-work.

'Community' and informal care therefore provide appropriate contexts within which to argue for the value of women's unpaid caring work to be recognised, as Land (1991) and Ungerson (1990) have recently done. The effects of care-giving on women's paid employment and living standards, as described below, lend further weight to this argument.

'*Community care*' – *the effects on women's employment and earnings*

Both national survey data and smaller in-depth studies now enable us to document at least some of the financial effects of care-giving on women, although we still know very little about the consequences for women who begin or continue to give care in their own old age, or about the experiences of Black women carers. The information which is available highlights the importance of disaggregating household-based data on incomes and expenditure patterns and looking at the consequences for the individuals *within* those households. By doing so, we can see how women carers can, and do, experience disproportionate reductions in their incomes and living standards; absorb extra care-related expenses through restricting their own personal expenditure; and experience increased financial dependency, not only on a male partner but also on the person they are caring for.

Labour market participation

Caring for a disabled or elderly person is clearly associated with lower rates of labour market participation among women. Baldwin's (1985) study of parents caring for a severely disabled child showed that the mothers' economic activity rates were almost half those of a control group of mothers who did not have a disabled child (33 per cent and 59 per cent respectively). This difference increased with the age of the youngest child in the family, so that by the time the latter had reached 11 years old still only 44 per cent of the mothers of disabled children were in paid work compared with 87 per cent of control group mothers. Similar differences in participation rates were revealed by the 1985 GHS and the OPCS disability surveys. Among women under 65 who were caring for more than twenty hours a week, only 40 per cent were employed, compared with 62 per cent of women generally (Green, 1988). Heavier caring responsibilities were clearly associated with lower rates of employment; only about one-fifth of working-age women providing more than fifty hours a week care for an elderly person were employed, compared with two-thirds of married women and half of all single (never-married) women caring for less than twenty hours a week (McLaughlin, 1989). In many instances it is likely that these lowered rates of employment are the direct result of providing care, although in some cases it is possible that a temporary withdrawal from the labour market (for example, because of redundancy or child-bearing) may enable some women to take on informal caring responsibilities and delay their return to paid employment. Two carers in one recent study described these different effects:

> I was working as a care assistant . . . I actually gave up work while [mother] was in hospital . . . when she first had her stroke . . . As long as mum is alive and as long as I'm able to look after her, there's no way I could hold down a job. (Married woman looking after her mother)

> I were applying for jobs . . . I'd just got [my daughter] into school . . . I said to the doctor 'Well that's the end of that then'. 'Do you work?' he said. I said 'No and I aren't going to now, am I?' (Married woman whose mother came to live with her after developing Alzheimer's disease) (Glendinning, 1992a)

Carers who do not withdraw altogether from the labour market nevertheless often have to reduce or restrict the hours they can work. Paradoxically, the widespread availability of part-time employment for women may enable them to remain in the labour market, even while providing substantial levels of care, whilst men appear more likely to have to choose between full-time employment and stopping work altogether (see Green, 1988, Table 2.9; Parker, 1992). Nevertheless, the experiences of women carers suggest that even these part-time opportunities may be restricted, with shift work bonuses, longer hours and training opportunities all forgone:

> If I didn't have me mother, I could have more hours [as a home help], if I had no ties. But I'm at work and I'm thinking 'I've got to get back'. (Widowed woman living with her frail elderly mother)

> I used to work like everyone else on this shift system . . . I couldn't cope with never knowing what days I was going to be there – you had to wait till the rota was up to see which days you'd be working . . . I was doing 20 hours . . . I reduced it to 14 and regular hours. (Married woman nursing auxiliary, caring for her father-in-law) (Glendinning, 1992a)

Care-giving can also have longer term effects on labour market participation. Both the 1985 GHS (Green, 1988) and McLaughlin's (1991) study of the invalid care allowance (ICA) found that women who had ceased to care within the previous twelve months were less likely to be in employment than their non-carer peers. Difficulties in returning to work after a period out of the labour market are particularly likely to be experienced by older women:

> I could only go out there and do what I was doing before, which is . . .

labouring. And labouring wages are pathetic . . . If anything happens to me mother – and it's not all that far off really – I'm expected to pick meself up, go back out there and start again. But the thing is, I was 36 when [mother] came here; I'm now 47. Is there anyone who's going to employ me? *I* can't see it happening. (Widowed woman, caring for her frail and confused mother) (Glendinning, 1992a)

Current and future earnings

Women who have to leave the labour market altogether, or who find the location, hours and other opportunities for employment restricted, will inevitably experience reduced earnings. Systematically comparing mothers with and without disabled children who had paid work, Baldwin (1985) found a £5 difference in mean weekly earnings. This difference increased to £16.30 among mothers whose youngest child was over 10 years old (1983 figures). A small-scale study of women caring for frail elderly relatives found average earnings losses of £87 a week among women who had given up or been unable to return to work and average weekly losses of £28 among those still in paid work (Nissel and Bonnerjea, 1982). One of Glendinning's (1992a) respondents described the financial effects of her switch from full- to part-time work as a store supervisor:

> Although I'm half time, I still run a full section . . . I reckon over the past two years I've probably lost about £8,000 with being at home, in lost earnings. (Unmarried woman living with her frail elderly mother)

However, it is not just current earnings which may be reduced by care-giving, but future earnings and pension entitlements too. As Heather Joshi has estimated (see Chapter 8 here), women returning to work after a period caring for children or at a later stage of the life cycle are likely to re-enter the labour market at lower rates of pay. McLaughlin's (1991) study showed clearly that the personal incomes of ex-carers were around £40 lower than the 1988 Family Expenditure Survey (FES) *per capita* average, while the incomes of two-adult households containing an ex-carer were £144 a week lower than their FES counterparts.

In the longer term, as Alan Walker and Dulcie Groves show in Chapters 12 and 13 here, current state, occupational and private pension schemes do not take adequate account of women's caring responsibilities and this is as true of women's care of disabled and elderly people as it is of young children. Unfortunately, there is little systematic evidence on this as yet, although one recent small-scale survey (Caring Costs, 1991) found a number of women expressing considerable anxiety about their own future old age:

> My national insurance stamp has not been paid since I gave up work to look after mother. Who pays for it? I can't afford to.

> I gave up my job at 60. I now have a reduced occupational pension because

of early retirement – one-third of my salary . . . I lost an income of £9,000 a year.

Coming on top of a period of reduced or forgone earnings towards the end of their working lives, the future prospects for carers such as these are indeed grim.

The extra costs of caring

There is a large body of evidence that disablement incurs extra expenditure (see for example Nissel and Bonnerjea, 1982; Glendinning, 1983; Baldwin, 1985; Martin and White, 1988), although the measurement of that expenditure is both problematic and controversial (Thompson *et al.*, 1988, 1990; Matthews and Truscott, 1990). However, two additional issues have only recently begun to be explored: first, the extent to which the work of informal care-giving *also* incurs extra expenditure, over and above any additional costs arising directly out of disablement; and, secondly, the extent to which the costs of disablement are in fact borne by carers and other members of their households, because the incomes of disabled and elderly people themselves are simply too low. In other words, just as the poverty experienced by women has largely been obscured by household-based studies of income and expenditure, so we need also to examine the patterns of expenditure and consumption *within* care-giving households, in order to assess the full costs to informal carers.

First, it is clear that some extra care-giving-related expenses can be identified. Glendinning's (1992a) study indicated that these may fall into four main groups. First, where an elderly person had moved into the household of a younger generation relative, the latter often made extra purchases, ranging from an extra bed or bedding through to the construction of an additional bedroom, in order to provide the necessary accommodation. Secondly, consumer durables, especially laundry equipment, microwaves, dishwashers and freezers were frequently purchased to save time or ease the work of care-giving. Thirdly, some carers regularly spent extra on transport and other services, again usually to save time. Fourthly, carers who were managing to retain full-time jobs often spent a considerable amount of money each week on substitute care, if statutory day care services were not adequate.

Even more widespread was extra spending by carers on items and services which were needed by the disabled or elderly person, but which were not covered by the financial contribution which the latter made to the household budget (even when this included both retirement or invalidity pensions and disability benefits). Extra spending by carers on heating, food and laundry for the disabled person were particularly common:

She couldn't cope on her own income, not with what she needs. The heating alone would swallow most of that. (Single woman living with her unmarried brother and their very frail elderly mother)

I do think that disabled people, unless they've had a big cash payment through an accident [compensation] . . . they don't get enough to live on . . . If she had a flat of her own, she would get more benefit but her quality of living would come down. (Married woman caring for a daughter disabled in adulthood) (Glendinning, 1992a)

The effects on carers' living standards

Lower incomes, extra spending on care-related equipment and services and extra expenditure arising from the disability of the person receiving care all lead to lowered standards of living among care-giving households. Using a number of different measures of inequality (quintile income distribution, median income levels and a 'poverty line' of 140 per cent of supplementary benefit), Evandron (1990) found that carers were consistently worse off than non-carers. Carers living in the same household as the person receiving care, female carers, those with sole responsibility for providing care and those who were not economically active were especially disadvantaged.

Two-thirds of current carers in McLaughlin's (1991) study reported that caring had had an adverse effect on their living standards, regardless of their household income level. Luxuries, treats and even basic necessities could be difficult to afford, a point emphasised by some of the respondents to the Caring Costs (1991) survey: 'We need a new kettle, iron, redecoration, freezer, tumble dryer, bedding, microwave. The whole family goes without clothes.' 'We need new fittings in the house, new carpets. There's lots of things I can't afford, you understand' (Caring Costs, 1991, pp. 5–6).

However, closer examination of how these deprivations were experienced within care-giving households suggests that it was often carers who bore the brunt of them, while trying to protect the living standards of the disabled or elderly person:

I go out less for drinks, less visiting friends, going to listen to music. I smoke less – I'm desperately trying to give up smoking. (Single woman receiving supplementary benefit, caring for a friend with a severe spinal injury)

I used to go out for a drink now and again. Well I don't do that any more. I can't get out and I haven't the money to do it. Smoking – I'm packing that up and all, that's too dear. My social life, you can say I've cut down on that. (Widowed woman receiving supplementary benefit, caring for her frail and confused elderly mother)

Whatever she [mother] needs, it's there regardless . . . if her money didn't amount to whatever she needed, she would get it, even if I had to borrow for it, she would get it from somewhere. (Woman, not employed, married to unemployed man and caring for her blind mother) (Glendinning, 1992a)

Social security provision for carers

Until very recently, Britain was the only country in the EC to have a social security benefit, the invalid care allowance (ICA), targeted at informal carers themselves. (A similar benefit was recently introduced in Eire.) Introduced in 1975, ICA is intended to replace the earnings lost or forgone by a working-age carer who is providing full-time (at least thirty-five hours a week) care to a severely disabled person. For the first eleven years following its introduction, ICA offered one of the most explicit examples of the assumption that married women are (or should be) economically inactive and financially dependent upon an earning husband – until 1986 they were excluded from the benefit on the grounds that 'they might be at home in any event' (DHSS, 1974, para. 60). However, despite the extension of ICA to working-age married women in 1986 following a successful appeal to the European Court, ICA is still received by less than one-tenth of all carers who are providing thirty-five hours' help a week (McLaughlin, 1991, p. 2).

This restricted coverage is largely the result of the complex eligibility criteria governing ICA. Thus the person being cared for must be receiving attendance allowance, in recognition that s/he is 'severely disabled'; the carer must not be in full-time education or earning (from April 1992) more than £40 a week; carers cannot take more than four weeks' holiday in any six-month period, nor can the disabled person be in hospital for more than four weeks at a time. Carers cannot receive another contributory or non-contributory benefit as well as ICA; and ICA is deducted in full from means-tested income support and housing benefits, so that some carers receiving these latter benefits may see no advantage to be gained from claiming ICA. Perhaps most crucially, ICA, as a non-contributory benefit, is very low – in 1991/2 less than 80 per cent of the basic minimum income support payable to a single adult.

All these factors contribute to the poverty experienced by many women caregivers. First, at £32.55 (1992/3), ICA is well below the incomes which many women can earn, even from low-paid part-time employment (see Susan Lonsdale's chapter here). As one of McLaughlin's respondents, who had been caring for her mother for seven years, pointed out: 'Well that really is a nonsense because the amount it is at the moment compared to anybody that's had the chance of a full-time job, you're talking of £24 as opposed to a job of about £98' (McLaughlin, 1991, p. 48).

The low level of ICA also means that many carers will still have to 'top up' the benefit with means-tested income support – if they are eligible. However, carers with savings above the limit for means-tested benefits have to rely entirely on

ICA plus income from their savings, a strategy which is likely to increase their risk of poverty in the longer term (Glendinning, 1990).

The limit on the amount which can be earned while receiving ICA effectively discourages carers from retaining contact with the labour market. Indeed, the earnings limit has a particularly harsh effect on women, who are more likely than men to be able to combine care-giving with continued part-time employment (McLaughlin, 1991, p. 50).

In addition to its low level and the discouragement of part-time work, ICA also plays an important role in structuring the financial dependency of women care-givers. First, the link between ICA eligibility and the receipt of attendance allowance by the person receiving care means that 'the disabled person acts as "gatekeeper" to income for the carer' (McLaughlin, 1991, p. 36). Yet over half of the disabled people being cared for in Glendinning's (1992a) study had apparently failed to claim the attendance allowance when they first became eligible, thereby potentially affecting their carers' benefit entitlement as well:

I heard about it from a neighbour this year . . . Then I went to the carers' meeting [at the day centre] and there was somebody there from CAB and they said 'You should have been getting it ages ago'. (Married woman with no earnings, caring for her confused elderly mother)

She [mother] didn't really know about it until one day the doctor came here and . . . she said . . . 'Do you get attendance allowance?' and I said 'No, I don't get anything', and she said 'Well jolly well apply for it!' (Single woman caring for her mother) (Glendinning, 1992a)

Secondly, married women whose earnings are curtailed (but nevertheless remain at a level above the ICA earnings limit) or who stop work altogether and claim ICA are likely to find their financial dependency on an earning spouse is increased. As one of Glendinning's (1992a) respondents explained: 'I gave up my job. I have given up a lot of my independence.'

Interestingly, two of the carers in Glendinning's study were single women who were sharing a household and some of the responsibilities of care-giving with an unmarried brother as well as their elderly parent. In both instances it was the sister whose earnings had been substantially restricted or reduced. When the patterns of resource allocation within these unmarried sibling households were examined, it was apparent that the brothers' higher earnings were making a substantially greater contribution to the housekeeping, thereby creating a degree of financial dependency for their unmarried sisters which was little different to the dependency of the married women carers on their earning husbands.

Thirdly, the very low level of ICA and the other restrictions on benefit entitlements for carers (see Glendinning, 1990) create a situation in which some carers are financially dependent on the person they are caring for. Single carers who have given up work to care appear to be especially likely to find themselves in this situation. Thus once incomes had been pooled and responsibilities for the various household outgoings apportioned, it was clear that some of the carers in Glendinning's study were being supported by the disabled or elderly person. This represented a return to the financial dependency on a parent which had characterised these carers' younger, pre-adult days:

> Me mother's kept me in food, she's looked after me dogs, she's paid the vet's bills . . . At 47 years of age I can't see why I should have to live off me mother . . . to that extent. What happens when she dies, who do I live off then? (Widowed woman receiving (then) supplementary benefit who had been caring for her frail mother for ten years)

This dependency and insecurity was of concern to other carers in similar situations:

> I've got to think – if anything happened to me mother, say she were to pass away tonight – I've no job and nothing coming in at all, only perhaps interest from savings which wouldn't keep me . . . The only thing I worry about is if I lose my mother at this time of life, before I'm due for a pension – what's going to happen to me? (Unmarried woman receiving only ICA who had given up her job as a local government clerk to care for her mother)

Conclusions

In short, the lowered or lost earnings of many women care-givers are likely to lead to poverty and to increased financial dependency – on a spouse, on an earning sibling, or on the person being cared for. The extra expenses which many carers also experience, on items needed by the disabled or elderly person or on equipment and services to ease the work of care-giving, are likely to add to these financial pressures. Moreover, as with studies of resource allocation and budgeting in households containing young children (Graham, 1987a, 1987b; Craig and Glendinning, 1990a), research has begun to uncover the unequal ways in which these pressures are experienced *within* care-giving households, with carers lowering their own standards of living in order to safeguard the needs of the person receiving care.

This situation is exacerbated by the inadequacy of current social security provision, for both disabled people and informal carers. The incomes of many disabled and elderly people are demonstrably inadequate, particularly when their extra needs are taken into account (Martin and White, 1988; Walker, 1990; see also Alan Walker's and Dulcie Groves' chapters in this volume). Consequently, for many carers, subsidising the living expenses of an elderly or disabled person in order to provide them with what the carer considers to be an acceptable standard of living is an integral part of care-giving. But social security provision for carers too is far from adequate. As Hilary Graham pointed out in the first edition of this book:

> Unlike other family dependants . . . women are economically dependent not because they need care but because they give it. Women's economic dependency within the family is created not by their own physical dependency but through the physical dependency of others . . . for women, economic dependency is the cost of caring. (Graham, 1987a, p. 223)

This conclusion is as pertinent to women caring for an elderly or disabled person as it is to their sisters caring for young, able-bodied children.

If 'community care' is not to result in increased impoverishment and dependency for women care-givers (with all the possible long-term adverse consequences for their own old age), then employment and social security policies and the provision of 'community care' services have to be integrated to a far greater extent than they are at present. Indeed, policy developments in each of these three areas have largely taken place in complete isolation from the others; only very recently has the importance of social security to the effectiveness of 'community care' been recognised in any official document (House of Commons Social Services Committee, 1990).

In the long term, enabling carers to retain contact with the labour market, through arrangements such as job-sharing, flexitime and entitlements to 'family leave' (Glendinning, 1992b) and through the removal of some of the present restrictions on ICA (McLaughlin, 1991, p. 50), represents one of the most effective ways of helping carers avoid poverty. Increasing the level of ICA and removing the 'gatekeeping' function exercised by the disabled person's receipt of attendance allowance would help to reduce the financial dependency currently experienced by many carers. Services such as day care can be important in enabling carers to retain paid employment, while other collective provision, both general and specialist – incontinence services, transport, special equipment, for example – will relieve carers of some of the extra expenses which are currently privately borne. However, until these issues are addressed, poverty, dependency and insecurity, in both the short and longer terms, will be the prices paid by women for their contribution to 'community care'.

12   *The poor relation: Poverty among older women*

Alan Walker[1]

Older people comprise a large proportion of those living in poverty in Britain and have done so ever since the systematic studies of Charles Booth (1894) at the end of the nineteenth century. But poverty is not evenly distributed among older people, and gender is one of the clearest lines along which the economic and social experience of old age is divided. Thus more than twice as many older women as older men live in poverty or on its margins. Among those in advanced old age (80 years and over) the ratio is around five to one. The dual purposes of this chapter are to describe and explain this major division in the distribution of resources in old age.

The main themes underlying this examination of poverty among older women may be summarised as follows. Poverty in old age is a function, first, of low economic and social status *prior* to retirement, which restricts access to a wide range of resources; and, secondly, of the imposition of depressed social status through the process of retirement itself. Within these social processes, which are responsible for the construction of poverty in old age (and, incidentally, the social construction of old age itself), the situation of older women is significantly different from that of older men. The economic and social status of women before retirement is, of course, closely related to the advantages secured by men in the social division of labour (see the chapters by Susan Lonsdale and Heather Joshi in this volume). This distorted access to resources in youth and middle age – institutionalised in segregative and discriminatory employment and other social

176

policies as well as in the domestic division of labour – is reflected, in due course, in the relative disadvantage of women in old age. The process of retirement too has a differential impact on men and women, but the experience of women has remained obscured because old age has been regarded, in Simone de Beauvoir's (1977, p. 101) terms, as 'a man's problem'. Women have been neglected in studies of the transition to retirement even though the proportion of women participating in the labour force, and therefore undergoing retirement from paid employment in their own right, has been growing steadily – an example of the patriarchal construction of retirement both in practice and in policy analysis and research. The situation of older Black women is even worse, suffering as they do exclusion based on both patriarchy and racism.

So, underlying this chapter is a theory of ageing based not on the analysis of biologically determined differences in senescence or individual adjustments to the ageing process but, instead, on the social creation of dependent status and on the structural relationships between older people and younger adults and between different groups of older people, especially men and women. (For a more detailed account of this approach see Walker, 1980, 1981; Phillipson and Walker, 1986.) The main practical implication of this theoretical position is that social policy is the primary focus of attention in explaining poverty in old age and in attempting to overcome it. Thus social policy must be critically evaluated not only for its failure to eradicate poverty among older women (and, to a lesser extent, men), but also because it occupies a central role in producing and legitimating both the poverty of a substantial proportion of older people and the marked inequalities between older women and men. The starting point for this analysis is a description of the current financial status of older women.

Poverty and low incomes among older women

The principal financial problem faced by older people is poverty. This fact has been demonstrated in official and independent research studies spanning the last century. Moreover, this pattern of poverty and financial insecurity among older women is common to all patriarchally organised societies, both developed and underdeveloped (Storey-Gibson, 1985). Poverty among older women in Britain has endured to the present day, despite the significant political commitment given to pensions in the 1970s, which culminated in the legislation in 1975 introducing the state earnings-related pension (SERP) scheme and in the series of pledges to uprate pensions in line with earnings or prices whichever was the greater (Walker, 1985a), policies which did result in some improvement in the relative position of older people in the national income distribution (see below). Poverty is one important aspect of the substantial inequalities in income and other resources between the majority of those under and those over retirement age (Townsend, 1979). While just under one in five (17 per cent) of all persons in Great Britain are over pension age, they comprise more than one in four of those living on incomes on or below the social assistance level (supplementary benefit between 1966 and 1988 and income support thereafter), and one in three of those living in poverty according to this definition or on the margins of poverty (i.e. with incomes of up to 40 per cent above the appropriate social assistance rates). The risk of experiencing poverty is twice as great for those over retirement age than it is for below retirement age (Johnson and Webb, 1990).

Within the generally impoverished status of older people, women and especially lone women (i.e. those living alone, including single, widowed, separated and divorced women) are often particularly disadvantaged (see Table 12.1). In 1987 (the most recent information available – see below) more than one in three older women (35 per cent) were living on incomes on or below the poverty line as defined by supplementary benefit levels, compared with less than one-quarter of older men (23 per cent). Just under half of lone older women compared with just under two-fifths of single older men had incomes on or below the poverty line. In all, more than three out of five older women were living in or on the margins of poverty.

Since the first edition of this volume, the government has discontinued the low-income families statistical series and substituted it with a new series showing households below average income. We are only able to present the figures for 1987 in Table 12.1 because the House of Commons Social Security Committee commissioned the Institute for Fiscal Studies to calculate them. The Committee also secured the publication of the 1988 households below average income data and these show that seven out of ten lone pensioners have below average incomes (after the deduction of housing costs) and that older women outnumber older men in this income group by three to one (House of Commons Social Security Committee, 1991, p. xxxix). In 1988 43 per cent of single pensioners were living on incomes below half of the average and more than two in three of them were women.

The preponderance of women among poor older people is, of course, partly due to the larger number of women than men in the elderly population as a whole. This results primarily from the greater longevity of women compared with men; life expectancy at birth is 78 years for women and 72 years for men, while at 65 it is 17 years for women and 16 years for men. (A century earlier these figures would have been 11 years and 10 years.) The main contributory factor here is the greater decline among older women than older men in mortality rates over the last forty years or so, with cancer and circulatory diseases now being the main causes of the higher mortality rate among men (Ermisch, 1983, 1990). Today more than 90 per cent of British women are expected to reach pension age (60) compared with three-quarters of men (65) (Ermisch, 1990, p. 20). Also, as a result of their greater longevity, elderly women are more than twice as likely as men to be widowed and, as a consequence of this and the lower propensity of the current generation (if not succeeding ones) to have married in the first place, they are three times as likely to be living alone. More women than men therefore

Table 12.1 Numbers and percentages of older women and men living in or on the margins of poverty, Great Britain, 1987

Family income in relation to supplementary benefit level	Women over 60 (000s)			Men over 65 (000s)		
	Lone	Married	Total	Lone	Married	Total
Below SB level	502	140	642	148	140	288
Receiving SB	1,043	260	1,303	307	260	567
Up to 140% SB	920	580	1,500	270	580	850
Total	2,465	980	3,445	725	980	1,705
Percentage of all pensioners in each group	77.8	39.6	61.1	61.9	39.6	46.8

Source: Johnson and Webb (1990) and author's own calculations.

survive into old age and advanced old age. But as Table 12.1 shows, the incidence of poverty among older women, especially lone women, is strikingly high compared with that of men.

Table 12.1 underestimates the poverty of older married women in two main respects. In the absence of more sophisticated data, the calculation of the numbers of married women and men living on low incomes has been forced to assume an equal division of income *within* the income unit. However, as Pahl (1980, 1989) and others have shown (and see Hilary Graham's chapter in this volume), the distribution of income within the family is likely to give women unequal access to total household resources. Secondly, it is not possible to distinguish in the aggregate figures either those married women who are not entitled to pensions until their husbands reach the age of 65 or those aged 60–4 whose husbands do not appear in the statistics. As a result the procedure of dividing the numbers of married persons by two artificially deflates the numbers and proportion of married women in poverty. If it is difficult to distinguish precisely the living standards of older women in official statistics, it is impossible to say anything at all about the position of older Black women (or men for that matter).

As a much greater proportion of women than men survive into advanced old age, they increasingly dominate the poverty profile of successively older age groups. For example, among income support recipients in 1989 the ratio of women to men increased from being roughly equal among those aged 60–9, to three to one in the 70–9 age group, to 4.6 to one for those aged 80 and over (DSS, 1991, p. 28). Women who have never married are over-represented among the very elderly. However, as Table 12.2 shows, it is *not* simply that there are more women in the older age groups. Older lone women are more likely than

Table 12.2 Percentage of pensioners supported by income support in 1989 by age, sex
and marital status

Age	Married couples	Lone men	Widows	Other lone women	All pensioners
60–4	—	—	14	27	19
65–9	3	12	16	24	7
70–4	3	11	23	29	10
75–9	9	21	37	32	21
80+	15	26	45	35	33
All pensioners	6	18	32	29	17

Note: Single people (i.e. widowed, unmarried, separated and divorced) are included in this table if
they are over pension age and married couples if the husband is 65 or above. Couples are classified
by age of husband.

Source: DSS (1989 ASE and OPCS population estimates).

Table 12.3   Average net income by age, sex and marital status, 1988: £ per
week

Age	Marital status		
	Married couples £	Lone men £	Lone women £
60–4	—	—	95
65–9	165	91	81
70–4	151	82	73
75+	135	86	70
All pensioners	152	86	76

Note: See note to Table 12.2.

Source: DSS (1988 FES).

lone men to have to rely on income support and widows are much more likely
than widowers to do so.

Further evidence of the disadvantaged position of older women in relation to
men can be gained from information on the distribution of income. Older women
in the bottom quintile of the income distribution have slightly lower incomes than
men in the same quintile and older men in the top quintile have much higher
incomes than women in the top quintile. Table 12.3 shows the inequalities in net
income between older women and men.

Two important features of Table 12.3 should be noted. The inequality
between lone men and lone women is greatest among those aged 75 and over.
Secondly, very elderly women are poorer than young ones.

The significant inequalities in income between older men and older women are mirrored in the distribution of other resources. For example, in his national survey of household resources and standards of living, Townsend found that a higher proportion of older lone women than lone men had less than £100 worth of assets and fewer than six consumer durables. The acute disadvantage experienced by widows was also noted by Townsend:

> Not only were there more of them than of other groups living in poverty or on the margins of poverty; more had no assets or virtually no assets, and fewer possessed substantial amounts of assets . . . According to a variety of indicators of economic situation, widowed women were least advantaged. (Townsend, 1979, p. 796)

A similar pattern of inequality was discovered in a local survey of all those aged 60 and over living in their own homes in the city of Aberdeen. Men had higher incomes and savings than women. Moreover, even when household income was controlled for marital status, women were still disadvantaged. These objective inequalities were reflected in subjective appraisals; for example, men envisaged less difficulty in obtaining emergency cash than women (Taylor and Ford, 1983, p. 190).

In addition to sex-based inequalities in income and household resources, older women, in general, are more disadvantaged than men according to a range of other indicators of deprivation. They are three times more likely than older men to be living alone and only half as likely to have a spouse. Older women report more illness and long-standing health problems and consult their GPs more frequently than men (OPCS, 1990). Even within broad socio-economic groupings there is a higher prevalence of reported acute sickness among older women than men. For example, among those aged 65 and over in non-manual socio-economic groups 12 per cent of men compared with 17 per cent of women report acute sickness and among manual groups the proportions are 16 per cent and 21 per cent respectively. The average number of days per year on which people in non-manual groups experience restricted activity due to illness are 32 among men aged 65 and over and 46 for women in the same age group. The figures for manual groups are 43 and 58 respectively (OPCS, 1990, p. 80; see also Victor, 1991). Older women are also more likely than older men to suffer from psychological problems such as loneliness and anxiety and to have lower levels of morale or life satisfaction (Atchley, 1976; Abrams, 1978).

The older person's experience of poverty is an enduring one and, because of their greater longevity, the poverty of older women is particularly long-lasting. In 1989 the proportion of pensioners who had been in receipt of income support for three years or more was nearly double that for younger adults (76 per cent as against 39 per cent) (DSS, 1991, p. 44).

It is important to emphasise before concluding this section that although flat-rate and earnings-related pensions imply that social *needs* are similar among older people – as, indeed, does the exclusion of older people from some benefits for people with disabilities (Walker, 1990) – the fact is that needs, as well as resources, are unevenly distributed in old age. For example, disability is a major indicator of the need for additional income and other resources among those both under and over retirement age (Townsend, 1981). People with disabilities are more likely than the non-disabled to experience poverty, have lower incomes and fewer assets. The combination of old age and disability substantially increases the risk of poverty (Townsend, 1979). Moreover, the more severe the disability, the higher the disability-related costs that are incurred and, therefore, those with the more severe disabilities are more likely to suffer financial hardship than those with less severe disabilities.

The national surveys of disability conducted by OPCS in 1985 revealed a higher prevalence of disability among women aged 75 and over than men in the same age group. Very elderly women were also more likely to experience severe disablement than their male counterparts. In the total population (including those in communal establishments) the prevalence of severe disability (OPCS categories 8–10) was 107 per 1,000 among men aged 75 and over and 154 among women in the same age group (Martin, Meltzer and Elliot, 1988, p. 22). The higher incidence of disability among older women is partly attributable to their greater longevity, but in addition some disabling conditions affect women more than men. For example, the number of women suffering from arthritis is more than three times that of men. The current generation of older women were more likely to have contracted poliomyelitis, are more likely to have strokes or develop multiple sclerosis. They also have a higher prevalence of high blood pressure and rheumatic complaints (Campling, 1981, p. 142). A significant proportion of women with these disabling conditions are also responsible for caring for a male spouse or other relative with a disability.

Primarily because of their greater experience of disability, the needs of older women are often greater than those of older men. In other words, it is not just that elderly women experience a higher incidence of poverty according to the social assistance measure of poverty. The gap between their needs and resources is likely to be even wider than the social security-based poverty line suggests.

Explanations of poverty among older women

Why are older women poor, and why is the incidence of poverty greater among this group than among older men? It would be wrong to conclude that it is simply because women live longer than men. We have already seen that even within age cohorts women are more likely to experience poverty and low incomes. An adequate explanation of the greater incidence of poverty among women in old age must reflect on the social and economic status of women *before* as well as after retirement and, therefore, the systems of distribution which determine status and access to resources. Chief among these are employment and, linked to it, the occupational pension system and social security. Inequalities forged or reinforced in the labour market are carried into retirement via occupational and state (earnings-related) pension schemes. Thus the poverty of older women is a function both of lifelong comparatively low access to resources (including the non-participation of some in the resource-generating potential of joint households via marriage); and of the restricted access to resources which is imposed by retirement and the assumptions about the level of state pensions which are allied to it. These factors imply that poverty in old age is not solely determined by gender; there are some acutely deprived groups of older men and some relatively affluent groups of older women. Nevertheless the severe disadvantage experienced by a large proportion of, in particular, very elderly women rests on the social production and distribution of resources in relation to the *combination* of social class, age, race and gender.

Some of the systematic disadvantages encountered by women in the labour market – especially working-class women, lone parents and those from ethnic minorities – are discussed elsewhere in this book and will only be mentioned here. Similarly, the role of occupational and private pensions is covered fully in the chapter by Dulcie Groves and it is therefore necessary only to highlight here the main features which disadvantage women and contribute to their greater likelihood of experiencing poverty in old age.

Occupational pensions

It is primarily through variations in access to the ownership of occupational pensions that inequalities forged or reinforced in the labour market are carried into retirement. Rights to occupational and private pensions are built up during the individual's employment. These schemes and the benefits they provide, in general, are organised hierarchically according to employment status and occupational class (James, 1984). Since women are much less likely than men to be employed full-time, to be in highly paid secure jobs or to hold managerial or professional posts, they are less likely to be members of occupational pension schemes. Those working in the public sector and those in jobs with strong union organisation are more likely to have occupational pensions.

Among full-time employees aged 16 and over, 54 per cent of women and 64 per cent of men are members of an occupational pension scheme. Women are more likely than men both not to be members of such schemes and to work for employers without them. The membership differential between men and women is particularly marked in engineering (65 per cent of men are in an occupational pension scheme and 48 per cent of women), hotels and catering (41 per cent of men and 28 per cent of women) and transport and communications (71 per cent and 54 per cent) (OPCS, 1990, p. 223).

Although over half of women employed full-time are members of employers' pension schemes, this represents only about one-fifth of adult women (Joshi and Davies, 1991). Thus the proportion of all men belonging to occupational pension schemes is more than double that of women. As a consequence, many women are reliant on their male partner's pension scheme to reduce the likelihood of their experiencing financial hardship in old age. This means, in turn, that divorce can have a devastating effect on the income prospects of, mainly, older women (Joshi and Davies, 1991).

Essentially, occupational pension schemes are designed by men with male 'family wage-earners' and male middle-class career patterns in mind, so not only do they exclude the majority of part-time workers, but they tend to assume that earnings peak in the final years of working life, which is much less often the case for women than for men. Part-time women workers are particularly disadvantaged here. Interestingly, membership of occupational schemes among women in the higher earnings groups is greater than that of men (86 per cent compared with 82 per cent among women and men with gross weekly earnings of £250 or more). This suggests a high propensity to join such schemes among women where their incomes and access to occupational pensions are on a par with men's.

The implications of this unequal access to occupational pension schemes during paid employment are that older married couples and lone men, *regardless of age*, are much more likely than lone women to have occupational pensions; three-fifths have income from such pensions compared with two-fifths of lone women. Among the very elderly (75 and over) the proportions of married couples, lone men and lone women with income from occupational pensions are 61 per cent, 49 per cent and 33 per cent respectively.

There are two forms of inequality related to occupational pensions which also serve to disadvantage very elderly women, especially widows. In the first place, there is the differential distribution of occupational schemes between men and women outlined above. Secondly, there is an inequality between younger and older women in their ability to gain access to the newly emerging occupational pension opportunities. Thus a half of lone women aged 60–4 receive income from occupational schemes compared with only a third of those aged 75 and over. This points to the changes in employment and related opportunities between the generations. Older women (55–9) in employment were more likely to have started their working lives in manual occupations, particularly semi-skilled factory work, than younger women and, therefore, their access to occupational pensions was more restricted (Martin and Roberts, 1984, p. 146).

Retirement policies

The growth of retirement and, more recently, early retirement has ensured that an increasing proportion of older people have been excluded from the labour force over the course of this century. This social process of exclusion has denied both older women and men access to earnings and the other economic, social and psychological aspects of the workplace. Partly because of the reliance of many older married women on their husband's state pension contributions, the proportion staying in the labour market beyond the age of 60 has remained fairly high (between a quarter and a fifth, compared with 8 per cent of men working beyond the age of 65). Furthermore, the proportion of older men remaining economically active fell by 50 per cent over the period 1975–88 while the rate for older women was relatively stable). There is, however, a sharp decline to only 4 per cent remaining economically active at the age of 65 or over (OPCS, 1990, p. 202). The position of non-married women is rather different. Their rates of economic activity over recent years have followed the male pattern of rapid decline in the 60–4 age group (from a third in 1973 to less than a fifth in 1988) with a similar decline in the 55–9 age group (60 per cent to 48 per cent).

The operation of this social process of exclusion from the formal economy (called retirement) has been closely related to the organisation of production and the demand for labour. Accounts of the emergence first of retirement and then of early retirement suggest that older people and, it must be said, particularly older men, have in fact been used as a reserve army of labour, to be tapped when labour is in short supply and to be shed when demand falls (Graebner, 1980; Phillipson, 1982; Walker, 1985b). The advent of large-scale unemployment in the 1930s was crucial to the institutionalisation of retirement, and its return in the mid-1970s and then again in the early 1980s resulted in two surges in the growth of early retirement (Walker and Taylor, 1991).

Like the experience of employment, attitudes towards retirement and the experience of retirement itself are socially divided. Although a significant proportion of women remain economically active until the age of 60 or even 65, retirement is still regarded as a predominantly male experience. Of course, with economic activity rates among women peaking at around two-thirds for married women in middle age and four-fifths for non-married women in their twenties and early thirties, there are a significant proportion who never experience 'retirement' from paid employment in their own right because they have withdrawn from the labour market long before formal retirement age. But since this proportion is relatively small, the main explanation for the neglect of women in the study of retirement is more likely to be a combination of two particular factors. First, women's labour market participation is regarded as marginal in comparison with that of men. Secondly, the vast majority of economically active women are engaged in at least two roles – formal and informal – and there is no such thing as retirement from the latter domestic role. The assumption appears to be, therefore, that women do not experience the same degree of loss as men do when they retire from paid work.

The experience of retirement is also divided on the basis of occupational class. There are those, mainly salaried, workers who are able to choose whether or not to leave work at the retirement age, leave prematurely, or perhaps work on. Then there are those, predominantly male workers, who are effectively coerced into retirement and sometimes early retirement by poor working conditions, ill-health, redundancy and unemployment (Walker, 1985b; Walker and Taylor, 1991). Thus for large numbers of older workers, poverty is experienced *prior* to the official pension ages. In fact, redundancy (or the threat of it) and ill-health are the main reasons why older people leave employment prematurely (S. Parker, 1980; Laczko *et al.*, 1988). So for some older workers the retirement age is effectively lowered by unemployment, sickness or injury. As with unemployment itself, semi-skilled and unskilled workers are over-represented among those who are 'discouraged' from economic activity by lack of employment opportunities, including some of the early retired.

Because the arbitrary pension ages of 60 and 65 have been adopted as customary retirement ages, women have been forced to retire five years earlier than men. In general, the earlier the retirement the sooner the imposition of poverty and, especially in the case of older women, the longer that poverty must be endured.

A series of legal rulings by the European Court of Justice and the House of Lords have pushed the British government towards the equalisation of retirement ages, if not pension ages. In 1986, the European Court ruled that the earlier retirement age for a woman employed by a health authority contravened the EC Equal Treatment Directive 76/207. As a result, the government added an amendment to the Sex Discrimination Bill (1986) to make it unlawful for a woman to be dismissed on grounds of age when a man would not be. In 1990, the European Court held that a 60-year-old man employed by an insurance company had been unlawfully discriminated against because when he had been made redundant his company pension scheme was deferred whereas a female member of the scheme could have drawn her pension immediately. This ruling mirrored the previous one but applied to occupational pension schemes as opposed to the then state retirement ages. Early in 1991, six women pensioners won a long-running case for compensation against their employer after being forced to retire from their jobs at 60. Their case began in an industrial tribunal in 1986, went to the European Court and was finally ruled on in April 1991. Despite these landmark judgments and the abolition of the earnings rule in 1989 (see below), the five-year differential in state pension age still remains at the time of writing. Moreover, the achievement of equal retirement ages, when it eventually comes, though significant, would do nothing to remove the tyranny of fixed age retirement for both women and men.

The main implications of age-barrier retirement are, first, that it results in an average fall in income of about a half. As a result, those who continue in employment after retirement age are less likely to experience poverty. Secondly, for those who do continue in employment, retirement age can produce a dramatic downward shift in occupational status (Walker, 1981, p. 82). So, for example, in the national survey of retirement conducted in 1977, between the age groups of 50–9 and 60–73, the proportion of women in junior and intermediate non-manual socio-economic groups fell from nearly half to nearly one-third, while the proportion in the unskilled group rose from one in ten to nearly one in four (S. Parker, 1980). Of course, these changes in employment and socio-economic status were reflected in earnings.

Pension and social security policies

The corollary of this social process of exclusion from the labour force, coupled with restricted access to alternative forms of post-retirement income, is that older people and women in particular are heavily dependent on the state for financial support. They are, in effect, trapped in poverty by virtue of their reliance on state benefits. We have seen that retirement has a differential impact on older people which depends primarily on their prior socio-economic status and the access which this grants to resources which might be carried into retirement. In addition, because of social pressures to limit the level of state pensions and other benefits for those outside the labour force, retirement imposes a lowered social status on the majority of older people in comparison with younger adults in the labour force (Walker, 1980, 1992).

The dependency relationship between older people, the state and the labour market was institutionalised by the 'retirement condition', introduced in 1949, whereby state pensions were conditional on retirement rather than age. Thus, until recently, the state pension was, in effect, a 'retirement' pension. This encouraged an end to labour force participation and established the two arbitrary ages as customary retirement ages. (Ironically, Beveridge (1942) had hoped that the retirement condition would encourage workers to defer retirement.) On 1 October 1989 the retirement condition was abolished along with the earnings rule which placed restrictions on what national insurance pensioners could earn. However, the state pension is still tied to the ages of 60 and 65, though it looks like this will change after the next general election, as a result of pressure from the European Court rulings outlined above and, in particular, their impact on the private pension industry. Whether this will mean a levelling up to 65 or down to 60 is not clear at this stage. The safest bet, actuarially and politically, is the age of 63 with its obvious implications for the extension of the working lives of women as a means of 'paying for' the reduction of those of men. The abolition of the earnings rule is likely to widen inequalities in income between older men and women as it will allow the former's higher earnings to be extended into old age.

The social security system is also one of the main mechanisms through which the income inequalities between older women and men are both generated and reinforced and by which the dependence of women on men is encouraged. Older married women are less likely than men to receive a National Insurance retirement pension in their own right. Thus, just under two-thirds of women in receipt of retirement pension have qualified on their partner's insurance contributions (DSS, 1991, p. 89).

The basic pension is payable according to a contributions formula which stipulates that to gain a full pension, sufficient contributions have to be paid in nine out of every ten years of a 'working life' (i.e. paid employment). So, if a person's paid employment lasts for forty years, she will need to have thirty-six qualifying years. Many women are unable to qualify for a full pension because of periods spent out of the labour force or in part-time work while caring for children or disabled relatives. Some limited home responsibilities protection was introduced in April 1978 in order to help women in this position, but in order to qualify for a full pension they still require twenty years' worth of contributions or credits. While single women receive a single person's pension, married and divorced women can choose to claim a pension in their own right (if they have sufficient contributions) or as a dependent wife. However, the dependent wife receives only 60 per cent of the single person's pension – a fact that reflects not only the dependent status of married women but also the failure of the social security system to adapt to the increase in economic activity (particularly in part-time jobs) among women since the Beveridge scheme was introduced.

The state earnings related pension (SERP) scheme also tends to disadvantage women as much as the basic pension, and recent changes to the SERP scheme have worsened their position. The SERP scheme was introduced in 1975. It applies only to those reaching pensionable age since April 1978 and will not reach full maturity until 1998. Because it is an earnings-related scheme, if women do qualify for a SERP, the pension they receive will reflect their tendency to earn less than men. Of course, because the scheme is in the process of maturation, the vast majority of current pensioners, both women and men, do not receive a SERP.

Ironically, the introduction of the SERP scheme did represent an attempt to improve the pension position of widows and other women. It allowed the surviving spouse to inherit the full SERP entitlement of a contributor, provided both were over retirement age. It also provided for home responsibility credits towards the basic pension. This relative 'generosity' to women was one of the main sources of official criticism of the scheme when it came under fire in the mid-1980s (Bornatt *et al.*, 1985, p. 31). The government's original proposal for the SERP scheme in the Green Paper on the Reform of Social Security was to abolish it altogether (DHSS, 1985a). However, the weight of influential opinion against this option, which included the Confederation of British Industry and the National Association of Pension Funds, and the public outcry which greeted the proposal, caused the government to modify its plans. Thus proposals in the White Paper (DHSS, 1985b) were intended instead to reduce the cost of the SERP scheme. Two of the measures enacted by the 1986 Social Security Act had a significant impact on women by reversing the main attempts of the 1975 scheme to begin, albeit very slowly, to adjust state pensions to the economic experiences of women.

In the first place it is proposed that the calculation of earnings-related pension is now based on 20 per cent of a lifetime's average earnings (forty years) rather than 25 per cent of the best twenty years. This had been considered to be 'over-generous' to those, especially women, who have shorter than average periods of employment or non-incremental earnings. Moreover, because SERPS provides the basis for the guaranteed minimum pension within occupational schemes, this measure also replicates in the private sector the disadvantage experienced by women in the public sector. Secondly, the proportion of SERPS that can be inherited by a spouse has been reduced to a half rather than the full amount under the original scheme (Walker, 1986, p. 193). The limited steps made by women towards more equal treatment in the provision of state earnings-related pensions were therefore reversed by the 1986 Act. Although these contentious measures were deferred until after the 1987 General Election, they were barely discussed during the campaign itself. The proposals made by the then DHSS for the rest of the social security system, including social assistance, were not deferred. On the basis of the government's own estimates, all of these changes made 1.9 million pensioners aged 60–79 and 350,000 of those aged 80 and over worse off, the vast majority of them being women (DHSS, 1985b).

Further changes introduced by the 1986 Social Security Act were intended to increase the numbers who contract out of the SERP scheme. In essence, these created rebates on contributions to occupational schemes and reduced the requirements they had to meet in order to be officially 'approved'. For the first time, money purchase schemes have been allowed to contract out (i.e. pension schemes that depend on the outcome of investments rather than a formula based on contributions). Again, because of their lower earnings and more precarious relationship to the labour market, women's access to this government subsidy and the most attractive occupational schemes is likely to be more restricted than men's (see Dulcie Groves' chapter in this volume).

This brief review of retirement and pension policies should be sufficient to indicate that the economic dependency – and therefore the poverty – of older people in general and older women in particular has been socially manufactured. Two sets of policies are in operation. On the one hand, age-restrictive social policies have been used by the state both to exclude older workers from the labour force and to legitimate that exclusion through the notion of 'retirement'. On the other hand, sex-discriminatory policies, particularly in the provision of pensions, have restricted the access of older women to even minimal income entitlements on a par with men. When coupled with the impact of lifelong low social and economic status resulting from the influence of social class, the effect of these policies is to impose the very severest deprivation on very elderly working-class women. For example, in the study of older people in Aberdeen, younger (60–74) middle-class men and older (75+) working-class women were the two groups at the extreme ends of the income distribution. None of the middle-class men had incomes below £30 per week and over half had incomes in excess of £60. By comparison, more than three in five of the older working-class women had an income of less than £30 per week and none had over £60 (Taylor and Ford, 1983, p. 192).

Conclusions

Because the widespread poverty of older women and the penury experienced by some groups among them derive to a considerable extent from the operation of social and economic policies within patriarchal capitalism, any major change in their status rests on the development of alternative policies. There is not space here to outline a full manifesto (see Bornatt *et al.*, 1985; Walker, 1986, 1990) but three fundamental sets of policies will be highlighted.

The practical implication of the analysis presented here is that the main determinants of the poverty of older women and the inequalities between them and older men have already been established long *before* retirement age. As in other spheres of women's lives, the key to their poverty and deprivation in old age is the socially constructed relationship between gender and the labour market. The labour market is the primary source of the inequalities which are carried into retirement. Major changes are required in the structure and organisation of work to give women in general, and older women in particular, equal access to paid employment and, in addition, a genuine choice about retirement. The promotion of *work* for all, regardless of gender, throughout the economy is the only realistic way that choice can be provided for women and older workers. This means that *both* paid *and* unpaid labour must be assessed in terms of their contributions to society and rewarded commensurately.

A broad focus on work is necessary because the concentration of policy on access to paid employment is unlikely to overcome the sexual division of labour in the home and the restrictions it imposes on women's role in paid employment. Care must be taken, however, to ensure that a broader-based policy does not simply confirm the subordinate position of women as the primary domestic workers. Equality of access must be promoted in all forms of work with the right not to take part in some roles as strongly guarded as the right of access to others. Furthermore, flexible retirement, with a minimum pension age of 60 for both women and men, would provide opportunities for older people to choose when precisely to retire (Walker and Laczko, 1982; Schuller and Walker, 1990).

Secondly, since many of the inequalities in pension provision derive from assumptions underlying the Beveridge social security system, an alternative approach is required if the poverty of older women is to be overcome. All pensioners have a need for income *regardless* of whether their previous employment was waged or unwaged. The priority is the provision of an adequate (in terms of social participation) flat-rate pension regardless of history or gender. This means that the contribution or employment test, which discriminates against substantial numbers of women, should be abandoned. The pension would be paid on an individual basis and at a level that enables older people to participate in the normal life of the community. The provision of an adequate flat-rate pension would also prove a better vehicle than pension-splitting for dealing with the problems that are likely to face older women in the future as a result of divorce. By the year 2025, some one in seven older women will be divorced (Joshi and Davies, 1991).

Thirdly, the special needs of the large proportion of very elderly people with disabilities, overwhelmingly women, must be recognised in the form of a disablement allowance paid *in addition* to the retirement pension. This would compensate for the extra costs and disadvantages of disability, and thereby help to reduce the disparity experienced by many older women between their needs and resources.

What chance is there that a start on such a package could be made in the near future? After all, the poverty of older people has been recognised by both official and independent research for over 100 years. Moreover, this account has demonstrated that social policies themselves reflect the paternalistic assumptions embedded in capitalist relations. The socially constructed relationship between age, gender and the labour market has not only been the cause of poverty in old age, but has also formed the basis for the spread of a more general dependency among older people and age discrimination in many aspects of public policy and social attitudes (Walker, 1990). Older women are especially prone to ageist assumptions and comments. Despite their preponderance in the population, they are usually ignored by the wider society and also to some extent by the women's movement (Peace, 1986). In the first edition of this volume I pointed, optimistically, to some signs that this situation was changing slowly with, for example, the establishment of the Older Feminists Network in 1982 and the recent Age Concern/EOC joint initiative on incomes in old age. But they remain merely hopeful signs. Moreover, Britain lags far behind developments in the USA, where older persons' organisations like the Gray Panthers are dominated by women, and where the shared interests between women and older people are recognised more commonly. Men, both young and old, and the social institutions they have constructed in their image, have proved consistently impervious to the longstanding case for equality between the sexes in the distribution of power and resources. There are very few hopeful signs of change on that front. Men are unlikely to be divested of power and advantage without a struggle.

Perhaps the combination of the growing strength of the feminist movement in this country and the expanding numbers of older women over the next twenty to forty years will provide the keys to political and social change. The women's movement in the USA has played a major role in exposing the similar processes which are responsible for the creation of sexism and ageism (and, for that matter, racism). Moreover, this broad focus has enabled older women to participate fully in the opposition to the twin evils of sex and age discrimination. Without a recognition of the common disadvantage experienced by women and older people, there is always a danger that proposals to eliminate sexism in certain aspects of social policy may unwittingly condone ageism by arguing that there is actually a conflict of interest between women (as carers) and older people (see, for example, Finch, 1984). Until the potential political power of the millions of women who are disadvantaged in relation to paid and unpaid labour and in retirement is realised, policies to combat the poverty of many of those aged 60 and over are not likely to be forthcoming. Unfortunately, the very poverty that afflicts older women so deeply is a major factor in their political acquiescence.

Note

1. I am very grateful to the Department of Social Security for providing the statistics contained in Tables 12.2 and 12.3.

13 Occupational pension provision and women's poverty in old age

Dulcie Groves

When in the 1960s poverty was 'rediscovered' in the UK, it became clear from research findings that those elderly people who had occupational retirement pensions derived from their previous employment were least likely to be living in poverty, as then defined. It also became clear that women were greatly under-represented among that minority of elderly people who had such occupational pensions. Furthermore, most female occupational pensioners were, in the language of the day, spinsters – mainly former teachers or civil servants. Few married women had occupational pensions derived from their own earnings. Surprisingly few widows had occupational pensions derived from their husbands' entitlements. Elderly non-married women were substantially over-represented among the poorest. 'Very elderly' women over 75 were among the poorest of all.

What are the links between female poverty in old age and access to occupational pension scheme benefits? Why was this early-1960s generation of older women, the youngest survivors of whom are, in the early 1990s, among the oldest within the current 'very elderly' female population, so under-represented among those with an employer's pension? How effective has occupational pension provision been in removing the present generation of 'young elderly' women, currently aged 60–75, from poverty? What are the prospects for the present generation of working-age women (16–60) with regard to occupational pension entitlements when they themselves reach pensionable age?

Women's access to occupational pension benefits, particularly those derived from their own (not a husband's) paid work record, is a crucial issue in the light of the major changes to retirement pension provision enacted in 1986 (see Groves, 1991). It is also important in the light of recent legal changes which have as their goal 'economic self-sufficiency' for divorced women. The aims of this chapter are, first, to explain why women now over pensionable age have benefited less than men from the existence of occupational pension provision, thus increasing their likelihood of being poor in old age. Secondly, it will comment on working-age women's access to membership of employers' pension schemes and the extent to which it appears that their risk of poverty in retirement may have lessened, both by increased access in their own right and through improved provision for widows. This critique, presented in an historical perspective, will focus both on women's opportunities to generate eventual occupational pension scheme benefits themselves via paid employment, and on issues relating to widows' benefits.

The modern 'occupational pension' (or employer's pension) derives from an early nineteenth-century civil service provision whereby elderly (or infirm) employees deemed to be suffering from physical or mental disabilities could be 'superannuated'; that is, 'retired' and awarded a replacement income or pension in an amount proportionate to the total number of years of service completed. By mid-century, a standard format had been devised which allowed a long-service civil servant to retire at a minimum age of 60 on a pension equal, at maximum, to two-thirds of his previous salary. The scheme was devised by men for men, since no women civil servants were at that time employed (Rhodes, 1965, Chapter 2).

These civil service pension arrangements were in due course copied, with modifications, by other public and private sector employers, though up to World War I it appears to have been a small minority of mainly the more prestigious employers who developed such formal occupational pension provision. Some schemes developed out of previous informal arrangements, characterised as *ex gratia* pensions, whereby an employer would award a retirement pension to a particularly long-serving or otherwise 'deserving' employee – a paternalistic, 'one-off' arrangement which could fail if the employer later ceased trading. All such pensions came to be known, in common parlance, as 'private pensions', to distinguish them from the state pensions first introduced in 1908 for indigent elderly people over 70, followed later (1925) by contributory state retirement and widows' pension schemes.

Strictly speaking, all these 'occupational' or employers' pensions were either 'public sector' pensions derived from formal arrangements made for central or local government employees or 'private sector' pensions. The latter were derived from commercial, industrial or other employment within the 'private sector' of the labour market. Banks and insurance companies were early providers of formal occupational pension schemes during the second half of the nineteenth century. After World War I there was an expansion of such private sector provision. Employers who might previously have paid *ex gratia* pensions to favoured employees began to set up formal schemes arranged through insurance companies (Rhodes, 1965, p. 87). The target beneficiary was the salaried 'family man' who, by reason of earning more than the £250 limit applied to non-manual workers, was excluded from participation in the new 1925 contributory state scheme, under which a retirement pension became payable at 65 and a modest pension became available to widows of any age (Groves, 1983, p. 41).

These early developments in occupational pension provision pre-dated the later nineteenth-century trend towards the employment of women in 'white-collar' occupations. Women were not, for instance, recruited into the civil service until the 1870s. They came on the scene when the private telegraph companies were 'nationalised' and integrated into the Post Office, the women literally being taken on as a 'job lot' with their male colleagues. These and later women were brought into the civil service pension scheme designed, as noted, for men. The civil service, like the private telegraph companies, found its female employees to be competent, 'docile' workers, with the additional advantage of being cheaper to employ than men. Women did not qualify for a 'family wage' since it was assumed (erroneously in some cases) that they lived at home with parents or relatives and that they did not have dependants to support financially. The crunch came when it was realised that these competent women had a propensity to marry (Martindale, 1939).

The civil service 'efficiency experts' of the mid-1870s quickly worked out that the retention of married women would be 'inefficient' in managerial terms, since the longer that female employees remained in government service, the more they would cost because of the modest incremental salary progression within their low-paid 'women's grades'. Furthermore, there was a danger that they would stay in service long enough to qualify for a retirement pension – an even more expensive proposition. Swiftly a 'marriage bar' was introduced, though its application does not appear to have been universal in the civil service until 1894 when government typists (hitherto an 'unestablished' all-female grade) obtained permanent, pensionable 'established' status by agreeing to a rule requiring automatic resignation on marriage. It was agreed that in lieu of the pension forgone, such women would qualify for a 'marriage gratuity' on leaving – a lump sum of a value relating to years of service not exceeding twelve (Martindale, 1939; Holcombe, 1973).

The 'marriage bar' became the rule in other forms of public sector employment and in many types of private sector employment, especially when unemployment rates were high between the two world wars. Thus up to the end of World War II (when the public sector marriage bar was abolished and young women retained paid jobs on marriage), in order to qualify for an occupational pension in old age derived from her own earnings a woman usually had to remain unmarried. The choice was marriage or career. Furthermore, salaried men were not expected to have 'working wives'. The development of widows' provision in occupational pension schemes is a reflection of this bourgeois family form (see Hall, 1979).

Holcombe (1973) has pinpointed five major occupations entered by women, from choice and/or financial necessity, in the late nineteenth century – teaching, the civil service, nursing, clerical work and employment in the retail trades. Women's occupational 'choices' were limited and these five occupations predominated up to the time of World War II and well beyond it. Elementary school teachers had access to a national pension scheme from 1898 so that teaching, along with the civil service, came to be thought of as a 'secure' pensionable occupation – a 'good job' for a single woman. Nursing in public hospitals was also pensionable, while the more prestigious voluntary hospitals were early pension providers. The Royal National Pension Fund for Nurses (1887) is an early example of the personal 'portable' pension, which entailed taking out an insurance policy so as to purchase an annuity on retirement. However, nurses were very badly paid, which may in part account for a seemingly low take-up of non-compulsory pension scheme provision for nurses (Maggs, 1983, p. 131).

In 1936 the Ministry of Labour carried out a pioneer survey of private sector employers' pension scheme membership, finding that women comprised about 20 per cent of the total membership of around 1.6 million persons. Nearly half the women were in the 'administration, clerical and sales' category, a minority being in sales. Private sector nurses were included and, indicative of an expansion of occupational pension provision into higher-status 'manual' employment during the inter-war period, just over half the women in private sector schemes were manual workers (*Ministry of Labour Gazette*, 1938). However, the 'progressive' employers who developed this form of occupational welfare, mainly after World War I (Jones, 1983), typically operated a 'marriage bar' and the 'women's pension scheme' doubled as a savings scheme which produced marriage gratuities.

The eventual pensions received by women who participated in these inter-war schemes would have reflected their low and unequal pay as well as conditions of service which typically required women to retire much earlier than men, especially in private sector employment. The Ministry of Labour survey showed that no fewer than 37 per cent of the 'administrative, clerical and sales' group were made to retire by 55 and a similar proportion by the age of 60, whereas 65 was the 'normal' retirement age for men (*Ministry of Labour Gazette*, 1938). Such practices reflect pre-war pension policies which, from the point at which women first began to enter white-collar employment, were clearly geared towards the recruitment of successive cohorts of low-paid young women for routine duties, a rapid turnover being ensured via the marriage bar. Employers were content to retain a cadre of single women who could supervise other women, though once into their fifties such women were at risk of being construed as 'too old'. Formal occupational pension provision was used 'in the managerial interest' to retire women early, a practice which could increase their risk of poverty in old age. Meanwhile, for men, such provision was a well-established device used to attract and retain competent male employees. Occupational pension scheme rules and related personnel policies helped to construct salaried men, in particular, as 'good providers', who typically served out a lengthy working life with one employer.

While occupational pension provision was originally intended as 'superannuation', it gradually came to incorporate provision for dependants, typically widows or dependent children including unmarried adult daughters. Again, *ex gratia* arrangements appear to have preceded the inauguration of formal schemes. The civil service in 1909 reduced the retirement pension from two-thirds to half salary in order to provide a lump sum in addition. By this means a male pensioner could choose to provide for any dependants after his death (Rhodes, 1965, p. 51). The police force was the first public sector occupation to achieve widows' pensions as such. By the mid-1930s male civil servants could choose to 'allocate' part of their pensions; that is, to opt for a lower pension on retirement, so that if they died first their wives would get a modest continuing pension (*ibid.*, p. 79). From 1937 male teachers could opt to take only one-third of the lump sum due to them on retirement so that an annuity would potentially be available to their widows (Gosden, 1972, p. 148). By the mid-1930s such 'option' arrangements were characteristic of private sector provision also; it was for the male breadwinner alone to decide whether he would so provide for his dependants or take his full pension on retirement. The new insurance-based schemes adopted by the private sector between the wars offered the possibility of a lump sum payment where a scheme member died in service (Owen, 1935, p. 88).

In the two decades between the outbreak of World War II and the poverty studies of the early 1960s there were changes both in patterns of female economic activity and in the nature of occupational pension provision. The latter expanded under favourable tax arrangements begun during the war (Pilch and Wood, 1979). However, although in wartime married women were positively encouraged and in some cases required to re-enter or remain in the labour market, working in those very occupations from which they had previously been 'barred', such women were often categorised as temporary workers, or were employed part-time. There is no evidence to suggest that they made substantial wartime gains in terms of occupational pension entitlements.

Nor, once the war had ended and formal marriage bars were removed, did the increasing presence of married women in the labour force mean that efforts were made to extend female access to membership of occupational pension schemes. Far from it. It was still the case that a white-collar woman employee within the public sector (including, now, the nationalised industries) had reasonably good pension prospects provided that she completed a lengthy period of full-time service. However, the early surveys of the Government Actuary's department show that in the private sector in 1956 there were only 34 per cent of 'salaried' women (71 per cent of men) and 23 per cent of 'waged' women (38 per cent of men) in schemes (Government Actuary, 1958, p. 4). By 1963 somewhat comparable proportions were 40 per cent of 'non-manual' women in schemes (80 per cent of men) and 15 per cent of 'manual' women (55 per cent of men) (Government Actuary, 1966, p. 12).

It was accepted practice for employers to admit women to schemes at older ages than men – 30 was not uncommon. In the post-war decades, the majority of women had married and subsequently left paid work to have children by the age of 30 (see Rimmer, 1981). However, they increasingly returned to work in both the public and private sectors once their children were in school, but tended to do so part-time (see Manley and Sawbridge, 1980). Nor, even if full-time, did they typically do the same type or level of paid work as that performed by the men who were included in the employers' pension schemes. The post-war National Insurance arrangements made it an unattractive proposition for married women, typically low-waged, to opt for paying full National Insurance contributions when a much cheaper 'married woman's option' was available. This option gave a married woman the right to a dependent wife's retirement pension at 60 per cent of a full single person's rate, once her husband had retired. Furthermore, even if a woman paid in for a full pension she had to pass the 'half test'; that is, she had to work for at least half of her married life before she could count in her contributions both before and after marriage (Groves, 1983, pp. 45–7). This rule resulted in only a small minority of married women becoming fully insured and helped to reinforce their financial dependence within marriage. It also helped to construct married women and, by extension, all young women, as employees who were 'not interested' in pensions, their wages typically being construed as 'pin money'. The technical pensions literature of the early 1960s advised employers to leave women out of pension schemes and give *ex gratia* (unfunded) pensions to that dwindling minority of single women who did become long-serving employees (Pilch and Wood, 1960, p. 80). Occupational pension providers were more interested in improving the benefits available to women as widows, rather than as scheme members in their own right. By 1960 widows' pensions were available in all public sector occupations apart from teaching, though they were still relatively uncommon in the private sector which continued to rely on 'allocation' options and lump sum provision (Government Actuary, 1958, 1966).

The above scenario helps to explain the part played by access to occupational pension scheme benefits in determining the income levels of the elderly women whose financial circumstances were studied between 1959 and 1965. Cole with Utting (1962, Chapter 5) estimated that 76 per cent of single and widowed women over pensionable age in Britain in 1959 were living in poverty (defined as less than £3.50 per week). Whereas 37 per cent of couples and 38 per cent of non-married men had an employer's pension, only 7 per cent of non-married women had one, including an even smaller percentage of widows. Likewise Townsend and Wedderburn (1965, Chapter 4), studying elderly people over 65 in Britain in 1962, found only 11 per cent of non-married women with occupational benefits – 18 per cent of single women and 9 per cent of widows, the older women being the poorest. By 1965 it appeared that 48 per cent of retired men over 65, but only 24 per cent of single women over 60 and 11 per cent of widows over pensionable age had employers' pensions, younger women predominating among those women who had a pension in their own right (Ministry of Pensions and National Insurance, 1966, p. 154). The single women had, on average, better pension levels than the men in all age groups, reflecting the levels of female employment in white-collar, public sector jobs. However, Townsend and Wedderburn (1965, Chapter 5) make it clear that the low level of many occupational pension payments sometimes served merely to keep their recipients off National Assistance, though still on the margins of poverty. Indeed, while it is not the brief of this chapter to comment on state pension provision, it must be remarked that in the early 1960s, as subsequently, it was chiefly the low level of state provision which made the presence or absence of entitlement to occupational pension benefits so crucial to many household budgets, not least to lone female households.

The introduction in the early 1960s of the state 'graduated' pension scheme, an earnings-related second-tier provision for lower income employees not in occupational pension schemes, opened up a growing gender gap in employee pension coverage. The lowest earners, seldom included in employers' pension provision and among whom women predominated, were excluded from the graduated scheme. Meanwhile employers continued to expand occupational provision for full-time salaried and some manual grades of staff, to the extent that full-time employment in the public sector became largely synonymous with access to occupational scheme membership. Employers, on the advice of specialists within the pensions 'industry', contracted out their better paid grades of full-time staff from the new graduated scheme (Heclo, 1974, p. 273). Hence the number of men in private sector schemes increased dramatically, by 3 million between 1956 and 1967, but among women by only half a million (Government Actuary, 1981, p. 6). From the late 1960s to the mid-1970s there was much political debate on pensions reform and two failed attempts at legislation before the Social Security Pensions Act 1975 was passed, becoming effective in 1978. The Labour Party favoured a major role for earnings-related state pension provision while the Conservatives wished for broad occupational coverage and a residual second-tier state pension, in which many employed women would have found themselves. The compromise was a system within which 'approved' occupational pension schemes were closely related to a new state earnings-related pension scheme (SERPS). Employers could contract 'occupational groups' of employees out of SERPS and into employers' provision (see Groves, 1983).

The Government Actuary's 1983 and 1987 surveys show that, during the years since the 1975 survey, about half of all men in private sector employment had access to occupational pension provision. However, whereas in 1975 17 per cent of women had access, the proportion increased to 25 per cent in 1979 (Government Actuary, 1978, p. 8; 1981, p. 4). By 1987 34 per cent of full-time private sector women were covered but only 7 per cent of part-timers

(Government Actuary, 1991, Table 2.4, p. 6). Since 1967 the number of women in public sector schemes had nearly doubled from 1 to 2 million, while the number of women in private schemes had risen from 1.3 to 1.4 million. Male membership, by contrast, fell by 35 per cent in the private sector and by 10 per cent in the public sector (*ibid.*, Table 2.1, p. 4). Female numbers partially reflect a major increase in female labour force participation since 1967, while male numbers reflect, among other factors, a declining number of men in the British workforce.

It might be thought that the present generation of 'younger' retired women have, by virtue of improved access to occupational pension benefits, greatly reduced their risk of poverty in old age, which for women officially begins five years earlier than men at the 'pensionable age' of 60. However, in 1982 only 40 per cent of lone (i.e. non-married) women aged 60–4 had their own and/or a widow's occupational pension and 25 per cent of that age group were drawing a supplementary (means-tested) state pension. Between the ages of 65 and 69, 37 per cent of lone women and 62 per cent of lone men had some sort of occupational pension. Only 20 per cent of the lone men drew supplementary pensions, along with 33 per cent of widows and 28 per cent of other lone women (DHSS, 1984, p. 17, Table 4; p. 19, Table 7). Married couples were most likely to have occupational pensions and least likely to have a supplementary pension. However, Hunt (1978, p. 28, Table 6.4.3) showed that employers' pensions were a very small component of elderly wives' incomes.

Analysis of data from the 1985 and 1986 General Household Surveys (Ginn and Arber, 1991) provides much detail on gender inequalities in occupational pension entitlements and in the actual value of pensions paid. Only 26 per cent of women over 65 had income from their own or a survivor's pension, as compared with 62 per cent of men. A further 2 per cent of women and 4 per cent of men had income from private pensions not derived from past employment (*ibid.*, Table I, p. 378). Only 12 per cent of married women had 'non-state pension' income from these two sources compared with 67 per cent of married men, as did 34 per cent of widows (60 per cent of widowers), 28 per cent of separated/divorced women (46 per cent men) and 47 per cent of single women (46 per cent men) (*ibid.*, 1991, Table II, p. 383). Single women are a very small proportion of the entire age cohort: among them it was the non-manual workers, notably those who had had professional or managerial jobs, who had non-state pensions. Furthermore, only 20 per cent of the women were getting more than £5 per week in non-state pension income, as compared with 50 per cent of the men. Only 7 per cent of the women were getting more than £25, though 26 per cent of the men were reaching this level. Women were severely under-represented among those pensioners with the highest non-state pension incomes.

Entitlement to a good occupational pension and access to any associated lump sum benefits is the key to a more adequate income in old age. To date, women have been greatly under-represented among those pensioners with such entitlements. The typically bi-modal career followed by women in Britain over recent decades (leaving aside the marriage bar which affected older women) has meant that married women and mothers of any marital status do not fit into structures of occupational pension provision designed for male breadwinners. Both the current generation of 'young elderly' women and women now of working age have been profoundly affected by the following aspects of women's employment and employers' pension provision.

Occupational pension provision has always served best the interests of employees who have a lifelong record of full time employment in the better paid occupations which offer an employer's pension as a fringe benefit. Outside public sector employment, which offers transferable pension rights, occupational pension benefits are maximised by minimal job changing or by an ability to compensate for any loss of pension rights on job change through a better remunerated new job. It is men rather than women who have, typically, been able to fulfil these requirements. Most women since World War II have had interrupted working lives. The Department of Employment's survey of women who were of working age in 1980 (Martin and Roberts, 1984) presents much evidence to explain why most women do not complete lengthy periods of pensionable service and why, where they have had access to occupational pension benefits, they tend to end up with lower weekly rates of pension and smaller lump sums than their male contemporaries. Most employers have required women to retire from their jobs at a 'normal' pensionable age of 60, whereas a much greater number of men are permitted to remain until 65, despite trends towards earlier retirement. While this practice has now been successfully challenged in the courts, the effects on pension scheme provision and older women's economic activity rates have yet to be seen (Davidson, 1990).

Women's limited access to employers' pension benefits are directly related to the traditional domestic division of labour which assigns the 'breadwinner' role to men, principally husbands, and the major responsibility for the unpaid work of the home (especially child care) to women. Joshi and Owen (1981, pp. 106–7) studied the labour force participation of successive cohorts of women in Britain from 1950 to 1974 and found that it was motherhood, rather than marriage, which determined the length of women's lives in paid work with Ms Average withdrawing from the labour market for seven years. Younger women had higher economic activity rates. Martin and Roberts (1984, pp. 11–12) found that older women, many of whom would not have been contributing to the state pension scheme in their own right, tended to leave the labour market in their mid-fifties. Caring for elderly relatives or an ailing husband is a common reason for such withdrawal (Finch and Groves, 1983).

A striking feature of women's economic activity (highlighted in the chapters by Susan Lonsdale and Heather Joshi in this volume) is the extent to which mothers and some childless women work part-time. This typically depresses their eventual income in old age. Only 12 per cent of part-time women workers (7 per cent of those in the private sector and 21 per cent of those in the public sector) were members of occupational pension schemes in 1987 (Government Actuary, 1991, Table 2.4, p. 6). Women working more than fifteen hours per week part-time are far more likely to be in an employer's pension scheme than those working less (OPCS, 1990, Table 10.14, p. 229).

In the past decade, employers have made increasing use of temporary and fixed-term 'short duration' contract staff. Meager (1986) showed that in 1984 such employment strategies were widely applied in relation to personal service, office and manual workers and to some extent to the recruitment of managerial, technical and professional staff. Two-thirds of the 'short duration' workers identified in the sample were women in non-professional categories. Case studies showed that employers made savings arising 'mainly from temporary workers having less beneficial (or no) entitlement to holiday and sickness pay, and particularly to occupational pensions' (Meager, 1986, p. 12). It was the larger employers of more than 200 workers who had greatly expanded their temporary recruitment since 1980. These were the very employers who, in the past, had been most likely to include their workers in occupational pension schemes (Government Actuary, 1958, 1966, 1968, 1972, 1978, 1981).

Women's work has always been highly segregated (Hakim, 1981), with important implications for female access to occupational pension benefits. The Social Security Pensions Act 1975 specifically allows employers to exclude workers from membership of occupational pension schemes by occupational category, thus facilitating the legal exclusion of women in vertically segregated occupational categories which are mainly or exclusively female. However, even where, as in many public sector occupations, membership of an employer's pension scheme was (until 1988) automatic for permanent full-time staff, including women, horizontal segregation ensured that women, typically, ended their working lives with lower pension benefits than their male colleagues.

Among women working full-time in the better paid jobs, there is a concentration of women in the lower grades of their particular type of employment. Martin and Roberts (1984, pp. 151–2 and Heather Joshi's chapter here) document the downward mobility experienced by women returning to paid work after a break, especially when returning to part-time work. Many full-timers have also had periods of part-time work or career breaks. Thus with their typically lower pay (see Susan Lonsdale's chapter in this volume) and lower lifetime earnings compared with men, the average woman ends up with a lower salary or wage on which to base her final salary for the purposes of working out occupational pension entitlements. Even if her scheme permits her to make additional pension contributions to make up for missing years of service, such payments will cost her more than would be the case for a man of the same age and salary status, since the arrangements assume that a woman will live longer and therefore claim benefits for longer than a man.

Study of the development of both state and occupational pension provision reveals arrangements which, especially until the 1975 legislation, endorsed the traditional domestic division of labour. It was difficult for married women to achieve a substantial basic retirement pension record within the state pension scheme and to gain access to an employer's pension scheme. The Social Security Pensions Act 1975 included an 'equal access' clause which entitles women to membership of an occupational scheme where this is available to men in the same category of employment. But as noted, this still leaves a substantial number of women with, over a working lifetime, limited access to occupational pension benefits in their own right. One way in which the 1975 legislation can be said to have further endorsed the domestic division of labour is by making provision of widows' pensions by occupational schemes one condition of approval by the Occupational Pensions Board. Indeed, the more recent history of pension provision shows more concern on the part of both governments and occupational pension providers to increase widows' benefits (themselves symbolic of the financial dependence of wives in marriage), than to help women build up their own occupational pension records. Some private sector occupational schemes are generous towards widows, especially if the death occurs in service. Such provision can reduce a widow's risk of poverty in old age not least because, unlike public sector schemes, private sector schemes are increasingly permitting widows to keep their pensions on remarriage and operate no cohabitation rules.

The preoccupation with providing for widows is one outcome of the high marriage rate for women which has persisted in Britain since World War II. Single (never married) women now form a very small proportion of the older working-age groups and a far smaller proportion of the 'young elderly' female population (OPCS, 1991, Table 1.1(b), p. 14). However, there are two groups of women whose marital status can put them at risk of poverty in old age because of their inability to qualify for dependants' benefits. An increasing number of couples are cohabiting, including older, previously married partners who in due course remarry. There is also an increasing number of women who have lost a potential occupational widow's pension, and associated benefits, on divorce.

If a man with occupational pension scheme entitlements dies leaving a female partner with whom he is living, it will depend on the rules of his pension scheme and the discretion of the scheme trustees (or manager) as to whether the woman qualifies as a female dependant with regard to any pension and/or lump sum for which her partner may have nominated her. The trustees may refuse to accept her as a beneficiary or may require any benefits to be divided with other individuals. One route to female poverty in old age is therefore through financial dependence in a marriage-like relationship which fails to deliver the occupational benefits to which a wife would have been entitled (see McGoldrick, 1984, Chapter 5). Pension providers are currently being challenged in this way by the existence of new family forms.

Divorce is likewise raising complicated issues of entitlement to dependants' occupational benefits, since on divorce a woman loses her potential right to a widow's pension and/or benefits. Section 5 of the Matrimonial Causes Act 1973 allows a wife to oppose divorce after five years' separation on the grounds that dissolution of the marriage would cause 'grave financial or other hardship', but very few such cases have succeeded (Cretney and Masson, 1990, pp. 130–1). It is the older wife in a divorce case, who has no recent contact with the labour market or a poor earning capacity, who has sometimes much to lose through the ending of her marriage. Older women are less likely to remarry than younger women (Ermisch, 1989, pp. 50–1) and are consequently at risk of poverty in old age unless, unusually, they have been able to generate an adequate income through their own resources.

The Matrimonial and Family Proceedings Act 1984 has as one goal the promotion of economic self-sufficiency for both parties on divorce. Any benefits such as pensions which the parties to the divorce will lose the chance of acquiring must be taken into consideration. However, the law does not normally allow for any order to be made which will directly affect pension entitlements (see Cretney and Masson, 1990, pp. 405–7). Although the courts do have wide powers to re-allocate property and can require an ex-husband to take out life assurance, such arrangements do not necessarily compensate for the loss of an index-linked widow's pension in old age or a lump sum and widow's pension payable on a husband's death in service. Such benefits can to some extent compensate a widow for lack of access to occupational scheme benefits in her own right and for financial disadvantage arising from the traditional domestic division of labour. Furthermore, it is commonly argued that the courts can fail to place a proper actuarial value on potential pension benefits and that (typically in pursuit of a 'clean break') a divorcing wife's loss of potential benefits can be 'traded off' or glossed over against her need for a home. Freedman *et al.* (1988, Chapter 6) address these issues, suggesting that pension rights should be jointly held by husband and wife for the duration of the marriage, allowing for a split on divorce. Loss of potential pension rights on divorce is now the subject of considerable debate as an unresolved issue of social policy and family law (see Joshi and Davies, 1991; Law Society, 1991).

Looking to the future, while the Social Security Act 1986 (operational from 1988) does not affect current pensioners or employees nearing retirement, it has profound implications for younger people (see Groves, 1991). Employers can no longer require membership of an occupational pension scheme as a condition of service. Employees can opt out of SERPS (with a generous financial rebate) into a modest 'appropriate personal pension' (APP) arranged commercially on an individual basis by a licensed financial provider. Additional personal pensions (PPs) may be purchased to supplement an APP, SERPS or an employer's pension (see Ward, 1990, Chapters 6 and 7). The SERPS has been severely downgraded (including widows' benefits) and will become a progressively less effective vehicle for compensating women in particular for their disadvantages in the labour market.

By 1991 over 4 million people, including a substantial number of women, had opted for a rebated APP instead of SERPS (Committee of Public Accounts, 1991). Marketers of personal pensions do appear to have discouraged exits from good occupational schemes and indicated that a return to SERPS may advantage employees as they get older. An APP (or PP) is a 'money purchase' (or 'defined contribution') scheme. The size of the eventual capital sum, which must be used in its entirety in the case of an APP for purchase of an annuity at 60 or later for women (at 65 or later for men), will depend on long-term investment performance and the state of the financial market, which dictates the current price of annuities. Personal pensions over and above APPs may be taken in part as a capital sum and at any age between 50 and 75 (see Wilson and Davies, 1988, Chapter 4). All money purchase schemes are potentially unpredictable, and are especially likely to lose value through monetary inflation (and not least if the annuitant lives a long time) unless the annuity is fully index-linked, which is not the case under present legislation.

For women, money purchase schemes are problematic in that early contributions are likely to promote the best returns, yet younger women typically leave the labour force for several years and/or work part-time on motherhood. Women (like men) may be tempted towards the cheapest option (an APP) rather than joining a good occupational scheme (if this is available) or paying the substantial personal pension contributions additional to the APP likely to be necessary to secure a really adequate personal pension in retirement. Furthermore, tradition dictates that married women should be dependent on their husbands for income in old age, his being the 'serious' earnings. Some employers, faced by likely future compulsion (under EC law) to include part-timers within occupational pension schemes where full-timers are eligible, are now taking up their rights under the Social Security Act 1986 to provide money purchase (rather than 'final salary'/'defined benefits') contracted-out occupational pension schemes or COMPS (see Ward, 1990, pp. 37–9) targeted at those occupational groups which include preponderantly female lower-paid staff. A study (Davies and Ward, 1992) for the Equal Opportunities Commission sheds light on the likely impact of personal pension provision on women. The Commission is already on record (1985, pp. 16–17) as having stated that, given women's typically discontinuous employment careers, 'personal pensions' are likely to be a recipe for female poverty in old age.

This chapter has attempted to explain why women have had unequal access to occupational pension benefits as compared with men. It can be argued, however, that neither a reformed employers' pension system, nor the new personal pension arrangements, are likely to guarantee an adequate income in old age for anyone (male or female) with a discontinuous employment record and/or a history of multiple job changes. A really well-designed state pension scheme (complete with lump sums) and not so closely tied to employment history as any of the current schemes on offer, could probably do as well or better than occupational or personal pension provision for most women. It can also be argued that all pension and retirement benefits schemes should be fully subject to sex discrimination law.

Women's greater share of unpaid domestic work and their labour market position, including low pay, have inhibited their ability to generate an adequate income for old age. Widows' pensions were designed as a partial replacement for loss of a 'family wage' or husband's retirement pension, but have become increasingly problematic as more women get divorced or prefer to remain unmarried. Meanwhile there is a real need to render women less invisible in debates on pensions and in statistics on pensions and poverty in old age. For the foreseeable future, occupational pension provision is likely to exist in some form. If women are in future to minimise their risk of poverty in old age, they will need to grasp their fair share of whatever is on offer in the admittedly inequitable sector of pension provision. Up to now, femininity has never been equated with financial self-sufficiency, but adult women will need to learn about the complicated world of personal finance and pension provision and exercise their choices so far as possible. To date, given the inadequate levels of state pension provision and the limited opportunities most women have had to save or invest for old age, their limited access to occupational pension scheme membership has been a major factor in the construction of female poverty in old age. Such poverty compounds the economic and domestic inequalities typically experienced by women over a lifetime and magnifies such inequalities in old age.

Note

Much material for this chapter is derived from a doctoral thesis on women and occupational pensions (Groves, 1986).

PART 5

Women, the family and poverty

14 Budgeting for health: Mothers in low-income households

Hilary Graham

This chapter reviews the research evidence which sheds light on the economic circumstances of mothers in low-income households. It looks, in particular, at the position of mothers in families on benefit. Thus, rather than developing a broad perspective on women's experiences of poverty, the chapter reviews what recent studies reveal (and obscure) about the impact of low household income on Black and white mothers caring for children.

The focus on households with children reflects recent trends in economic welfare in Britain. Households with children have borne the brunt of the widening inequalities in income; they have been hard hit, too, by changes in the social security system which offers a minimum income for an increasing number of families. Looking at the experiences of mothers in these households provides an insight into what life is like at the sharper end of economic and social change in Britain.

The chapter begins by exploring some of the limitations of the data on low-income households. It then turns to examine evidence which illuminates the economic circumstances of households, drawing out what these data suggest about families headed by Asian and Afro-Caribbean parents. The second part of the chapter sets the concept of poverty within the gendered organisation of family life. Against the backdrop of mothers' health responsibilities, it suggests that budgeting strategies represent the everyday routines through which many mothers seek to reconcile financial commitments with health needs.

Researching women and poverty: some limitations of the data

Four limitations of the data should be noted. First, social trends and policy changes are affecting low-income families in ways that leave studies rapidly out of date. The pace of change means that insights culled from even the most up-to-date research may still miss crucial dimensions of how mothers cope with poverty. For example, there is little evidence about the effects of the recent round of changes in the social security system, introduced in April 1988, on claimant households.

Secondly, much of the available data relate, not to women, but to the households in which they live. In both the large national surveys and the smaller scale studies, data tend to be collected and analysed at a household level (for example, Bradshaw and Holmes, 1989; Ritchie, 1990; DE, 1990c; DSS, 1990b). As a result, knowledge about women's experiences is often derived indirectly from studies which describe household patterns of income, expenditure and consumption.

Thirdly, household studies adopt different measures of 'low income' and 'poverty'. Some data sources place households into income bands which do not contain an obvious low income/poverty line (as, for example, in the government's *Households Below Average Income* – DSS, 1990b). Other data sources, most notably the small-scale studies, identify households on benefit or with benefit-level incomes, and describe coping strategies in this context (see, for example, Evason, 1980; Graham, 1987b; Ritchie, 1990; Phoenix, 1991). As these different income measures suggest, there is no common population of low-income households to which the various data sets refer. The data which they provide are thus not strictly comparable. What they suggest, however, are the broad parameters within which the lifestyles of mothers in low-income households take shape.

In trying to tease out these broad parameters, we hit a fourth problem. Since the early 1980s, debates within feminism and anti-racism have highlighted differences among women. Particular attention has been given to 'race' and racism as structures which mediate gender divisions (and divide women), with these differences always cross-cut by other dimensions of identity and experience (by sexuality, social class and the oppressions associated with disability, for example). Recent studies have described how racism shapes both the distribution and experience of poverty and the patterns of physical and mental ill-health associated with it (see the chapter here by Juliet Cook and Shantu Watt; also Gordon and Newnham, 1985; Eyles and Donovan, 1990).

Such arguments sit uneasily within a tradition of British poverty research where data are constructed in ways which prevent 'race' (let alone racism) being a focus of analysis. For example, the national surveys of income and expenditure include Black and other ethnic minority households, but typically do not describe respondents in terms of ethnic identity (see Brown, 1984, as an exception). In most small-scale studies, too, the ethnic identities of respondents remain undeclared (see, for example, Burghes, 1980; Bradshaw and Holmes, 1989; Ritchie, 1990; Craig and Glendinning, 1990a). In feminist research on poverty and resources within households, respondents again tend to be given no ethnic identity. Indeed, where studies have provided this information, it is typically only to note that the majority of the sample were white (for example, Wilson, 1987; Graham, 1987b).

If, as Phoenix suggests (1988a, p. 154), 'race' is seen as something that only influences Black women, this silence about 'race' is likely to signal an absence of Black people in the populations of most poverty studies. It suggests, too, that feminist research on resources within households has grounded its analyses in the accounts that white women have given white researchers about their lives. It is only the most recent studies, where detailed findings are still awaited, which clearly include a significant proportion of Asian and Afro-Caribbean parents (Cohen, 1991a, 1991b; Craig, 1991; Sadiq, 1991). In these studies, racism is also a more explicit part of the research agenda.

Further, most studies have focused primarily on heterosexual couples in nuclear households (see, for example, Burghes, 1980; Bradshaw and Holmes, 1989; Pahl, 1989; Ritchie, 1990). While some studies of resources within households have included one-parent households, information from women living in other kinds of household have not informed the typologies that researchers have built to explain how households run their financial affairs. These typologies may well not capture the patterns found in lesbian relationships or in multi-family households. One in ten households with children with South Asian heads are multi-family households. Among families with white, West Indian and African heads of household the proportion is one in forty (Haskey, 1989). The money-management systems identified in studies of white couples may not capture, either, the 'moral economy of kin' described by the respondents in Afshar's study of Pakistani women. This study, of three-generational households in West Yorkshire, notes the expectation felt by women to contribute their labour and their income to a family unit beyond the household (Afshar, 1989).

These four limitations of the research literature on mothers' experiences of poverty – the lack of up-to-date evidence, the lack of data on women, the variability of measures of low income/poverty, and the eclipsing of 'race' and other dimensions of difference among women – set limits on what is known about mothers in low-income households. They suggest that our understanding of mothers' experiences has to be gleaned from studies employing a variety of income measures, which collect and analyse their data in ways which obscure differences both within and between households. Specifically, while poverty disproportionately affects Black families, studies which address women's experiences of poverty focus disproportionately on white families.

Taken together, these problems raise the issue of whether anything useful can be said about Black women from a research tradition which has failed to engage with their lives. While clearly not capable of resourcing an anti-racist perspective on women's poverty, it may none the less be possible to provide some insights into experiences which Black and white mothers share.

As a number of commentators have noted, 'Black' and 'white' do not represent fixed group identities which stand in contrast to each other. Gilroy, for example, has argued against catch-all terms like 'Black', 'Asian' and 'Afro-Caribbean' which imply homogeneous groups of people whose culture and way of life stands in contrast to some white norm (Gilroy, 1990). Emphasising specific minority group needs among women can obscure their common material needs, for housing and income, for example (Nanton, 1989).

Some recent studies have drawn attention to these common material circumstances. For example, Phoenix, in her study of women who had their first child between the age of 16 and 19, argued that contrasting the lives of Black and white women did little to illuminate their experiences of becoming a mother (Phoenix, 1991). Pointing to the way in which poverty structured the lives of the majority of her respondents, she concluded that 'young Black women and young white women become pregnant for the same sorts of reasons, and this is because they share the same socio-economic contexts' (Phoenix, 1988a, p. 154).

The economic position of low-income households: some recent trends

The economic contexts in which mothers care for their children have been deeply affected by the widening of income inequalities in Britain in recent decades. The economic welfare of many families has been directly affected, too, by changes in the social security system. This section reviews the trends in income and income maintenance while the next section examines what these trends suggest about the position of families headed by Asian and Afro-Caribbean parents.

Three trends are shaping the living standards of households with children. First, there has been a sharp reversal of the trend towards greater income equality in Britain which characterised the decade from 1939. The evidence suggests that income differentials between households at the top and bottom of the income scale narrowed during the war years of 1939–45 and that, through the late 1940s, the poorest households found basic necessities increasingly affordable. It was around 1950 that the gap in living standards between rich and poor was at its narrowest (Wilkinson, 1989). From this point, living standards have widened, decade by decade, up to and including the 1980s (Wilkinson, 1989; Townsend, 1991a).

Data on household income point to a second trend in the distribution of income in Britain: a shift in the composition of households in the low-income groups. They point, in particular, to a sharp deterioration in the economic position of households with children through the 1970s and 1980s (O'Higgins, 1989). As a result, families represent an increasing proportion of households with the lowest standards of living. In the late 1980s, only a third of households contained children (OPCS, 1990). However, households with children made up nearly 60 per cent of households with incomes in the lowest 10 per cent of the income distribution (Oppenheim, 1990).

Thirdly, there has been a widening of income inequalities among households with children. The majority of families experienced a sustained rise in living standards through the 1970s and 1980s. However, the overall rise masked a decline in living standards for a minority (O'Higgins, 1989). Among this minority, a high proportion are one- and two-parent households headed by parents without a full-time job. Data for 1987 suggest that nearly 80 per cent of families where the head of household is unemployed have incomes below 50 per cent of average income (Oppenheim, 1990).

Recent changes in the social security system are likely to have intensified these widening income inequalities among families with children. Combined with changes introduced earlier in the decade, the 1986 Social Security Act has worked to increase the financial responsibilities of parents on benefit and reduce their access to additional sources of financial support for expenses that they are unable to meet from their regular benefit. For example, the 1986 Act removed the right to benefit for most 16- and 17-year-olds and made it a requirement that claimants pay 20 per cent of their rates/poll tax and 100 per cent of their water rates. At the same time, it replaced the regulated system of single payments for claimants in financial difficulties. Families were major beneficiaries of the single payments system, which provided one-off payments as a matter of entitlement to claimants who qualified for help. The new scheme, the Social Fund, offers only limited help through grants with the result that most families have to look to discretionary loans to cope with large items of expenditure or with an emergency.

Reviewing the impact of these changes on claimant households, Svenson and McPherson (1988) calculated that the majority of lone-parent families (74 per cent) and couples with children (81 per cent) lost out financially in the shift from supplementary benefit to income support.

Black households with children

The patterns of post-war immigration provide the context in which the income trends outlined in the previous section have impacted on Black households with children. In reviewing the limited evidence, it should be noted that households are typically defined by the ethnic group into which the head of household is classified. Other adults and children thus assume the ethnic group identity ascribed to the designated 'head of household'. Such an approach masks diversity within households. For example, analyses of the 1984–6 Labour Force Survey suggest that over a quarter of married and cohabiting Afro-Caribbean women (and Afro-Caribbean men) aged under 30 had white partners (CSO, 1988).

Post-war immigration from the New Commonwealth developed through the 1950s and 1960s, at a time when income trends were shifting from increasing equality to increasing inequality. Most Asian and Afro-Caribbean men and women were drawn into low-paid occupations which placed them at the lower rather than the upper limits of these widening inequalities. For example, a study of earnings in Leicester suggests that, in 1990, 86 per cent of Asian women in employment had gross earnings of less than £150 a week. Among white women, the proportion was 55 per cent (Duffy and Lincoln, 1990).

Reflecting these patterns of post-war immigration, most ethnic minority groups have a higher proportion of young adults and children than the population as a whole. Data from the Labour Force Survey for the late 1980s indicate that around a half of Afro-Caribbean households and over 70 per cent of Pakistani and Bangladeshi households contained children, compared with around one-third of white households (Haskey, 1989). As these statistics suggest, Asian and Afro-Caribbean women are significantly more likely than white women to live in households with children (Duffy and Lincoln, 1990).

The age and household composition of ethnic minority communities means that they have been more affected by the fall in the relative income position of households with children during the 1970s and 1980s than the white population. It means, too, that these communities have been disproportionately affected by social security changes relating to families, like the change in the benefit position of 16- and 17-year-olds (Oppenheim, 1990). Further, the limited evidence points to both indirect and direct discrimination within the social security system. For example, the social security system sets conditions which can make it hard for families to support family members who live elsewhere. Data from the early 1980s indicate that 40 per cent of Afro-Caribbean households and 30 per cent of Asian households send money to dependants, compared with 5 per cent of white households (Brown, 1984, p. 232). However, the social security system (including child benefit) does not recognise such financial obligations (Gordon and Newnham, 1985).

Change and complexity in the social security system can further disadvantage claimants whose first language is not English (NACAB, 1991). In one recent survey of income support claimants in Bradford, Asian respondents made up nine out of ten of those who had not heard of the Social Fund (Craig, 1991). It has been argued, too, that the emphasis on discretion within the Social Fund could give greater scope for the individual racism displayed by some social security staff (Cooper, 1985; Atkin and Robbings, 1991).

The evidence suggests that the trends which are adversely affecting the living standards of families with children have hit Black households hard. If social research always followed in the wake of social trends, there should be a rich vein of studies in which Black families, and Black women within these families, describe their poverty. Yet, as noted earlier, studies of poor families have dealt primarily with white households. The emerging feminist perspectives on poverty, too, have been resourced primarily by the accounts provided by white women.

As the next sections scan the literature, it is important to remember how few studies have given Black as well as white parents an opportunity to tell researchers about the realities of their lives.

Poverty: an income that undermines care

Both the major definitions of poverty – as an absolute and as a relative condition – turn on the question of individual health. The two concepts define poverty in ways which, explicitly or implicitly, call attention to people's physical, social and emotional welfare.

Health is the pivot around which an absolute concept of poverty revolves. Poverty is defined as an income insufficient to keep members of the family in a state of physical well-being. As Rowntree put it, life on the poverty line is governed by the regulation that 'nothing must be bought but what is absolutely necessary for the maintenance of physical health' (Rowntree, 1941, p. 103). An absolute conception of poverty thus alerts us to the fact that health – for some or all of the family – will be bartered in the struggle to meet basic needs.

A relative concept highlights not only costs to physical health. It also draws attention to the social and economic isolation of poor families; to their exclusion from the experiences of parenthood and childhood that others take for granted and from the cultural and political life of the communities to which they belong. As Townsend notes, 'their resources are so seriously below those commanded by the average individual that they are, in effect, excluded from ordinary living patterns, customs and activities' (Townsend, 1979, p. 31). Relative poverty is often experienced as the difference between 'living' and 'existing'. As mothers in a 1988 study of forty-five white, Asian and Afro-Caribbean families on benefit put it (Cohen, 1991a, p. 28):

> We're not living on the dole. We're just existing barely . . . Going into the butcher's shop and asking 'You got some bones for the dog?' and then making a pot of soup . . . Living is where I could go into a shop and say . . . 'I'd like a pair of shoes, fit them on my bairn and we'll take them'.

In their different ways, both absolute and relative concepts suggest that the struggle to make ends meet is fought out in and against the routines which sustain health; in the routines of buying bones from the butcher and not buying new shoes for the children. While it is unlikely that a feminist politics informed their development, these concepts draw attention to routines which, in many households, are deeply gendered. In most households, it is the culturally defined role of women which includes responsibility for family and individual welfare.

Research suggests that, irrespective of ethnic affiliation, women are primarily responsible for the health and care of children, and that this figures as a central and defining source of their identity (Mayall, 1986; Warrier, 1988; Afshar, 1989; Phoenix, 1991). Women's caring responsibilities frequently include the welfare of male partners as well as children. These responsibilities, in turn, are associated with domestic duties, with the preparation of food and the serving of meals, the maintenance of the home and the washing, ironing and repair of clothes. Reflecting this gendered division of care, in over 80 per cent of households, women are 'mainly responsible for general domestic duties', which include cleaning, washing and ironing, shopping and cooking (Jowell *et al.*, 1988, p. 184).

In many households, 'the cycle of caring' rolls forward to include not only young children and partners but frail older parents and adult children and siblings with illnesses and disabilities. Studies suggest that those needing help with everyday health tasks are concentrated among households with low incomes. The rates of disability, physical illness and poor psycho-social health are all higher among those living in low-income households (Blaxter, 1990). Underlining these patterns, a recent study of ninety-one claimant households with children found that the majority reported that at least one member had a chronic illness or disability (Craig, 1991).

As the context in which many mothers experience poverty, the gendered organisation of care gives the experience a particular edge. It means caring in circumstances which threaten both the well-being of family members and the economic survival of the household. In meeting these responsibilities, some mothers play little part in household budgeting. In Cohan and Sadiq's study where most of the Asian families were Mirpuri Muslims, a number of the women were not involved in the day-to-day management of money, particularly with respect to transactions involving outside agencies (bills, mortgage repayments and the DSS, for example) (Sadiq, 1991). However, in the majority of households, responsibility for looking after the family and home goes hand-in-hand with money management. Studies of (white) low-income households have described how women commonly manage the weekly budget and take the major responsibility for making ends meet. In Bradshaw and Holmes' study of two-parent families on benefit, the majority (58 per cent) of the couples reported that the woman was responsible for managing the money (Bradshaw and Holmes, 1989).

While money may be under female management, it is not necessarily under the woman's control. Where their partners control what they manage, women can find their attempts to meet health needs and financial commitments thwarted. The comments of one respondent in a mid-1980s' study of mothers with pre-school children which I conducted reflected a theme identified in other studies of family life (see Brannen and Wilson, 1987). She noted:

> His hobby is fishing and do-it-yourself things and he'll just go out and buy the tools and I think, 'Oh that money, what I could have done with that money!' So I will budget and go around the markets and that, and find the best buys and he'll just go to the best shops because it is convenient.

Her comments also shed an indirect light on the experiences of some lone mothers. Over 80 per cent of lone mothers depend on social security benefits for some or all of their income, and have average incomes well below the average for two-parent households (Millar, 1989; see also her chapter here). Despite their greater poverty, lone mothers may not always see marriage or cohabitation as improving their access to resources. For example, some respondents in Phoenix's (1991) study of white and Afro-Caribbean mothers aged under 20 pointed to their increased control of household resources as one reason why they felt they fared better economically by staying single. Lone mothers in other studies have described how their greater control of resources can offset the lower incomes they are able to secure for their families (Evason, 1980; Graham, 1987b; Bradshaw and Millar, 1991). In my study, a white mother, previously married to a full-time skilled manual worker and now living on benefits, described her changed economic circumstances like this:

> Money was *the* issue, because he used to spend his money on hobbies and I'd never know what I'd be getting from week to week and some weeks I'd not get anything. He wanted me to handle all the money side and do the bills but some weeks I had nothing for food, nothing for bills, nothing for the children. So I'm much better off. Definitely. I know where I am now, because I get our money each week and I can control what I spend. Oh, he was earning more than I get but I was worse off then than I am now.

Her comments set the divisions of caring responsibilities and material resources in particularly sharp relief. In a less extreme way, however, gender divisions provide the everyday context in which many mothers confront household poverty. Set within this context, poverty is a daily struggle to meet health needs without jeopardising financial survival.

Meeting health needs and making ends meet

This section explores how mothers resist the impact of poverty on the health of their children, their partners and themselves while, at the same time, working to meet the financial commitments of the household. Budgeting often embraces both dimensions: it marks out the routines through which mothers confront, and struggle to contain, the conflict between individual health and economic survival. It is through their budgeting strategies and skills that many mothers seek to maximise health opportunities without (further) threatening economic survival. In exploring these strategies, the section draws primarily on studies which pre-date April 1988 when the major changes introduced in the 1986 Social Security Act came into force. As yet, there are few studies which describe the economic circumstances of households since April 1988.

The section describes budgeting strategies in households on benefit under two broad headings. The first set of strategies seeks to meet health needs and make ends meet within household income. The second set of strategies looks to outside sources of support. In practice, these strategies are often pursued in tandem. Separating them out, however, signals the priority given by most parents to managing the economic dependency of living on state benefits as independently as possible.

Meeting health needs and financial responsibilities without recourse to others

Low-income households devote a higher proportion of their weekly income to basic and collective necessities, such as food and fuel, than better-off households (Bradshaw and Holmes, 1989; CSO, 1991a). Alongside the priority given to food and fuel goes a restriction of expenditure on items which are – or can be treated as – individual and less essential, like clothes, shoes, private transport and leisure. In Bradshaw and Holmes' study of two-parent, two-child households on benefit, about three-quarters of the women and men lacked more than two items of basic clothing, with women's clothing tending to be in the worst condition and children's in the best (Bradshaw and Holmes, 1989).

While statistics on household expenditure suggest that families give priority to health needs, in practice many mothers find themselves cutting back on basic necessities. Spending on current health needs is often constrained by the serving of financial commitments taken on in the past to secure basic health resources. Credit and debt repayments for housing, fuel, furniture and children's clothes tend to have first call on the income, being deducted from benefit at source or paid early in the weekly budgeting cycle.

Because of the priority given to these 'fixed costs', mothers typically draw on the household income when it is at its most depleted. The residual income has to cover a range of items which are directly related to caring like food, clothes, services and transport for mothers and children. As one white respondent noted in my study of mothers in low-income households, 'The bills come first, they've got to, then the meters (for fuel) and then food.' It was a theme reiterated by other mothers in the study:

As I see it, you get your bills in for a certain amount and you've got to pay it. You can't sort of say – well, I know some people do – but I can't say 'I won't pay that bill because I've got to buy some food.' I put away the money to pay that bill and if I haven't got anything left over to buy food with, then we have to manage.

As this comment suggests, food is the major item to be paid for within the family's residual income. It is also the item of expenditure over which a mother is most likely to exert control. As a result, the conflict between health-keeping and house-keeping is often experienced in a particularly acute form in the diet she can give her children. One white lone mother in my study, living with her two pre-school children on benefit, noted:

Food's the only place I find I can tighten up. The rest of it, they take it before you can get your hands on it really. So it's the food . . . The only place I can cut down is food . . . You've got to balance nutrition with a large amount of food which will keep them not hungry. I'd like to give them fresh fruit, whereas the good food has to be limited. Terrible, isn't it, when you think about it?

The evidence suggests that, through the 1980s and 1990s, financial commitments to outside agencies, and in particular credit repayments and debt obligations, have exerted an increasing pressure on low-income families. As families find themselves giving more priority to fixed costs, spending on other resources is squeezed further. A range of personal items – new clothes, underwear, make-up, haircuts, public transport, leisure services – rarely appear in the expenditure diaries of mothers in low-income households. However, cutting back on personal items does not always produce the necessary economies. In these circumstances, mothers have described how they turn to collective items where they can restrict what they consume. For example, mothers report how they cut back on their own consumption of food in order to protect the living standards of children and partners. As one mother in Ritchie's study of families on benefit noted: 'I buy half a pound of stewing meat or something and give that to Sid and the kiddies and then I just have the gravy – before I used to buy soya things and substitutes to meat but I can't afford that now' (Ritchie, 1990, p. 35). Other studies too have described how mothers regularly cut down or miss out on meals in order to provide a better diet for their children. As one mother described: 'I've seen me going three or four days without anything to eat . . . I've always been the one that ends up just going without' (Cohen, 1990, p. 28).

The 'individualising' of the family's lifestyle is apparent, too, in other areas of consumption, including clothes, fuel and transport. A mother in Craig and Glendinning's study described the different standards of dress which she set within her family:

I'll go to jumble sales for my clothes. I won't go to a catalogue for mine. But I'm not seeing me kid and me husband walk to town in second-hand clothes. I'll make do for myself but I won't make do for them. (Craig and Glendinning, 1990a, p. 31).

Her approach to clothes was matched by a mother in Ritchie's study who noted that the cost of fuel meant that she did not light the fire during the day when her children were at school but saved the limited fuel supplies to protect their standard of living. As she put it, 'as long as it's warm when the children get home, I'm not bothered about myself' (Ritchie, 1990, p. 36). It was an approach also adopted by mothers in my study of low-income households. For example, two lone mothers, one white and one Asian, described the scope for savings in personal fuel consumption in the following ways:

> I put the central heating on for one hour before the kids go to bed and one hour before they get up. I sit in a sleeping bag once they've gone to bed.

> When the children are in bed, I turn the heating off and use a blanket or an extra cardigan. (Graham, 1985, p. 246)

These personal cost-cutting measures, like the other approaches outlined in this section, are mediated through the wider household distribution of resources. The financial control exercised by a partner or by other members of the household may constrain a mother's attempts to look after health within the limits of the resources available to her. For example, a white mother with two children in my study described her strategies for budgeting on benefit in great detail, ending her account by noting how these strategies floundered: 'Because he spends his money and we could do with it. On benefit you never have enough money. We need it all but he has to have his bit' (Graham, 1985, p. 89).

The control that partners exercise over other household resources, like food or fuel, can also limit the scope for savings in collective and personal consumption. For example, women have described to researchers how it is difficult to cut down on food when cooking for a partner who expects meat with his main meal (Charles and Kerr, 1986). Partners' preferences can also make it more difficult to control household fuel consumption and to effect cutbacks in personal consumption. As a respondent in my study commented about economising on the heating: 'I turn it off when I'm in on my own and put a blanket on myself. Sometimes we both do in the evening but my husband doesn't like being cold and puts the heating back on' (Graham, 1985, p. 246). With or without a supportive partner, managing independently remains a common goal for many mothers searching for ways of meeting health needs while cutting back on health resources. However, studies have documented how increasing economic dependency is the cost of trying to keep families in health and in credit. One respondent in Cohen and Sadiq's study of white, Asian and Afro-Caribbean families on benefit summed up how both physical and financial survival is threatened by poverty with the comment, 'You have to incur debt to live' (Cohen, 1991b).

Looking to additional sources of help for survival

For mothers faced with the task of reconciling an inadequate income with the health needs of their children, small additional sources of income can take on a significance disproportionate to their size. The major source of independent income available to mothers is child benefit, which, Brown's survey suggests, reaches almost all eligible white, Asian and Afro-Caribbean households (Brown, 1984, p. 233). However, the value of this additional source of income has been falling in real terms over the last decade. Beyond this universal benefit lie the discretionary sources of help from the informal and formal sectors of welfare. While many mothers rely on both, it is helpful to look briefly at each in turn.

Studies have highlighted the importance of families and friends as sources of mutual support for parents who have access to them. They have highlighted, too, how this system of exchange is mediated through women, reflecting and reinforcing the gendered organisation of care within the families. Thus, most of the day-to-day help received by mothers comes from other women, from female friends and female relatives (Graham, 1986; Willmott, 1987). Their mothers and their partners' mothers play a particularly important part in this informal economy of care, providing both practical help with child care and material support, typically in kind rather than cash. Gifts of food, children's clothes and toys give tangible expression to mothers' health-keeping and housekeeping responsibilities.

For mothers struggling to meet these responsibilities, such gifts can help to protect the living standards of their children (Craig and Glendinning, 1990a; Ritchie, 1990). One Afro-Caribbean mother in my study, who was living on benefits with her partner, described how it was her grandmother who bought her daughter's shoes, while her mother

> is always buying things. If she sees a nice dress for her, she'll buy it. A couple of times she's sent money for Easter eggs and school photos. Occasionally, she's given me £5 or £10 if I go down to see her and says 'Treat yourself and don't tell Paul. Treat yourself'. (Graham, 1985, pp. 167–8)

Material support from kin can be more deeply woven into mothers' budgeting strategies, providing essential health resources on a regular basis. Two white lone mothers in my study described their economic dependency on kin in this way:

> We have three good meals a day at my mum's, Saturday, Sunday and Monday, and we always have meat and fresh vegetables then. It would worry me if I was having to feed her all the time but knowing that three days out of seven she's getting good meals, it doesn't worry me so much. And more often than not, when I come back from me mum's, I find little

bits in the bottom of the bag because she feels sorry for us. (Graham, 1985, p. 141)

If I've had a big bill, occasionally I've had to say to my mum 'I've no money left, can I come down for the week?' and I've had to go down there. Somehow or other I manage to get through and I think it's because my parents help me. (Graham, 1985, p. 249)

As the last comment suggests, mothers, and families more generally, can be an important source of financial help in emergencies. In Bradshaw and Holmes' 1986 study of two-parent households on benefit, two-thirds of the respondents said they would turn to their families for money in an emergency. Mothers were the single most frequently cited source of help (Bradshaw and Holmes, 1989).

While parents provide a lifeline for many women in poverty, they are not always an unproblematic source of help. First, women may not have access to relatives who are able or willing to respond. In Morris' study of the households of forty redundant steelworkers, kin were providing extra help – mostly in the form of food and clothes for the children – for less than a third of the families (Morris, 1983). The poverty of parents can limit what they can provide. One white lone mother in my study noted that her mother was also a woman coping alone on a very limited income: 'she'd rather put us first but I don't want to see her go without.'

Secondly, asking relatives for help can undermine the moral base on which relations with kin are built. Loans and gifts of money provided by older relatives can often run counter to the expected patterns of support. As one single mother noted about the financial support she received from her mother, 'it's not very nice her doing it because I feel I should be helping her' (Cohen, 1991a, p. 40).

Receiving such help can undermine further an already-fragile self-esteem. An Asian single parent interviewed in Cohen and Sadiq's study conveyed the sense of distress felt about having to turn to relatives for financial help:

This is the first time in my working life I have to go to the family to ask them for money. I've never asked them for anything before . . . then all of a sudden, you become partly dependent on them . . . it's very difficult. (Cohen, 1991a, p. 40)

Many parents also have reservations about turning to outside agencies for financial help. There is some evidence to suggest that Asian claimants are particularly reluctant to become indebted to agencies beyond the family (Cohen, 1991b). However, borrowing to meet health and financial commitments has become a fact of life for many mothers on benefit. In Bradshaw and Holmes' study, 96 per cent of claimant households with children had debts averaging £441, and with an average weekly repayment which represented 12 per cent of their weekly income (Bradshaw and Holmes, 1989, p. 44). In Cohen and Sadiq's 1989/90 study of forty-five single parents and couples with children, two-thirds had debts, most commonly for housing, fuel and children's clothes (Cohen, 1991a).

Some mothers turn to 'tick' credit from local shops, primarily for food and clothes. Most of the Asian claimants in Cohen and Sadiq's study were able to buy goods on credit from local Asian shops where they were known (Sadiq, 1991). Mail-order catalogues were less commonly used by Asian mothers than by white mothers in their study. Other studies confirm the significance of mail-order catalogues for white mothers (Bradshaw and Holmes, 1989; Craig and Glendinning, 1990a). Among poor households as a whole, they represent the major source of credit (Berthoud, 1989). Catalogues can offer a more flexible system of credit than commercial loans and Social Fund loans, allowing mothers sometimes to miss repayments when money is particularly tight. Because catalogues are typically run by someone the mother knows, they can also link a mother to the networks beyond her home (Cohen, 1991a).

Little is yet known about the impact of the Social Fund scheme on the patterns of borrowing. While the scheme makes some provision for grants, most of the payments are in the form of loans to those deemed eligible and able to meet the repayments. Thus, rather than an additional source of money, the Social Fund represents an additional fixed cost and one, moreover, which is repaid by direct deductions from benefit. The limited evidence suggests that knowledge about the new scheme – particularly among Asian claimants – can be limited (Craig, 1991; Craig and Glendinning, 1990a; Cohen 1991b). For those with access to a Social Fund loan, it can prove a too-expensive form of debt. While interest-free, the weekly repayments can be pitched above what parents can afford (Craig, 1991; Cohen, 1991b).

Rather than increasing claimants' economic independence, studies tracking the impact of the new social security regulations point to increasing debt and increasing dependency on kin (Craig, 1991; Craig and Glendinning, 1990a, 1990b; Cohen, 1991a, 1991b). Craig and Glendinning (1990b) point to a 'transfer of dependency', away from state support and towards relatives and friends. As families face greater financial hardship, the health threats that poverty represents become starker. As one Asian claimant interviewed in Cohen and Sadiq's study put it, 'to borrow from someone to eat is very bad. But when you're desperate you have to' (Cohen 1991b).

Conclusions

The chapter has focused on one group of women in poverty, scanning the research literature for information on mothers in low-income households. Within the limits of the data, it has sought to identify the trends affecting the economic circumstances of low-income households, looking within claimant households for information on how Black and white mothers cope with family poverty.

A number of interlocking themes emerge from the chapter. First, the economic circumstances of poor families have worsened relative to the rest of the population in recent decades. The early 1990s seem to be intensifying this pattern, with claimants reporting that each year is worse than the previous one and the hardest they have ever experienced (Cohen, 1991b).

Secondly, because of their position in the family economy, deepening poverty has a particular significance for women. For most mothers, the experience of poverty is one which is structured by the need to protect the health as well as financial security of the family. 'Budgeting' is therefore not simply about money management: it is about health care management as well. It represents the strategic space in which mothers work to resist the impact of poverty on individual health while trying, at the same time, to prevent their families slipping further into debt. It is thus in their budgeting strategies that the conflict between health needs and financial survival is often most acutely felt.

Thirdly, the chapter has suggested that, in seeking to reconcile these conflicting objectives, mothers (and fathers) have to look to others for help. They have looked to relatives, and to mothers in particular, to credit agencies and to the social security system. Until the mid-1980s, the single payments scheme provided a particularly important resource for claimant households.

Studies conducted in the early and mid-1980s described how mothers weave informal and formal sources of support into their budgeting strategies in ways which, at least in part, served to protect the living standards of their families (Graham, 1986; Bradshaw and Holmes, 1989). However, economic trends and social security changes appear to have undermined these strategies. Studies conducted since April 1988 convey mothers' powerful sense that, as their poverty deepens, strategies which once gave some protection to their families are crumbling under the weight of increasing debt (Cohen, 1990, 1991a,b; Craig and Glendinning, 1990a, 1990b; Craig, 1991).

In reviewing patterns of survival in lower income families, the chapter has drawn its evidence from an established research tradition which has paid little attention to gender. It has drawn its evidence, too, from a more recent feminist literature which has rooted its perspectives in the lives of white women living with men. Findings gleaned from these research literatures provide only partial insights into the issues confronting mothers caring in poverty. These partial insights are likely to prove to be provisional insights, understandings in the process of revision. They are likely to be revised as the circumstances of mothers' lives change through the 1990s. The themes identified in the chapter are also likely to be re-worked as poverty research engages with feminist debates about diversity and difference. Looking forward, I anticipate new understandings of how gender and poverty connect. And I anticipate new perspectives on how these connections are reflected in the lives of mothers working for the health and survival of their families.

15 Making ends meet: Women, credit and debt

Gillian Parker[1]

At the end of 1990, some £52.9 billion was owed by UK residents on credit sale, hire purchase agreements and personal loans (CSO, 1991b). Recent estimates suggest that the level of consumer credit has grown in real terms by a factor of 2.25 between 1981 and 1987 (Office of Fair Trading, 1989). At the same time, the proportion of people who use credit has grown. In 1969 just over a fifth of the adult population was currently using credit; by 1977 this had risen to just over half, and by 1987 was well over a half (Office of Fair Trading, 1989). Early findings from a national survey of credit use in 1989 suggest that nearly three-quarters of British households had used some form of credit in the previous year (Berthoud and Kempson, 1990) and that over 4 million households had four or more different commitments.

Estimates suggest that consumers will encounter difficulties paying at least 5 per cent of the credit outstanding nationally and that at least 1 per cent of this credit will remain irrecoverable (NCC, 1980). This means that around 2.4 million households would have experienced difficulty repaying credit during 1991 (Berthoud and Kempson, 1990). The work of the County Courts shows clearly how the incidence of indebtedness has risen in recent years. In 1978 1.5 million proceedings were started; in 1989 this number had increased to 2.6 million, the majority of which were for the recovery of debt or land (Judicial Statistics, 1990).

In addition to consumer default, debt has been growing in other areas. In

1989, it was estimated that local authority (LA) housing arrears in England and Wales stood at around £450 million (a similar estimate in 1983 had judged this figure to be around £240 million) and that over 40 per cent of LA tenants were in arrears, with an average debt of £116 (Audit Commission, 1989). At the same time mortgage arrears have risen. Recent figures from the Building Societies Association show that in the middle of 1990 over 1 per cent of the mortgages lent by its members were at least six months in arrears (*Housing Finance*, November 1990). Berthoud and Kempson (1990) suggest that around 3 per cent of mortgagors will have experienced some difficulty with repayments over the past year.

Fuel debt is also a problem for many households. Around 2 per cent of the population experience difficulty paying fuel bills in a year (Berthoud and Kempson, 1990) while about 90,000 consumers have their electricity supply disconnected each year. Until recently, when disconnection policy was altered, around 60,000 gas consumers were also disconnected each year (Berthoud, 1989). Beyond this, there is a substantial 'hinterland' of householders who have difficulty paying their electricity bills but who do not suffer disconnection. Some make special repayment arrangements while others pay their fuel bills but borrow elsewhere or miss other regular payments to do so. It is possible that as many as 5.5 per cent of electricity consumers and 6.5 per cent of gas consumers, including those who are disconnected, may experience difficulty of one sort or another in meeting their fuel bills each year (Parker, 1988a, 1988b).

Even if there were considerable overlap between households experiencing different forms of financial difficulty, it is clear that a substantial proportion of the inhabitants of England and Wales, and by extension the UK as a whole, experiences considerable financial distress.

To talk of 'households', of course, disguises the reality of where the burden of indebtedness lies. By virtue of the position they hold within two-partner households, many women carry responsibility for budgeting (Pahl, 1980, 1989) and, thereby, for making ends meet in times of financial crisis. Further, by virtue of the position they hold in society, women, though apparently equal users of credit with men (NCC, 1980; Equal Opportunities Commission, 1989), are likely to have unequal access to certain types of low-cost credit, including mortgages. As is so often the case, a legislative framework which appears to enshrine equality (in this instance the Consumer Credit Act 1974) is unable to redress those structural inequalities which actually determine access to resources. Finally, if the dissolution of marriage or a partnership brings with it a reduced income, women may be particularly susceptible to debt in their own right, including housing arrears, with the subsequent risk of losing their homes. They may also be left to carry responsibility for arrears and debts which were jointly incurred before the ending of the relationship.

This chapter will examine, in turn, women's responsibility within the household for financial management (budgeting); women's access to consumer credit; and the impact and consequences of indebtedness for women. It will draw on historical accounts of women's lives as well as on empirical evidence, including a study of clients of the Birmingham Money Advice Centre (Parker, 1990c).

Budgeting

Concern about the budgeting practices of the poor or 'labouring classes' has a long history, although it was not until Rowntree's study of families in York (Rowntree, 1902), and subsequent studies in other parts of the country (e.g. Lumsden, 1905; Rathbone, 1909), that any kind of objective or scientific approach was applied to this concern. Despite the best, and usually philanthropic, intentions of those who carried out these surveys, their concentration on description rather than explanation led to a failure to examine household expenditure in its wider economic, social and cultural context. Most significantly, the constraints under which working-class women struggled to keep their families fed, clothed and housed were almost totally ignored.

These failings led the authors of budget studies to suggest remedies which were far removed from the realities of everyday life of those they sought to help. Perhaps the most glaring example of this, and one which even now recurs every time debate on the adequacy of social security benefits is raised, was the reformers' obsession with porridge and pulses. For example, Lumsden (1905, p. 141) claimed that 'a diet of a much higher nutritional value could be purchased for the money now spent, i.e. oatmeal porridge, beans, peas, lentils, etc.'. Rathbone (1909) raised some doubts about Rowntree's emphasis on the importance of 'farinaceous foods', but it took the Fabian Women's Society's more detailed and involved examination of the lives of women budgeting on a pound a week to show why such foods played so little part in the diets of working people:

> The visitors in this investigation hoped to carry with them a gospel of porridge to the hard-worked mothers of families in Lambeth. The women of Lambeth listened patiently, according to their way, agreed to all that was said, and did not begin to feed their families on porridge. Being there to watch and note rather than to teach and preach, the visitors waited to hear ... what the objection was. It was not one reason, but many. Porridge needs long cooking; if on the gas, that means expense; if on an open fire, constant stirring and watching just when the mother is most busy getting the children up. Moreover, the fire is often not lit before breakfast. (Pember Reeves, 1913, p. 57)

The visitors then pointed out that the porridge could be made the day previously and warmed up in the morning – still no porridge:

> It seemed after further patient waiting on the part of the visitors, that the

husbands and children could not abide porridge . . . Why? Well – cooked the day before, and eaten with milk and sugar, all children liked porridge. But the mothers held up their hands. Milk! Who could give milk – or sugar either, for that matter. Of course, if you could give them milk and sugar, no wonder! They might eat it then even if it was a bit burnt. (*ibid.*, pp. 57–8)

The women pointed out that porridge quickly burnt in the old pots and pans they had available, and that porridge took the taste of whatever had been cooked last in the pan. To compound their difficulties, these women were bound by the likes and dislikes of their husbands. One woman wound up a long and patient explanation of why she did not give her husband porridge with: 'An' besides, my young man, 'e say, "Ef you gives me that stinkin' mess, I'll throw it at yer"' (Pember Reeves, 1913, p. 58). This passage is worth quoting because it demonstrates so clearly how the lack of financial resources limited (and limits) not only the amount of any commodity that could be consumed but, more importantly, the type of commodity bought. Furthermore, the Lambeth investigation showed that while men might carry the outward, public burden of low wages, it was women who carried the real and essentially hidden burden. Moreover, this burden was hidden not just from public scrutiny but *within* the household itself. Women were driven to extraordinary shifts in order to stretch the available resources to meet the needs of their households and the whims of their husbands:

> Old flour bags were used as pillow cases and towels; old sacks and old coats were used to make peg rugs. Old clothes were very frequently made up into patchwork quilts; some women converted bacon or orange boxes into furniture . . . old shoes were converted into clogs by the dozen; tailors' samples were begged and made into woollen patchwork blankets; brown paper was put between blankets to provide extra warmth in the winter. (Roberts, 1984, p. 151)

Yet, as Tebbut has indicated, even the most sympathetic of husbands was so far removed from the everyday reality of his wife's existence that he was 'at a loss to understand the shortsighted methods [his wife was] forced to employ just to get by':

> A woman's management of the family budget was a world entirely separate from that of her husband, necessity forcing it to encompass a thriving sub-culture of credit activities. Men were quite insulated from these strains. (Tebbut, 1983, pp. 38–9)

'When husbands were *not* sympathetic and wives failed to make the money stretch, violence against the wife – or the threat of it – might follow' (Ayers and Lambertz, 1986).

The rigid sexual division of labour within households made it the woman's responsibility to keep the household solvent, regardless of the inadequacy of the money she was 'allowed' by her husband and regardless of the personal deprivation that she might endure in doing so:

> Poverty increases the housewife's difficulties in relentless geometric progression and it is not surprising that she takes one comparatively easy way out by eating much less than any other member of her family. By saving the necessity to plan for herself, the difficulties of the budget are somewhat reduced. (Spring-Rice, 1939, p. 157)

Even in the 1930s when Spring-Rice was writing, it was made clear that it was the woman's own fault if her family was not better fed:

> Very few of these women know how to make the best of their slender resources by the wise expenditure either of money or time ... every opportunity, if not *compulsion* to learn her trade would immediately release her from much of her present bondage. (*ibid.*, p. 107, my emphasis)

This compulsion to 'learn their trade' was to be inflicted on women on the basis that, by doing so, much could be done to relieve them 'even without dealing with the basic evil of poverty and without disintegrating the sacred edifice of the home ...' (*ibid.*, p. 106)! One has to look very hard in any of these historical accounts for a similarly damning analysis of the women's husbands, who often retained substantial proportions of their earnings for their own use.

Time and social change have not materially altered the patterns of responsibility within households, especially where income is low. The meticulous, 'penny-pinching' budgeting required has been described in Edwardian households (Pember Reeves, 1913; Roberts, 1973); between the two world wars (Spring-Rice, 1939; Hoggart, 1958); in the 1960s (Land, 1969; Marsden, 1973); and in the 1980s (Burghes, 1980; Bradshaw and Holmes, 1989). Most significantly, Jan Pahl's unpacking of the 'black box' of household income has demonstrated the persistence of women's burdens in financial management (Pahl, 1978, 1980, 1982, 1984, 1989). Despite the changes in women's position in the labour market (Hunt, 1968; Martin and Roberts, 1984), in many two-partner households it is still the man who is the main wage-earner and the women who assumes major responsibility for housekeeping. Within this framework, various patterns for the allocation of money and domestic responsibilities are possible (Gray, 1976; Edwards, 1981; Pahl, 1982, 1984, 1989; Vogler, 1989).

Some men pay all their wages to the woman for housekeeping and take no other part in family finances (the whole wage system). Others may pay all or some of the major commitments such as the rent or mortgage, rates or fuel bills and leave the remainder to the woman to be met out of his allowance to her and, where appropriate, her own income (the allowance system). Some men may take a very active part in all aspects of housekeeping and budgeting, sharing decision-making and sometimes even the tasks equally (the pooling system). More rarely, some couples maintain independent financial arrangements, each taking responsibility for previously agreed commitments (independent management system).

These patterns of allocation and responsibility are determined by many factors: age, stage of the life cycle, family size, income, cultural background, socio-economic class and reliance on state benefits (Land, 1969; Gray, 1979; Edwards, 1981; Pahl, 1980, 1982, 1989). Among low-income and 'working-class' households, the whole wage and allowance systems, which put the major burden on the woman, still predominate (University of Surrey, 1983). Although the whole wage system puts a considerable burden of responsibility on the woman (Pahl, 1980), it could be argued that, in circumstances where resources are very limited, it is more sensible for one person to have total financial control (Land, 1969). Evidence from a study of indebted households (Parker, 1990c) suggests, indeed, that patterns of financial management may be implicated in the genesis of debt. Of fifty-six households studied in depth, thirty consisted of two partners, with or without dependent children. Among these, the allowance system was the most common pattern of allocating resources, used by just under a half. This was followed by the whole wage system, used by just under a third. Only a fifth used the pooling system. The pattern of allocation systems in this group was thus atypical, even compared with 'blue-collar' local authority tenants (University of Surrey, 1983). There was, in total, more reliance on the allowance and whole wage systems than would be expected. However, given the low income level of the households studied and their heavy reliance on state benefits, an even higher proportion of whole wage systems would have been anticipated (Land, 1969; Gray, 1979; Pahl, 1980; Edwards, 1981).

The relationships between the allocation system used, the proportion of the man's income used for the housekeeping allowance, and the number of major household expenses met by the man were also examined. In eight of the fourteen two-partner households where the allowance system was used, the man met none of the major household expenses (rent, fuel, food, clothing, hire-purchase). When major expenses were met out of the man's retentions, these were usually electricity bills, rent or mortgage, or hire-purchase payments. Overall, the less responsibility the man took for meeting major expenses, the more likely he was to devote more than 90 per cent of his income to the housekeeping allowance. However, the eight men who used the allowance system and met no major expenses out of their retentions were still keeping 10 per cent or more of their income as personal spending money.

Even in households where there were considerable debts, then, some men retained considerable portions of their own incomes (from earnings or benefits), giving women housekeeping allowances which in some cases were quite inadequate. Beyond this, few men were closely involved in household financial management. This disengagement usually meant that men were less aware of the cost of running a home and were thus less likely to update housekeeping allowances in line with price rises (NCC, 1975; Young, 1977). Women in such partnerships were left with all the decision-making and all the anxiety of making ends meet. If financial problems occurred, they might remain concealed within the household for a long time, causing considerable stress to the women as they struggled to keep their families fed and clothed while trying to fend off the consequences of indebtedness. Conversely, men who gave a housekeeping allowance but remained responsible for certain outgoings sometimes incurred debts without the women knowing of them.

From first principles it would seem sensible in indebted households either to pool all resources and make joint decisions about expenditure or for one partner to take charge of all income and outgoings. Yet many in the study continued with the allowance system even when it was no longer (if it ever was) a sensible approach. Some men may have done this without fully realising the implications for their partners; others may have been hidebound by cultural and historical attitudes towards their role as breadwinner; yet others may have been mean or selfish or using the allocation of financial resources as a way of retaining power over their wives. Regardless of the reasons, it is highly likely that the mismatch between the needs of the household and the allocation pattern adopted contributed to the financial difficulties being experienced.

Access to consumer credit

While the use of consumer credit has grown substantially since the 1950s, and particularly since the mid-1970s, and while the major proportion of the population now chooses credit as its preferred method of obtaining household and other goods, access to and use of credit is not evenly spread.

Contrary to what might be expected, those who make the most use of consumer credit are those whose jobs place them in the higher socio-economic groups. Socio-economic status can also influence the type of credit which people use. Those in professional and managerial occupations use bank loans, credit cards and store budget accounts. Skilled manual workers use finance company loans and hire-purchase, while shopping and trading check use is almost exclusive to those in semi-skilled jobs (OFT, 1979; Ison, 1979; NCC, 1980).

Age also influences credit use. Older people are more likely to use cash and least likely to have used credit or to have current commitments. By contrast, those in the 30–9 age group make the greatest use of credit (Berthoud and Kempson, 1990). Although socio-economic status and income are linked, income seems to be a more important influence on credit use overall and on the type of credit used. Those with the highest incomes use bank loans, credit cards, credit and budget accounts at shops, and second mortgages for home improvements. Those in the middle-income groups use hire-purchase, mail order, finance house loans and credit sale. The poorest rely on check and voucher trading, the tallyman and, to a substantial extent, their relatives (NCC, 1980; OFT, 1989; Berthoud and Kempson, 1990).

Although the above account emphasises use of credit, it also essentially describes access to credit. This is not an area in which free choice operates, but is closely determined by income, occupation, tenure, sex, age, home address and culture (Baldwin, 1975; NCC, 1980). Further, these variables determine access to particular types of credit and thereby influence the cost of credit to different sections of the community. Paradoxically it is those groups who can least afford expensive credit who pay the most for it (Piachaud, 1974; Masey, 1977). Shopping checks and vouchers can attract interest rates of up to 200 per cent (Ford, 1991). By contrast, bank personal loans cost around 26.4 per cent per annum and loans from major stores around 30.2 per cent (*Which?*, June 1991).

It hardly needs to be pointed out that women are disadvantaged both in obtaining access to any credit, and in relation to the type and therefore the cost of the credit which they can obtain. Occupational status and low income, and the low incidence of owner-occupation among single, divorced and separated women in particular ensure that bank loans, credit cards and other forms of 'cheap' credit are beyond their reach. Further, the arrangements made within two-partner households for financial control mean that many women have no option but to seek credit from those who provide weekly repayment arrangements. Inevitably, these are the most expensive forms of credit.

The reasons why men and women seek credit are likely to vary, too. The Crowther Committee (1971) drew the distinction between credit for improvement (i.e. for the acquisition of consumer goods and services that would not otherwise have been obtained) and credit for adversity (i.e. when used to tide a household or individual over a financial crisis). This latter strategy is one employed in low-income households with few or no other resources to enable them to ride out a difficult time. Again, the combination of women's overall economic status and the burden which they often carry within the household will ensure that it is they who most often seek 'credit for adversity'.

This, of course, is not a new phenomenon. Women's role in keeping the family housed and fed in the nineteenth century led them to pawnbrokers and sometimes to the (usually illegal) moneylender. As Tebbut has suggested, these women were even more bound by their class and culture than were their husbands. In the close-knit communities beyond which women rarely travelled, the options for financial help at a time of crisis were friends and relatives, the pawnbroker and the moneylender. When not in straitened circumstances, the tallyman or 'scotch draper', the burial club and the clothing club were the extent of most working-class women's credit activities. Familiarity with these 'credit and retail expedients . . . tended to mitigate the pull of more economical alternatives' (Tebbut, 1983, p. 65).

Today, women, particularly in working-class households, still use forms of credit with which they are familiar, even when they might be able to obtain cheaper credit elsewhere (Parker, 1980). The weekly 'callers' from shopping check companies and small-scale moneylenders are often from well-established 'family' firms and this influences the way in which they are regarded by their customers. Women do business with the company that their mothers, and even grandmothers, used and the callers come to be seen as family friends. Inevitably, the personalisation of a business transaction makes it particularly difficult when customers become financially distressed. Women are often reluctant to reduce payments to their callers, even if the electricity is about to be disconnected or a notice to quit has been received, because by doing so they feel they would be 'letting down' the caller or getting him or her into trouble.

Further, some women are reluctant to cut themselves off from this source of credit by missing or reducing payments, when no other form of credit may be available or acceptable. A shopping check or small money loan may be relatively expensive but it is at least legal; the alternative for increasing numbers of people is the extortionate and illegal loan secured on a child benefit book (Crossley, 1984; Ford, 1991).

Credit as a form of insurance figured often in the responses of householders interviewed in the debt study (Parker, 1990c). The group as a whole were relatively isolated from family members or even friends and had little or no savings. With no safety barrier of informal sources of loans or 'nest-eggs', the credit trader or moneylender often formed the only line of defence against fuel disconnection or eviction when times were hard. The fact that borrowing might only compound their difficulties was usually far from the front of respondents' minds when they took out loans in these circumstances. In this they were little different from the women of the nineteenth century, who were keen to keep in with their local pawnbroker for fear of losing a financial lifeline which might keep them and their families out of the workhouse (Tebbut, 1983).

The introduction of the Social Fund might have provided a lifeline for women in such circumstances, offering them the opportunity of interest-free loans to meet urgent needs. Indeed, some recipients of Social Fund loans do value them because of this (Craig and Glendinning, 1990a). However, when items which might previously have been obtained with the help of a grant (a single payment under the pre-1988 social security system) are now purchased with a loan – albeit interest-free – which has to be repaid from benefits, there is an inevitable negative impact on household finances. As Becker has pointed out, a device which 'might have been able to help some women escape the burden of debt-related poverty' has failed 'because it forces those who are "successful" in getting loans to pay for that success through lower levels of future benefits. Their success is also at the expense of other applicants, other women' (Becker, 1989, pp. 71–2).

Geting into and being in debt

There appear to be two main ways in which households find themselves in debt. First, there are those households which have enjoyed an income adequate for their needs and which have taken on credit commitments for household and other goods in anticipation of that income continuing to be adequate. When this expectation fails, usually through loss of the main breadwinner's income, these commitments become burdensome. If outgoings on these commitments cannot be reduced, then, sooner or later, other aspects of household finances – housing costs, fuel, food – will be put under pressure.

Secondly, there are those households which have chronically low incomes because they are dependent on low-paid work or on state benefits. Lone parents in particular will be represented in this group. There will also be some in this group where the household is 'poor' because the main breadwinner retains a large proportion of his income for his own use. For such households, the normal expectations of life as a late twentieth-century consumer cannot be sustained *other* than by recourse to credit or, occasionally, a Social Fund loan from the DSS.

From information reviewed in earlier sections of this chapter, it is clear that, whatever the initial cause of household indebtedness, women are both more likely to be involved in coping with it and may also experience its effects more keenly than do men. Regardless of who takes out credit arrangements for household durables, it is usually women who take responsibility for stretching the budget to meet these and other demands. If income falls, it is women who bear the brunt of responsibility again. In households where income is chronically low, women will be involved in a daily battle not just to make money available for household durables but, more basically, to ensure that a roof is kept over the household's head, that fuel continues to be readily available and that adequate supplies of food are obtained. This struggle may lead women to become involved in clandestine credit activity, taking out loans from legal or illegal sources unknown to their partners in an attempt to tide them over financial crises.

At the lowest level of income, distinctions between budgeting, access to credit and becoming indebted are blurred. Indeed, the literature on low incomes and poverty, and studies of indebted households, indicate a certain inevitability about debt, particularly in low-income households with dependent children (Parker, 1986, 1990c). Land (1969), for example, showed how buying clothes caused particular difficulties for large families with low incomes. Unemployment, single parenthood and reliance on supplementary benefit (now income support) have also been shown to be associated with difficulty in obtaining clothing and household durables and with getting into debt (Burghes, 1980; Berthoud, 1989; Parker, 1990c).

The Birmingham Money Advice Centre study of indebted households (Parker, 1990c) showed clearly how these budgeting pressures could easily develop into full-blown indebtedness. For example, respondents were twice as likely to mention using credit for their children's clothes and shoes as for their own.

Women often found themselves having to buy their children new clothes and shoes at a time when their household budget could not sustain the expense outright. Using credit, especially in the form of shopping checks or mail order catalogues, allowed them to meet these needs fairly promptly. In contrast, adults waited until the cash was available (if ever) or found other, usually second-hand, sources. This was especially the case for women. Jumble sales, 'nearly new' shops and clothes passed on from friends and relatives figured prominently in these women's accounts of their own clothes buying.

The presence of dependent children clearly put pressure in other ways on the households studied. Not only were households with children significantly more likely than others to have credit commitments for clothing, but they were also more likely to be repaying small cash loans. Such loans were obtained to pay fuel bills, to meet Christmas expenses, and in a few cases to meet everyday expenses. Recourse to these loans often represented the thin end of the financial wedge.

Purchasing household goods also put a strain on the households studied. A fifth never bought new furniture or carpeting and the remainder relied very heavily on credit. Some households used credit for even relatively small goods, such as pots and pans, bedding and curtains.

Once households on low incomes or reliant on state benefits begin to experience difficulty making repayments, they have few options open to them which would enable them to recover solvency. Over a half of the households studied had incomes at or below 120 per cent of their supplementary benefit entitlement, and over two-thirds at or below 140 per cent. Thus few had much scope for reducing expenditure, but despite this some had attempted to do so, usually by cutting back on food. Opportunities for increasing income were also limited; out of thirty-nine households with dependent children, seven lone parents and five (female) spouses said that they could not increase their income because of lack of adequate child care facilities.

This complex interrelationship of low income and debt, and the impact on women, can be highlighted by some examples from the debt study:

> Mrs B. had first run into financial difficulties sixteen months before she was interviewed, when her husband was receiving a very low wage and they moved into a new house. Before this they had always paid for fuel through pre-payment meters and had kept up with their rent. The combination of a higher rent, quarterly credit meters and the need for extra furnishings, albeit secondhand, made it increasingly difficult to cope. Soon after she had sought advice for her difficulties, Mrs B.'s husband left home, leaving her in an even more difficult financial position and with sole responsibility for their jointly incurred debts.

> Mrs R. said that she had 'always' had money problems, not triggered by any particular event but rather as a result of long-term dependence on state benefits. Twelve years before being interviewed, Mrs R.'s common-law husband had died, leaving her with three young children. A subsequent relationship produced two more children before Mrs R.'s

partner left to marry a younger woman. Mrs R. soon found herself in difficulties again, when the pressure of feeding and clothing five children mounted. She might miss a rent payment to enable her to buy a pair of shoes but once one payment was missed she found it almost impossible to catch up.

Mrs E. had been experiencing financial problems for around three years when she was interviewed. Most of these problems had been caused by her husband's inability or reluctance to pay bills on time; although Mr E. had assumed responsibility for paying the rent and fuel bills, he had not always done so. In addition, he always kept Mrs E. very short of housekeeping money. Despite suffering from a serious stomach ailment, Mrs E. had taken a part-time cleaning job to try to improve the household's financial position. This household's indebtedness was not caused by any apparent or objectively measured lack of money; Mrs E. had never known how much her husband earned but suspected with good reason that it was considerably more than he ever gave her. Neither were the debts caused by any 'inadequacy' or profligacy on Mrs E.'s part, yet it was she who had to deal with unpaid rent and fuel bills and she who had to seek help. Thus she took on public responsibility for a situation that was none of her making.

This one-sided shouldering of responsibility was evident in many two-partner households. Women in such households were more likely than men to report that their health, mental or physical, had been affected by their financial problems. For example, Mrs L. reported that her nerves were 'in a state' because she felt that she carried far more responsibility than did her husband.

Women were affected by the hopelessness as well as the drabness of a life spent always counting pennies and dreading the arrival of bills. Mrs G. said that she was more irritable than she had been because she had little to look forward to; she could no longer have her hair done or give her children a treat. Mrs W. felt that she had deteriorated 'in herself', losing interest in her appearance and feeling 'let down'. Mrs M., who had been deserted by her husband and had experienced considerable problems with the payment of benefits, had lost several stones in weight through stress and not being able to afford to eat as she had previously done. Her experiences, however, had also made her more tolerant and understanding of others. She felt she could now appreciate why some women turned to prostitution or why people committed suicide, because she had been tempted by both 'solutions' to her financial problems.

Conclusions

Despite the social and economic developments of the last 100 years, the responsibility which women carry for household financial management remains essentially unchanged. Even in households where women now share control of financial matters the burden of management or budgeting is still with them. In more traditional household financial arrangements this responsibility remains where it has always fallen.

The effects of this continuing imbalance in responsibility are at least twofold. First, in households where income is low the impact is transferred from the main earner or claimant (i.e. the man) to the woman, who is responsible for making it stretch to meet household needs. Secondly, where income may be adequate but where the main earner retains a large proportion of it for his own use, household poverty is disguised. In both situations, a sleight of hand is achieved which takes these issues out of the public domain.

Inability to cope on a low income or on an inadequate housekeeping allowance thus becomes a matter not of public policy but of private failure. By this process it becomes the housekeeper's (i.e. the woman's) fault that the household cannot pay the rent or meet the fuel bills or clothe the children. If women then turn to credit to stretch inadequate resources, they risk the disapproval of those, both within and without the household, who observe their behaviour without understanding its root cause.

Women experience further disadvantage in the type and cost of the credit they can obtain. This is not always a result of direct discrimination against women, but follows indirectly from their relative poverty, lack of secure employment and low levels of owner-occupation. It is these characteristics which determine access to the increasingly important resource of cheap credit:

> While the wealthy use credit as a clever expedient it remains an essential part of the lives of the poor, for whom the ability to borrow continues to offer an illusory freedom. Their only way of participating in the consumer society has been to buy goods on credit, but it is a second class participation since the most advantageous forms remain closed to the unemployed, low paid and single parents. (Tebbut, 1983, p. 201)

Note

1. This chapter is based, in part, on research carried out by the author at the Birmingham Money Advice Centre. The research was funded by the Esmee Fairburn Charitable Trust.

References

Abbot, E. and Bompass, K. (1943) *The Woman Citizen and Social Security* (London: by the authors).

Abel-Smith, B. and Townsend, P. (1965) *The Poor and the Poorest* (London: Bell).

Abrams, M. (1978) *Beyond Three Score Years and Ten* (Mitcham: Age Concern).

Adams, P. (1981) 'Social control or social wage: on the political economy of the "welfare state"' in R. Dale, G. Esland, R. Fergusson and M. Macdonald (eds), *Education and the State: Politics, patriarchy and practice* (Basingstoke: Falmer Press).

Afshar, H. (1989) 'Gender roles and the "moral economy of kin" among Pakistani women in West Yorkshire', *New Community* vol. 15, no. 2, pp. 211–25.

Ahmed, S. (1978) 'Asian girls and culture conflict', *Social Work Today* vol. 9, no. 47, pp. 14–16.

Ahmed, S., Cheetham, J. and Small, J. (1986) *Social Work with Black Children and their Families* (London: Batsford in association with the British Association for Adoption and Fostering).

Allen, S. and Wolkowitz, C. (1987) *Homeworking: Myths and realities* (London: Macmillan).

Anderson, A. (1981) *Redundancy Provisions Survey*, Manpower Commentary no. 13, Institute of Manpower Studies (Brighton: University of Sussex).

238

Anderson, M. (1983) 'What is new about the modern family: an historical perspective'. British Society for Population Studies Conference Papers, *The Family* (London: OPCS).

Anderson, M. (1985) 'The emergence of the modern life cycle in Britain', *Social History* vol. 10, no. 1, pp. 69–87.

Anwar, M. (1979) *The Myth of Return* (London: Heinemann).

Arber, S. and Gilbert, N. (1989) 'Men: the forgotten carers', *Sociology* vol. 23, no. 1, pp. 111–18.

Arber, S., Gilbert, N. and Evandron, M. (1988) 'Gender, household composition and receipt of domiciliary services by the elderly disabled', *Journal of Social Policy* vol. 17, no. 2, pp. 153–75.

Arnot, M. (1983) 'An analysis of the forms of transmission of class and gender relations' in S. Walker and L. Barton (eds), *Gender, Class and Education* (Sussex: Falmer Press).

Atchley, R.C. (1976) 'Selected social and psychological differences between men and women in later life', *Journal of Gerontology* vol. 31, no. 2, pp. 204–11.

Atkin, K. and Robbings, J. (1991) *Informal Care and Black Communities* (York: University of York Social Policy Research Unit).

Atkinson, A.B. and Micklewright, J. (1989) 'Turning the screw: benefits for the unemployed, 1979–1988' in A.B. Atkinson (ed.), *Poverty and Social Security* (Hemel Hempstead: Harvester Wheatsheaf).

Audit Commission (1989) *Survey of Local Authority Housing Rent Arrears* (London: HMSO).

Ayers, P. and Lambertz, J. (1986) 'Marriage relations, money and domestic violence in working-class Liverpool, 1919–1939' in J. Lewis (ed.), *Labour and Love: Women's experience of home and family* (Oxford: Blackwell).

Baldock, J. and Ungerson, C. (1991) 'What d'ya want if you don' want money? – a feminist critique of paid volunteering' in M. Maclean and D. Groves (eds), *Women's Issues in Social Policy* (London: Routledge).

Baldwin, S. (1975) 'Credit and class distinction' in K. Jones (ed.), *The Yearbook of Social Policy 1974* (London: Routledge).

Baldwin, S. (1985) *The Costs of Caring* (London: Routledge).

Baldwin, S. and Glendinning, C. (1983) 'Employment, women and their disabled children' in J. Finch and D. Groves (eds), *A Labour of Love: Women, work and caring* (London: Routledge).

Baldwin, S. and Twigg, J. (1991) 'Women and community care' in M. Maclean and D. Groves (eds), *Women's Issues in Social Policy* (London: Routledge).

Ballard, R. (1989) 'Social work with black people: what's the difference' in C. Rojeck, G. Peacock and S. Collins (eds), *The Haunt of Misery: Critical essays in social work and helping* (London: Routledge).

Barron, R.D. and Norris, G.M. (1976) 'Sexual divisions and the dual labour market' in D.L. Barker and S. Allen (eds), *Dependence and Exploitation in Work and Marriage* (London: Longman).

Baxter, C. (1988) *The Black nurse: An endangered species* (Cambridge: National Health Service Training Authority).

de Beauvoir, S. (1977) *Old Age* (Harmondsworth: Penguin).

Becker, S. (1989) 'Women's poverty and social services' in H. Graham and J. Popay (eds), *Women and Poverty: Exploring the research and policy agenda* (London: Thomas Coram Research Unit/Coventry: University of Warwick).

Berthoud, R. (1989) *Credit, Debt and Poverty*, Social Security Advisory Committee Research Paper no. 1 (London: HMSO).

Berthoud, R. and Kempson, E. (1990) *Credit and Debt in Britain: First findings from the PSI survey* (London: Policy Studies Institute).

Beveridge, W. (1942) *Social Insurance and Allied Services*, Cmd 6404 (London: HMSO).

Bingley, P., Symons, E. and Walker, I. (1991) *The Labour Supply of UK Lone Mothers: The effects of maintenance and the welfare system* (London: Institute of Fiscal Studies).

Bissett, L. and Huws, U. (1984) *Sweated Labour: Homeworking in Britain today*, Low Pay Pamphlet no. 33 (London: Low Pay Unit).

Black Faith (1990) Channel 4 TV.

Blair Bell, W. (1931) 'Maternal disablement', *Lancet* 30 May, pp. 1171–7.

Blaxter, M. (1990) *Health and Lifestyles* (London: Tavistock).

Booth, C. (1889) *London Life and Labour* vol. 1 (London: Williams and Norgate).

Booth, C. (1894) *The Aged Poor: Condition* (London: Macmillan).

Bornatt, J., Phillipson, C. and Ward, S. (1985) *A Manifesto for Old Age* (London: Pluto Press).

Bradshaw, J. and Holmes, H. (1989) *Living on the Edge: A study of the living standards of families on benefit in Tyne and Wear* (Newcastle: Tyneside Child Poverty Action Group).

Bradshaw, J. and Millar, J. (1991) *Lone-parent Families in the UK*, Department of Social Security Research Report no. 6 (London: HMSO).

Bradshaw, J. and Piachaud, D. (1980) *Child Support in the European Community* (London: Bedford Square Press).

Brannen, J. and Moss, P. (1991) *Managing Mothers* (London: Unwin).

Brannen, J. and Wilson, G. (eds) (1987) *Give and Take in Families: Studies in Resource Distribution* (London: Allen and Unwin).

Bransbury, L. (1991) 'Two steps forward and one a half backwards: improving the position of women through the social security system', *Benefits* no. 2, September/October, pp. 10–13.

Breughel, I. (1989) 'Sex and race in the labour market', *Feminist Review* no. 32, pp. 49–68.

Broad, R. and Fleming, S. (eds) (1983) *Nella's Last War* (London: Sphere).

Broadbridge, A. (1991) 'Women and retailing' in N. Redcliff and M. Sinclair (eds), *Working Women* (London: Routledge).

Brook, L., Jowell, R. and Witherspoon, S. (1989) 'Recent trends in social attitudes', *Social Trends* no. 19.

Brown, C. (1984) *Black and White in Britain: The third PSI survey* (Aldershot: Gower).

Brown, J. (1989) *Why Don't They Go to Work?* (London: HMSO).

Brown, J.C. and Small, S. (1985) *Occupational Benefits as Social Security* (London: Policy Studies Institute).

Brown, P. (1987) *Schooling Ordinary Kids* (London: Tavistock).

Bryan B., Dadzie, S. and Scafe, S. (1985) *The Heart of the Race* (London: Virago).

Bulmer, M. (1986) *Neighbours: The work of Phillip Abrams* (Cambridge: Cambridge University Press).

Burghes, L. (1980) *Living from Hand to Mouth: A study of 65 families living on supplementary benefit*, Poverty Pamphlet no. 50 (London: Family Service Units and Child Poverty Action Group).

Buswell, C. (1984) 'Sponsoring and stereotyping in an English secondary school' in S. Acker, J. Megarry, S. Nisbet and E. Hoyle (eds), *Women and Education* (London: Kogan Page).

Buswell, C. (1985) 'Employment processes and youth training' in S. Walker and L. Barton (eds), *Youth, Unemployment and Schooling* (Milton Keynes: Open University Press).

Buswell, C. (1991) 'The gendering of school and work', *Social Studies Review* vol. 6, no. 3, pp. 108–11.

Cadbury, E., Matheson, C.M. and Shann, G. (1906) *Women's Work and Wages* (London: T. Fisher Unwin).

Caine, B. (1982) 'Beatrice Webb and the Woman Question', *History Workshop Journal* no. 14, Autumn, pp. 23–43.

Callender, C. (1985) 'Unemployment: the case for women' in M. Brenton and C. Jones (eds), *The Yearbook of Social Policy 1984–5* (London: Routledge).

Callender, C. (1986a) 'Women seeking work' in S. Fineman (ed.), *Unemployment: Personal and social consequences* (London: Tavistock).

Callender, C. (1986b) 'Women and the redundancy process: a case study' in R.M. Lee (ed.), *Redundancy, Layoffs and Plant Closures: The social impact* (London: Croom Helm).

Callender, C. (1988) *Gender and Social Policy: Women's redundancy and unemployment*, Unpublished PhD thesis. University of Wales.

Callender, C. (1989) 'Through the grapevine', *Guardian*, 4 October, p. 23.

Callender, C. and Metcalf, H. (1991) *The Impact of the 1989 Social Security Act on Recruitment and Job Search: The employer's perspective* (Brighton: Institute of Manpower Studies).

Campbell, B. (1984) *Wigan Pier Revisited: Poverty and politics in the 1980s* (London: Virago).

Campling, J. (1981) 'Women and disability' in A. Walker and P. Townsend (eds), *Disability in Britain* (Oxford: Martin Robertson).

Caradog Jones, D. (ed.) (1934) *Social Survey of Merseyside* (Liverpool: Liverpool University Press).

Carby, H.V. (1982) 'White women listen!: Black feminism and the boundaries of sisterhood' in Centre for Contemporary Cultural Studies, *The Empire Strikes Back: Race and racism in 70s Britain* (London: Hutchinson).

Caring Costs (1991) *Taking Care, Making Do: The costs of caring for a disabled person at home* (London: Caring Costs).

Castle, B. (1980) *The Castle Diaries 1974–1976* (London: Weidenfeld and Nicolson).

Castle, B. (1981) 'Sex and the social wage', *Over 21*, April, p. 21.

Central Statistical Office (1986) *Social Trends 16* (London: HMSO).

Central Statistical Office (1988) *Social Trends 18* (London: HMSO).

Central Statistical Office (1991a) *Social Trends 21* (London: HMSO).

Central Statistical Office (1991b) *Financial Statistics, July 1991* (London: HMSO).

Charles, N. and Kerr, M. (1986) 'Eating properly, the family and state benefit', *Sociology* vol. 20, no. 3, pp. 412–29.

Child, J., Loveridge, R., Harvey, J. and Spencer, A. (1985) 'The quality of employment in services' in T. Forrester (ed.), *The Information Technology Revolution* (Oxford: Blackwell).

Child Poverty Action Group (1991) *Welfare Rights Handbook* (London: CPAG).

Cmnd 372 (1988) *The Single European Act* (London: HMSO).

Cockburn, C. (1987) *Two-Track Training* (London: Macmillan).

Cocking, J. and Athwal, S. (1990) 'A special case for treatment', *Social Work Today* nos 21/22, pp. 12–13.

Cohen, R. (1990) 'The money jugglers', *Social Work Today* vol. 21, no. 25, pp. 12–13.

Cohen, R. (1991a) 'If you have everything second-hand, you feel second-hand: bringing up children on income support', *FSU Quarterly* vol. 46, pp. 25–41.

Cohen, R. (1991b) *Debt and the Social Fund: The experience of families on income support* (London: Family Service Unit).

Cole, D. with Utting, J. (1962) *The Economic Circumstances of Old People* (Welwyn: Codicote Press).

Collins, P.H. (1990) *Black Feminist Thought – Knowledge, Consciousness and the Politics of Empowerment* (Boston: Unwin Hyman).

Commission of the European Communities (CEC) (1989) *Who Cares for Europe's Children?* (Brussels: CEC, European Childcare Network).

Commission of the European Communities (CEC) (1990) *Community Charter of the Fundamental Social Rights of Workers* (Brussels: CEC).

Commission of the European Communities (CEC), Directorate General V (DGV) (1991) *Employment in Europe* (Luxembourg: OOPEC).

Commission of the European Communities (CEC), Directorate General V (DGV) (1991) *Employment in Europe* (Luxembourg: OOPEC).

Commission of the European Communities (CEC), Equal Opportunities Unit (1991) *The Third Community Action Programme on the Promotion of Equal Opportunities for Women, 1991–1996* (Brussels: CEC).

Commission of the European Communities (CEC), Network of Employment

Coordinators (NEC) (1991) *Shortage of Information Technology Professionals in Europe; Shortage of Jobs and Labour in the Construction Industry* (Brussels: CEC).

Commission on Industrial Relations (1974) *Retail Distribution*, Report no. 89 (London: HMSO).

Committee of Public Accounts (1991) *Eighth Report*, Session 1990–91, House of Commons Paper (London: HMSO).

Community Relations Commission (1975) *Who Minds?* (London: CRC).

Conroy-Jackson, P. (1990) *The Impact of the Completion of the Internal Market on Women in the European Community* (Brussels: CEC, Equal Opportunities Unit).

Cooper, S. (1985) *Observation in Supplementary Benefit Offices* (London: Policy Studies Institute).

Coote, A. (1981) 'The AES: a new starting point?', *New Socialist* no. 2, November/December, pp. 4–7.

Coyle, A. (1984) *Redundant Women* (London: The Women's Press).

Cragg, A. and Dawson, T. (1981) *Qualitative Research Among Homeworkers*, Research Paper no. 21 (London: Department of Employment).

Cragg, A. and Dawson, T. (1984) *Unemployed Women: A study of attitudes and experience*, Research Paper no. 47 (London: Department of Employment).

Craig, C., Garnsey, E. and Rubery, J. (1985) *Payment Structures and Smaller Firms: Women's employment in segmented labour markets*, Research Paper no. 48 (London: Department of Employment).

Craig, G. (1991) 'Life on the Social', *Social Work Today* vol. 22, no. 28, pp. 16–17.

Craig, G. and Glendinning, C. (1990a) *Missing the Target: A report on the impact of the 1988 social security changes on families using Barnado's services* (Barkingside: Barnado's).

Craig, G. and Glendinning, C. (1990b) 'Parenting in poverty', *Community Care* vol. 24, no. 7, pp. 24–5.

Cretney, S.M. and Masson, J.M. (1990) *Principles of Family Law*, 5th edn (London: Sweet and Maxwell).

Cross, M., Wrench, J. and Barnett, S. (1990) *Ethnic Minorities and the Careers Service*, Department of Employment Research Paper no. 73 (London: HMSO).

Crossley, M. (1984) 'Tackling the scandal of illegal money lenders', *Municipal Review* no. 647, p. 56.

Crowther, A. (1982) 'Family responsibility and state responsibility in Britain before the Welfare State', *Historical Journal*, vol. 25, no. 2, pp. 131–45.

Crowther Committee (1971) *Report of the Committee on Consumer Credit*, Cmnd 4596 (London: HMSO).

Curran, M. (1985) *Recruiting Gender Stereotypes for the Office*, EOC Research Bulletin no. 9, Spring (Manchester: Equal Opportunities Commission).

David, M. (1983) 'The new right, sex education and social policy: towards a new moral economy in Britain and the USA' in J. Lewis (ed.), *Women's Welfare, Women's Rights* (London: Croom Helm).

David, M. (1986) 'Morality and maternity: towards a better union than the moral right's family policy', *Critical Social Policy* vol. 6, no. 1, pp. 40–56.

Davidson, F. (1990) 'Occupational pensions and equal treatment', *Journal of Social Welfare Law* vol. 5, pp. 310–31.

Davies, B. and Ward, S. (1992) *Women and Personal Pensions*, Research Report for the Equal Opportunities Commission (London: HMSO).

Davies, H.B. and Joshi, H.E. (1990) 'The forgone earnings of Europe's mothers', *Birkbeck Discussion Paper in Economics 90/24*. Publication of extended version forthcoming in O. Ekert-Jaffe (ed.), *Levels of Life and Families* (Paris: Editions INED).

Davis, A. (1982) *Women, Race and Class* (London: The Women's Press).

Department of Employment (1980) *Family Expenditure Survey 1979* (London: HMSO).

Department of Employment (1984) *Family Expenditure Survey 1983* (London: HMSO).

Department of Employment (1986) *Financial and Explanatory Memorandum to the Wages Act 1986* (London: Department of Employment).

Department of Employment (1988) *Employment for the 1990s*, Cmnd 540 (London: HMSO).

Department of Employment (1990a) *New Earnings Survey 1990* (London: HMSO).

Department of Employment (1990b) *Family Expenditure Survey 1989* (London: HMSO).

Department of Employment (1990c) *Family Expenditure Survey 1990* (London: HMSO).

Department of Employment (1990d) *Regional Trends 1990* (London: HMSO).

Department of Employment and Productivity (1971) *British Labour Statistics, Historical Abstract 1886–1968* (London: HMSO).

Department of the Environment (1987) *Housing: The government's proposals*, Cmnd 214 (London: HMSO).

Department of the Environment (1991) *Annual Report*, Cmnd 1508 (London: HMSO).

Department of Health and Social Security (1974) *Social Security Provision for Chronically Sick and Disabled People*, HC 276 (London: HMSO).

Department of Health and Social Security (1981) *Growing Older*, White Paper on Services for Elderly People, Cmnd 8173 (London: HMSO).

Department of Health and Social Security (1984) *Population, Pension Costs and Pensioner's Incomes*, Background Paper for the Inquiry into Provisions for Retirement (London: HMSO).

Department of Health and Social Security (1985a) *The Reform of Social Security*, vols 1–4, Cmnd 9517–9520 (London: HMSO).

Department of Health and Social Security (1985b) *Reform of Social Security: Programme for action*, Cmnd 9691 (London: HMSO).

Department of Health and Social Security (1986) *Social Security Statistics 1985* (London: HMSO).

Department of Health and Social Security (1988) *Social Security Statistics 1988* (London: HMSO).

Department of Health and Social Security (1989a) *Caring for People: Community care in the next decade and beyond*, Cmnd 849 (London: HMSO).

Department of Health and Social Security (1989b) *Social Security Statistics 1989* (London: HMSO).

Department of Social Security (1990a) *Children Come First*, Cmnd 1263 (London: HMSO).

Department of Social Security (1990b) *Households Below Average Income 1981–1987* (London: Government Statistical Services).

Department of Social Security (1991) *Social Security Statistics 1990* (London: HMSO).

Dex, S. (1984) *Women's Work Histories: Analysis of the Women and Employment Survey*, Research Paper no. 46 (London: Department of Employment).

Dex, S. (1985) *The Sexual Division of Work* (Brighton: Wheatsheaf Books).

Docksey, C. (1987) 'The European Community and the promotion of equality' in C. McCrudden (ed.), *Women, Employment and European Equality Law* (London: Eclipse).

Drake, B. (1920) *Women in Trade Unions* (London: Labour Research Department).

Duffy, K.B. and Lincoln, I.C. (1990) *Earnings and Ethnicity* (Leicester: Leicester City Council).

Dyhouse, C. (1977) 'Good wives and little mothers: social anxieties and schoolgirls' curriculum, 1880–1920', *Oxford Review of Education* vol. 3, no. 1, pp. 21–36.

Edmonds (now Cook), J. (1981) 'Asian girls, English assumptions', *Youth in Society*, no. 60, November.

Edwards, M. (1981) *Financial Arrangements Within Families* (Canberra, Australia: National Women's Advisory Council).

Elias, P. and Main, B. (1982) *Women's Working Lives: Evidence from the National Training Survey* (Coventry: University of Warwick Institute for Employment Research).

Employment Gazette (1984) vol. 92, no. 12, p. 559 (London: HMSO).

Employment Gazette (1988) vol. 96, no. 8 (London: HMSO).

Employment Gazette (1990) *Women in the Labour Market*, Results from the 1989 Labour Force Survey, December (London: HMSO).

Employment Gazette (1991) Issue of 1 April, p. 182 (London: HMSO).

Equal Opportunities Commission (1979) *Health and Safety Legislation* (Manchester: Equal Opportunities Commission).

Equal Opportunities Commission (1985) *Reform of Social Security: Response of the EOC* (Manchester: Equal Opportunities Commission).

Equal Opportunities Commission/Research Surveys of Great Britain Ltd (1989) *A Sound Investment? The treatment of women by financial institutions* (London: HMSO).

Erens, B. and Hedges, B. (1990) *Survey of Incomes In and Out of Work* (London: Social and Community Planning Research).

Ermisch, J. (1983) *The Political Economy of Demographic Change* (London: Heinemann).

Ermisch, J. (1989) 'Divorce: economic antecedents and aftermath' in H. Joshi (ed.), *The Changing Population of Britain*, Centre for Economic Policy Research (Oxford: Blackwell).

Ermisch, J. (1990) *Fewer Babies, Longer Lives* (York: Joseph Rowntree Foundation).

Esam, P. and Berthoud, R. (1991) *Independent Benefits for Men and Women* (London: Policy Studies Institute).

Eurostat (1990a) *Demographic Statistics*, Population and Social Conditions, Theme 3, Series C (Luxembourg: Eurostat).

Eurostat (1990b) *Poverty in Figures: Europe in the early 1980s* (Luxembourg: Eurostat).

Eurostat (1990c) *Inequality and Poverty in Europe (1980–1985)*, Rapid Reports – Population and Social Conditions, July (Luxembourg: Eurostat).

Eurostat (1990d) *Earnings 1989: Marked differences persist between the Member States*, Rapid Reports – Population and Social Conditions, August (Luxembourg: Eurostat).

Evandron, M. (1990) *Challenging the Invisibility of Carers: Mapping informal care nationally*, Working Paper no. WSP/49 (London: LSE SunTory–Toyota International Centre for Economics and Related Disciplines).

Evason, E. (1980) *Just Me and the Kids: A study of single parent families in Northern Ireland* (Belfast: Equal Opportunities Commission for Northern Ireland).

Evason, E. (1991) 'Women and poverty' in C. Davies and E. McLaughlin (eds), *Women, Employment and Social Policy in Ireland: A problem postponed* (Belfast: PRI).

Eyles, J. and Donovan, J. (1990) *The Social Effects of Health Policy* (Aldershot: Avebury).

Fabian Women's Group (1911) *How the National Insurance Bill Affects Women* (London: Fabian Women's Group).

Family Policy Studies Centre (1991) *Family Policy Bulletin*, August.

Feinstein, C.F. (1972) *National Income, Expenditure and Output of the UK, 1855–1965* (Cambridge: Cambridge University Press).

Fiegehen, G.C., Lansley, P.S. and Smith, A.D. (1977) *Poverty and Progress in Britain 1953–1973* (Cambridge: Cambridge University Press).

Field, F. (1989) *Losing Out: The emergence of a British underclass* (Oxford: Blackwell).

Finch, J. (1984) 'Community care: developing non-sexist alternatives', *Critical Social Policy* vol. 3, no. 3, pp. 6–19.

Finch, J. (1990) 'The politics of community care in Britain' in C. Ungerson (ed.), *Gender and Caring* (Hemel Hempstead: Harvester Wheatsheaf).

Finch, J. and Groves, D. (eds) (1983) *A Labour of Love: Women, work and caring* (London: Routledge).

Finer, M. (1974) *Report of the Committee on One-Parent Families*, Cmnd 5629 (London: HMSO).

Ford, J. (1991) *Consuming Credit: Debt and poverty in the UK* (London: Child Poverty Action Group).

Forest, R. and Murie, A. (1988) 'The social division of housing subsidies', *Critical Social Policy* vol. 8, no. 2, pp. 83–93.

Freedman, J., Hammond, E., Masson, J. and Morris, N. (1988) *Property and Marriage: An integrated approach*, IFS Report Series no. 29 (London: Institute for Fiscal Studies).

Freeman, C. (1982) 'The understanding employer' in J. West (ed.), *Work, Women and the Labour Market* (London: Routledge).

GB (1909) *Report of the Royal Commission on the Poor Laws and the Relief of Distress*, Cmnd 4499 (London: HMSO).

Gilroy, P. (1990) 'The end of anti-racism' in W. Ball and J. Solomos (eds), *Race and Local Politics* (London: Macmillan).

Ginn, J. and Arber, S. (1991) 'Gender, clan and income inequalities in later life', *British Journal of Sociology* vol. 12, no. 3, pp. 369–96.

Ginsberg, N. (1989) 'The Housing Act 1988 and its policy context: a critical commentary', *Critical Social Policy* vol. 9, no. 1, pp. 56–81.

Glendinning, C. (1983) *Unshared Care: Parents and their disabled children* (London: Routledge).

Glendinning, C. (1990) 'Dependency and interdependency: the incomes of informal carers and the impact of social security', *Journal of Social Policy* vol. 19, no. 4, pp. 469–97.

Glendinning, C. (1992a) *The Costs of Informal Care: Looking inside the household* (London: HMSO).

Glendinning, C. (1992b) 'Employment and community care', *Work, Employment and Society* vol. 6, no. 1, pp. 103–11.

Glendinning, C. and Millar, J. (eds) (1987) *Women and Poverty in Britain* (Hemel Hempstead: Harvester Wheatsheaf).

Glendinning, C. and Millar, J. (1989) 'New directions for research on women and poverty: challenges to our thinking and practice' in H. Graham and J. Popay (eds), *Women and Poverty: Exploring the research and policy agenda* (London: Thomas Coram Research Unit/Coventry: University of Warwick).

Glendinning, C. and Millar, J. (1991) 'Poverty: the forgotten Englishwoman' in M. Maclean and D. Groves (eds), *Women's Issues in Social Policy* (London: Routledge).

Gohil, V. (1987) 'DHSS service delivery to ethnic minority clients', *Leicester Rights Bulletin* no. 32.

Gordon, D.M., Edwards, R. and Reich, M. (1982) *Segmented Work, Divided Workers* (London: Cambridge University Press).

Gordon, P. (1986) 'Racism and social security', *Critical Social Policy* no. 17, pp. 23–40.

Gordon, P. and Newnham, A. (1985) *Passport to Benefits? Racism in social security* (London: Child Poverty Action Group and the Runnymede Trust).

Gosden, P.H.J.H. (1972) *The Evolution of a Profession* (Oxford: Blackwell).

Government Actuary (1958) *Occupational Pension Schemes – a Survey* (London: HMSO).

Government Actuary (1966) *Occupational Pension Schemes – a New Survey* (London: HMSO).

Government Actuary (1968) *Occupational Pension Schemes – Third Survey* (London: HMSO).

Government Actuary (1972) *Occupational Pension Schemes 1971 – Fourth Survey* (London: HMSO).

Government Actuary (1978) *Occupational Pension Schemes 1975 – Fifth Survey* (London: HMSO).

Government Actuary (1981) *Occupational Pension Schemes 1979 – Sixth Survey* (London: HMSO).

Government Actuary (1991) *Occupational Pension Schemes 1987 – Eighth Survey* (London: HMSO).

Graebner, N. (1980) *A History of Retirement* (New Haven: Yale University Press).

Graham, H. (1983) 'Caring: a labour of love' in J. Finch and D. Groves (eds), *A Labour of Love: Women, work and caring* (London: Routledge).

Graham, H. (1985) *Caring for the Family*, Unpublished Research Report from the Faculty of Social Science, Open University.

Graham, H. (1986) *Caring for the Family*, Research Report no. 1 (London: Health Education Council).

Graham, H. (1987a) 'Women's poverty and caring' in C. Glendinning and J. Millar (eds), *Women and Poverty in Britain* (Hemel Hempstead: Harvester Wheatsheaf).

Graham, H. (1987b) 'Being poor: perceptions and coping strategies of lone mothers' in J. Brannen and G. Wilson (eds), *Give and Take in Families: Studies in resource distribution* (London: Allen and Unwin).

Gray, A. (1976) 'Family budgeting systems: some findings from studies in Edinburgh and Portsmouth' in N. Newman (ed.), *In Cash or Kind: The place of financial assistance in social work*, 3rd edn (Edinburgh: Edinburgh University).

Gray, A. (1979) 'The working-class family as an economic unit' in C. Harris (ed.), *The Sociology of the Family*, Sociological Review Monograph no. 28 (Keele: University of Keele).

Green, H. (1988) *Informal Carers: General Household Survey 1985* (London: HMSO).

Griffin, C. (1982) *The Good, the Bad and the Ugly* (Birmingham: Birmingham University Centre for Contemporary Cultural Studies).

Griffin, C. (1985) *Typical Girls?* (London: Routledge).

Groves, D. (1983) 'Members and survivors: women and retirement pensions legislation' in J. Lewis (ed.), *Women's Welfare, Women's Rights* (London: Croom Helm).

Groves, D. (1986) *Women and Occupational Pensions 1870–1983: An exploratory study*, Unpublished PhD thesis, University of London.

Groves, D. (1991) 'Women and financial provision for old age' in M. Maclean and D. Groves (eds), *Women's Issues in Social Policy* (London: Routledge).

Hadjivarnava, E. (1988) *Migration and the Special Problems of Elderly People and Women* (Athens, Greece: National Welfare Organisation).

Hakim, C. (1978) 'Sexual divisions within the labour force: occupational segregation', *Employment Gazette* vol. 86, no. 11, pp. 1264–8.

Hakim, C. (1980) 'Homeworking: some new evidence', *Employment Gazette* vol. 88, no. 10, pp. 1105–10.

Hakim, C. (1981) 'Job segregation: trends in the 1970s', *Employment Gazette* vol. 89, no. 12, pp. 521–9.

Hakim, C. (1984) 'Homework and outwork', *Employment Gazette* vol. 92, no. 1, pp. 7–12.

Hakim, C. (1989) 'Workforce restructuring, social insurance coverage and the black economy', *Journal of Social Policy* vol. 18, no. 4, pp. 471–503.

Hall, C. (1979) 'The early formation of Victorian domestic ideology' in S. Burman (ed.), *Fit Work for Women* (London: Croom Helm).

Haskey, J. (1989) 'Families and households of the ethnic minority and white populations of Great Britain', *Population Trends* vol. 57, pp. 8–19.

Haskey, J. (1991) 'Estimated numbers and demographic characteristics of one-parent families in the UK', *Population Trends*, vol. 65, September.

Heclo, H. (1974) *Modern Social Politics in Britain and Sweden* (New Haven and London: Yale University Press).

Henwood, M. and Wicks, M. (1984) *The Forgotten Army: Family care and elderly people*, Briefing Paper (London: Family Policy Studies Centre).

Henwood, M., Rimmer, L. and Wicks, M. (1987) *Inside the Family* (London: Family Policy Studies Centre).

Higgs, M. (1910) *Where Shall She Live? The homelessness of the working woman* (London: P.S. King).

Hoel, B. (1982) 'Contemporary clothing "sweatshops", Asian female labour and collective organization' in J. West (ed.), *Work, Women and the Labour Market* (London: Routledge).

Hoggart, R. (1958) *The Uses of Literacy* (Harmondsworth: Penguin).

Holcombe, L. (1973) *Victorian Ladies at Work: Middle-class working women in England and Wales, 1850–1914* (Newton Abbot: David and Charles).

Hollands, R.G. (1990) *The Long Transition: Class, culture and youth training* (London: Macmillan).

Holtby, W. (1936) *South Riding* (London: Collins, republished Glasgow: Fontana, 1954).

HM Treasury (1990) *Economic Progress Report: Public spending in the 1980s* (London: HMSO).

Hooks, B. (1991) *Yearning, Race, Gender and Cultural Politics* (London: Turnaround).

Houghton, H. (1973) *Separated Wives and Supplementary Benefit* (London: Department of Health and Social Security).

House of Commons Social Security Committee (1991) *Low Income Statistics: Households below average income tables 1988*, HC401 (London: HMSO).

House of Commons Social Services Committee (1989) *Ninth Report* (London: HMSO).

House of Commons Social Services Committee (1990) *Community Care: Carers*, Fifth Report, Session 1989–90 (London: HMSO).

House of Lords Select Committee on the European Communities (1990) *Part-Time and Temporary Employment*, Second Report, Session 1990–1, HL Paper No. 7 (London: HMSO).

Housing Finance: The quarterly economics of the Council of Mortgage Lenders (1990) no. 8 (London: Council of Mortgage Lenders).

Hunt, A. (1968) *A Survey of Women's Employment* (London: HMSO).

Hunt, A. (1978) *The Elderly at Home: A study of people aged sixty-five and over living in the community in England in 1976* (London: HMSO/OPCS).

Industrial Research and Development Advisory Committee (IRDAC) (1990) *Skill Shortages in Europe* (Brussels: IRDAC Comett Technical Assistance Office).

Ison, T. (1979) *Credit, Marketing and Consumer Protection* (London: Croom Helm).

Jamdagni, L. (1980) *Hamari Rangily Zindagi (Our Colourful Lives)* (Leicester: National Association of Youth Clubs).

James, C. (1984) *Occupational Pensions: The failure of private welfare* (London: Fabian Society).

James, E. (1962) 'Women at work in twentieth-century Britain: the changing structure of female employment', *The Manchester School of Economic and Social Studies Quarterly* vol. XXX, no. 3, pp. 282–300.

Jenkins, S. (1991) 'Poverty measurement and the within household distribution', *Journal of Social Policy* vol. 20, no. 4, pp. 457–83.

Johnson, P. and Webb, S. (1990) *Poverty in Official Statistics: Two reports* (London: Institute for Fiscal Studies).

Johnson, P. and Webb, S. (1991) *UK Poverty Statistics: A comparative study* (London: Institute for Fiscal Studies).

Jones, H. (1983) 'Employers' welfare schemes and industrial relations in inter-war Britain', *Business History* vol. XXV, no. 1, pp. 61–75.

Joshi, H.E. (1984) *Womens' Participation in Paid Work: Further analysis of the Women and Employment Survey*, Research Paper no. 45 (London: Department of Employment) to be read, if possible, in conjunction with 'Research Paper no. 45: Author's note on an error' (Department of Employment 1985).

Joshi, H.E. (1986a) 'Participation in paid work: evidence from the Women and Employment Survey' in R. Blundell and I. Walker (eds), *Unemployment, Search and Labour Supply* (Cambridge: Cambridge University Press).

Joshi, H.E. (1986b) 'Gender inequality in the labour market and the domestic division of labour' in P. Nolan and S. Paine (eds), *Rethinking Socialist Economics* (Cambridge: Polity Press in association with Basil Blackwell, London).

Joshi, H.E. (1989) 'The changing form of women's economic dependency' in H. Joshi (ed.), *The Changing Population of Britain*, Centre for Economic Policy Research (Oxford: Blackwell).

Joshi, H.E. (1990) 'The cash opportunity cost of childbearing: an approach to estimation using British evidence', *Population Studies* vol. 44, March, pp. 41–60.

Joshi, H.E. (1991) 'Sex and motherhood as sources of women's econmic disadvantage' in M. Maclean and D. Groves (eds), *Women's Issues in Social Policy* (London: Routledge).

Joshi, H.E. and Davies, H.B. (1991) *The Pension Consequences of Divorce*, CEPR Discussion Paper no. 550 (London: Centre for Economic Policy Research).

Joshi, H.E. and Newell, M.-L. (1987) 'Job downgrading after childbearing' in M. Uncles (ed.), *Longitudinal Data Analysis: Methods and applications*, London Papers in Regional Science no. 18 (London: Pion).

Joshi, H.E. and Newell, M.-L. (1989) *Pay Differentials and Parenthood: Analysis of men and women born in 1946*, Centre for Economic Policy Research Discussion Papers nos 156 and 157 (Coventry: University of Warwick Institute for Employment Research).

Joshi, H. and Owen, S. (1981) *Demographic Indicators of Women's Work Participation in Post-War Britain* (London: Centre for Population Studies).

Jowell, R., Witherspoon, S. and Brook. L. (eds) (1988) *British Social Attitudes: 5th Report* (Aldershot: Gower).

Judicial Statistics (1990) *Annual Report 1989*, Cmnd 1154 (London: HMSO).

Kaluzynska, E. (1980) 'Wiping the floor with theory – a survey of writings on housework', *Feminist Review* no. 6, pp. 27–54.

Knight, I. (1981) *Family Finances*, OPCS Occasional Paper no. 26 (London: HMSO).

Kumar, K. (1978) *Prophecy and Progress* (Harmondsworth: Penguin).

Laczko, F. (1988) *Poverty and the Elderly in the European Community*, Working Paper no. 24 for the 2nd European Programme to Combat Poverty (Bath: University of Bath).

Laczko, F., Dale, A., Arber, S. and Gilbert, G.N. (1988) 'Early retirement in a period of high unemployment', *Journal of Social Policy* vol. 17, no. 3, pp. 313–33.

Land, H. (1969) *Large Families in London*, Occasional Papers on Social Administration no. 32 (London: Bell).

Land, H. (1975) 'The introduction of family allowances: an act of historic justice?' in P. Hall, H. Land, R. Parker and A. Webb, *Change, Choice and Conflict in Social Policy* (London: Heinemann).

Land, H. (1978) 'Who cares for the family?', *Journal of Social Policy* vol. 7, no. 3, pp. 357–84.

Land, H. (1980) 'The family wage', *Feminist Review* vol. 6, pp. 55–7.

Land, H. (1983) 'Who still cares for the family?' in J. Lewis (ed.), *Womens' Welfare, Women's Rights* (London: Croom Helm).

Land, H. (1986) 'Women and children last: reform of social security?' in M. Brenton and C. Ungerson (eds), *The Yearbook of Social Policy in Britain 1985–6* (London: Routledge).

Land, H. (1990) 'Eleanor Rathbone and the economy of the family' in H. Smith (ed.), *British Feminism in the Twentieth Century* (Aldershot: Edward Elgar).

Land, H. (1991) 'Time to care' in M. Maclean and D. Groves (eds), *Women's Issues in Social Policy* (London: Routledge).

Law Society (1991) *Maintenance and Capital Provision on Divorce* (London: The Law Society).

Layard, R., Piachaud, D. and Stewart, M. (1978) *The Causes of Poverty*, Royal Commission on the Distribution of Income and Wealth, Background Paper no. 5 (London: HMSO).

Leat, D. and Gay, P. (1987) *Paying for Care: A study of policy and practice in paid care schemes* (London: Policy Studies Institute).

Lee, D. (1991) 'Poor work and poor institutions' in P. Brown and R. Scase (eds), *Poor Work* (Milton Keynes: Open University Press).

Lee, D., Marsden, D., Rickman, P. and Duncombe, J. (1990) *Scheming for Youth: A study of Y.T.S. in the enterprise culture* (Milton Keynes: Open University Press).

Lee-Cunin, M. (1989) *Daughters of Seacole: A study of Black nurses in West Yorkshire* (Batley: West Yorkshire Low Pay Unit).

Leicester City Council (1988) *Language and Benefits: A study of DHSS service delivery to ethnic minority communities* (Leicester: City Council).

Leicestershire Child Poverty Action Group (1983) *Poverty Pay* (Leicester: CPAG).

Levie, H., Gregory, D. and Callender, C. (1984) 'Redundancy pay: trick or treat' in H. Levie, D. Gregory and N. Lorentzen (eds), *Fighting Closures* (Nottingham: Spokesman).

Lewis, J. (1984) *Women in England, 1870–1940* (Hemel Hempstead: Harvester Wheatsheaf).

Lewis, J.C. (1985) 'Technical change in retailing: its impact on employment and access', *Environment and Planning* vol. 12, part A, pp. 165–91.

Lipsky, M. (1981) *Street Level Bureaucracy* (New York: Russell Sage Foundation).

Lister, R. (1987) 'Future insecure: women and income maintenance under a third Tory term', *Feminist Review* no. 27, Autumn, pp. 7–16.

Lister, R. (1990) 'Women, economic dependency and citizenship', *Journal of Social Policy* vol. 19, no. 4, pp. 445–67.

Littler, C. and Salaman, G. (1984) *Class at Work* (London: Batsford).

Llewellyn Davies, M. (1915) *Maternity: Letters from working women* (London: Bell).

Lonsdale, S. (1985) *Work and Inequality* (London: Longman).

Lonsdale, S. and Byrne, D. (1988) 'Social security from state insurance to private uncertainty' in M. Brenton and C. Ungerson (eds), *The Yearbook of Social Policy 1987–88* (London: Longman).

Low Pay Unit (1991) *The New Review* no. 10, June/July.

Luckhaus, L. (1990) 'The Social Security Directive: its impact on part-time work' in M. O'Brien, L. Hantrais and S. Mangen (eds), *Women, Equal Opportunities and Welfare* (Birmingham: Aston University).

Lumsden, D. (1905) *An Investigation into the Income and Expenditure of Seventeen Brewery Families and a Study of their Diets* (Dublin: Guinness and Son Ltd).

Mack, J. and Lansley, S. (1985) *Poor Britain* (London: Allen and Unwin).

MacLennan, E. (1980) *Minimum Wages for Women* (London: Equal Opportunities Commission/Low Pay Unit).

Maggs, C. (1983) *The Origins of General Nursing* (London: Croom Helm).

Main, B.G.M. (1988) 'Women's hourly earnings: the influence of work on rates of pay' in A. Hunt (ed.), *Women and Paid Work: Issues of equality* (London: Macmillan).

Mama, A. (1989) *The Hidden Struggle: Statutory and voluntary responses to violence against Black women in the home* (London: Race and Housing Research Unit/ Runnymede Trust).

Manley, P. and Sawbridge, D. (1980) 'Women at work', *Lloyds Bank Review* no. 135, pp. 29–40.

Marks, P. (1976) 'Femininity in the classroom' in J. Mitchell and A. Oakley (eds), *The Rights and Wrongs of Women* (Harmondsworth: Penguin).

Marsden, D. (1973) *Mothers Alone: Poverty and the fatherless family*, revised edition, first published in 1969 (Harmondsworth: Penguin).

Marti, J. and Zeilinger, A. (1985) 'New technology in banking and shopping' in T. Forrester (ed.), *The Information Technology Revolution* (Oxford: Blackwell).

Martin, J. (1986) 'Returning to work after childbearing: evidence from the Women and Employment Survey', *Population Trends* no. 43, Spring, pp. 23–30.

Martin, J. and Roberts, C. (1984) *Women and Employment: A lifetime perspective. The report of the 1980 DE/OPCS Women and Employment Survey* (London: HMSO).

Martin, J. and White A. (1988) *The Financial Circumstances of Disabled Adults Living in Private Households* (London: HMSO/OPCS).

Martin, J., Meltzer, H. and Elliot, D. (1988) *The Prevalence of Disability Among Adults* (London: Gower).

Martin, R. (1983) *Women and Unemployment: Activities and social contact*, paper given at SSRC Labour Markets Workshop, Manchester, December.

Martin, R. and Wallace, J. (1984) *Working Women in Recession: Employment, redundancy and unemployment* (Oxford: Oxford University Press).

Martindale, H. (1939) *Women Servants of the State 1870–1938: A history of women in the civil service* (London: Allen and Unwin).

Masey, A. (1977) 'Savings, insurance and credit' in F. Williams (ed.), *Why the Poor Pay More* (London: National Consumer Council/Macmillan).

Matthews, A. and Truscott, P. (1990) *Disability, Household Income and Expenditure*, Department of Social Security Research Report no. 2 (London: HMSO).

Mayall, B. (1986) *Keeping Children Healthy* (London: Allen and Unwin).

McGoldrick, A. (1984) *Equal Treatment in Occupational Pension Schemes: A research report* (Manchester: Equal Opportunities Commission).

McLaughlin, E. (1989) *'Community' Care and Solo Women in Europe*, Unpublished Research Report (York: University of York Social Policy Research Unit).

McLaughlin, E. (1991) *Social Security and Community Care: The case of the invalid care allowance*, Department of Social Security Research Report no. 4 (London: HMSO).

McRae, S. and Daniel, W.W. (1991) *Maternity Rights in Britain: First findings* (London: Policy Studies Institute).

McRobbie, A. (1978) 'The culture of femininity' in Centre for Contemporary Cultural Studies (ed.), *Women Take Issue* (London: Hutchinson).

Meager, N. (1986) 'Temporary work in Britain', *Employment Gazette* vol. 94, no. 1, pp. 7–15.

Meehan, E. (1987) 'Women's equality and the European Community' in F. Ashton and G. Whitting (eds), *Feminist Theory and Practical Policies*, Occasional Paper no. 29 (Bristol: University of Bristol School for Advanced Urban Studies).

Meulders, D. and Plasman, R. (1989) *Women and Atypical Employment, Women in the Labour Force Network*, DG V, V/1426/89 (Brussels: Commission of the European Communities).

Millar, J. (1989) *Poverty and the Lone-Parent Family* (Avebury: Gower).

Millar, J. (1991a) 'Mothers, employment and poverty' in R. Davidson and A. Erskine (eds), *Poverty and Deprivation* (London: Jessica Kingsley).

Millar, J. (1991b) *The Socio-Economic Situation of Solo Women in Europe* (Brussels: European Commission).

Millar, J. (1991c) 'Bearing the cost' in S. Becker (ed.), *Windows of Opportunity* (London: Child Poverty Action Group).

Millar, J. and Glendinning, C. (1989) 'Gender and poverty', *Journal of Social Policy* vol. 18, no. 3, pp. 363–81.

Millar, J. and Whiteford, P. (1991) *Child Support in Australia: Lessons for the UK?* (Bath: Centre for Analysis of Social Policy, University of Bath).

Ministry of Labour Gazette (1938) 'Schemes providing for pensions for employees on retirement from work', *Ministry of Labour Gazette* vol. XXX, no. 5, pp. 172–4.

Ministry of Pensions and National Insurance (1966) *Financial and Other Circumstances of Retired Pensioners* (London: HMSO).

Morokvasic, M. (1983) 'Women in migration: beyond the reductionist outlook' in A. Phizacklea (ed.), *One Way Ticket: Migration and female labour* (London: Routledge).

Morris, L. (1983) 'Redundancy and patterns of household finance', *Sociological Review* vol. 32, no. 3, pp. 492–523.

Morris, L. and Llewellyn, T. (1991) *Social Security Provision for the Unemployed: Report to the Social Security Advisory Committee* (London: HMSO).

Moss, P. (1988) *Consolidated Report of the European Childcare Network* (Brussels: Commission of the European Communities).

Moss, P. (1991) 'Day care for young children in the UK' in E. Melhuish and P. Moss (eds), *Day Care for Young Children* (London: Routledge).

Moss, P. and Melhuish, E. (1991) *Current Issues in Day Care for Young Children* (London: HMSO).

Murray, C. (1990) *The Emerging British Underclass* (London: IEA).

Nanton, P. (1989) 'The new orthodoxy: racial categories and equal opportunity policy', *New Community* vol. 15, no. 4, pp. 549–75.

Nathan, R.P. (1986) 'A welfare revolution', *Washington Post* 4 October.

National Association of Citizens' Advice Bureaux (NACAB) (1991) *Barriers to Benefit: Black claimants and social security* (London: NACAB).

National Consumer Council (1975) *For Richer for Poorer: Some problems of low income consumers* (London: HMSO).

National Consumer Council (1980) *Consumers and Credit* (London: NCC).

National Economic Development Office (1989) *Defusing the Demographic Timebomb* (London: NEDO/The Training Agency).

Newman, C. (1989) *Young Runaways* (London: The Children's Society).

Nissel, M. and Bonnerjea, L. (1982) *Family Care of the Handicapped Elderly: Who pays?* (London: Policy Studies Institute).

O'Donnell, C. (1984) *The Basis of the Bargain* (London: Allen and Unwin).

O'Donovan, K. (1985) *Sexual Divisions in Law* (London: Weidenfeld and Nicolson).

Office of Fair Trading (1989) *Overindebtedness: A Report by the Director General of Fair Trading* (London: OFT).

Office of Fair Trading/NOP Surveys Ltd (1979) *Consumer Credit Survey 1977* (London: OFT).

Office of Population Censuses and Surveys (1984) *Population Census: Economic activity tables* (London: HMSO).

Office of Population Censuses and Surveys (1987) *Labour Force Survey 1987* (London: HMSO).

Office of Population Censuses and Surveys (1989) *Population Trends* no. 55 (London: HMSO).

Office of Population Censuses and Surveys (1990) *General Household Survey 1988* (London: HMSO).

Office of Population Censuses and Surveys (1991) *Marriage and Divorce Statistics 1989* (London: HMSO).

Official Journal of the European Commission (1989) Council Decision of 18 July 1989, no. L.224/10, 2 August.

O'Higgins, M. (1987) *Lone Parent Families in the European Community: Numbers and socio-economic characteristics*, Consultancy Paper for the 2nd European Programme to Combat Poverty (Bath: University of Bath).

O'Higgins, M. (1989) 'Inequality, social policy and income distribution in the United Kingdom' in J.-P. Jallode (ed.), *The Crisis of Redistribution in European Welfare States* (Stoke-on-Trent: Trentham Books).

O'Higgins M. and Jenkins, S. (1989) *Poverty in Europe*, Consultancy Paper for the 2nd European Programme to Combat Poverty (Bath: University of Bath).

Oppenheim, C. (1990) *Poverty: The facts* (London: Child Poverty Action Group).

Orakwue, S. (1990) 'High income, low profile', *Guardian* 7 November.

Owen, A.P.K. (1935) 'Employers' retirement pensions in Great Britain', *International Labour Review* no. XXII, pp. 80–99.

Owen, S.J. and Joshi, H.E. (1990) 'Sex, equality, and the state pension', *Fiscal Studies* vol. 11, no. 1, pp. 53–74.

Pahl, J. (1978) *A Refuge for Battered Women* (London: HMSO).

Pahl, J. (1980) 'Patterns of money management within marriage', *Journal of Social Policy* vol. 9, no. 3, pp. 313–35.

Pahl, J. (1982) *The Allocation of Money and the Structuring of Inequality Within Marriage* (Canterbury: University of Canterbury Health Services Research Unit).

Pahl, J. (1984) 'The allocation of money within the household' in M. Freeman (ed.), *The State, the Law and the Family* (London: Tavistock).

Pahl, J. (1985) *Private Violence and Public Policy: The needs of battered women and the response of the public services* (London: Routledge).

Pahl, J. (1989) *Money and Marriage* (Basingstoke: Macmillan).

Parker, G. (1980) 'Birmingham Money Advice Centre clients' in National Consumer Council, *Consumers and Credit* (London: NCC).

Parker, G. (1986) 'Unemployment, low income and debt' in I. Ramsey (ed.), *Creditors and Debtors: A socio-legal perspective* (London: Professional Books).

Parker, G. (1988a) 'Credit' in R. Walker and G. Parker (eds), *Money Matters: Income, wealth and financial welfare* (London: Sage).

Parker, G. (1988b) 'Indebtedness' in R. Walker and G. Parker (eds), *Money Matters: Income, wealth and financial welfare* (London: Sage).

Parker, G. (1990a) 'Whose care? Whose costs? Whose benefits?', *Ageing and Society* vol. 10, no. 4, pp. 459–67.

Parker, G. (1990b) *With Due Care and Attention: A review of research on informal care*, Occasional Paper no. 2 (London: Family Policy Studies Centre).

Parker, G. (1990c) *Getting and Spending: Consumer credit and debt in Britain* (Aldershot: Avebury).

Parker, G. (1992) *With This Body: Caring and disability in marriage* (Milton Keynes: Open University Press).

Parker, S.R. (1980) *Older Workers and Retirement* (London: OPCS/HMSO).

Parmar, P. (1982) 'Gender, race and class: Asian women in resistance' in Centre for Contemporary Cultural Studies, *The Empire Strikes Back: Race and racism in 70s Britain* (London: Hutchinson).

Patel, N. (1990) *Race Against Time* (London: Racial Equality Unit).

Payne, J. (1987) 'Does unemployment run in families? Some findings from the General Household Surveys', *Sociology* vol. 21, no. 2, pp. 199–214.

Payne, S. (1991) *Women, Health and Poverty* (Hemel Hempstead: Harvester Wheatsheaf).

Peace, S. (1986) 'The forgotten female: social policy and older women' in C. Phillipson and A. Walker (eds), *Ageing and Social Policy* (London: Gower).

Pember Reeves, M.S. (1913) *Round About a Pound a Week* (London: Bell, reprinted by Virago, 1979).

Phillipson, C. (1982) *Capitalism and the Construction of Old Age* (London: Macmillan).

Phillipson, C. and Walker, A. (eds) (1986) *Ageing and Social Policy* (London: Gower).

Phizacklea, A. (1983) 'In the front line' in A. Phizacklea (ed.), *One Way Ticket: Migration and female labour* (London: Routledge).

Phizacklea, A. (1990) *Unpacking the Fashion Industry* (London: Routledge).

Phoenix, A. (1988a) 'Narrow definitions of culture: the case of early motherhood' in S. Westwood and P. Bhachu (eds), *Enterprising Women: Ethnicity, economy and gender relations* (London: Routledge).

Phoenix, A. (1988b) 'The Afro-Caribbean myth', *New Society* 4 March.

Phoenix, A. (1991) *Young Mothers?* (London: Polity Press).

Piachaud, D. (1974) *Do the Poor Pay More?* Poverty Research Series no. 3 (London: Child Poverty Action Group).

Piachaud, D. (1985) *Round About Fifty Hours a Week: The time costs of children*, Poverty Pamphlet no. 64 (London: Child Poverty Action Group).

Pilch, M. and Wood, V. (1960) *Pension Schemes* (London: Hutchinson).

Pilch, M. and Wood, V. (1979) *Pension Schemes: A guide to principles and practice* (Farnborough: Gower).

Popay, J. and Jones, G. (1990) 'Patterns of health and illness among lone parents', *Journal of Social Policy* vol. 19, no. 4, pp. 499–535.

Price, J. (1991) *Low Pay and Women Homeworkers*, Unpublished undergraduate dissertation, Edge Hill College of Education, Ormskirk, Lancashire.

Prondzynski, I. (1989) 'The social situation and employment of migrant women in the European Community', *Policy and Politics* vol. 17, no. 4, pp. 347–54.

Purvis, J. (1981) 'The double burden of class and gender in the schooling of working-class girls in nineteenth-century England' in L. Barton and S. Walker (eds), *Schools, Teachers and Teaching* (Sussex: Falmer Press).

Purvis, J. (1983) 'Towards a history of women's education in nineteenth century Britain' in J. Purvis and M. Hales (eds), *Achievement and Inequality in Education* (London: Routledge).

Quadagno, J. (1982) *Ageing in Early Industrial Society* (London: Academic Press).

Qureshi, H. (1990) 'Boundaries between formal and informal care-giving work' in C. Ungerson (ed.), *Gender and Caring* (Hemel Hempstead: Harvester Wheatsheaf).

Qureshi, H. and Walker, A. (1986) 'Caring for elderly people: the family and the state' in C. Phillipson and A. Walker (eds), *Ageing and Social Policy* (London: Gower).

Qureshi, H. and Walker, A. (1989) *The Caring Relationship* (Basingstoke: Macmillan).

Ramazanoglu, C. (1989) *Feminism and the Contradictions of Oppression* (London: Routledge).

Rathbone, E. (1909) *How the Casual Labourer Lives* (Liverpool: The Northern Publishing Company for The Liverpool Economic and Statistical Society).

Rathbone, E. (1924) *The Disinherited Family* (London: Edward Arnold).

Rathbone, E. (1925) *Widows, Orphans and the Old Age Contributory Pensions Bill* (London: National Union of Societies for Equal Citizenship).

Raynsford, N. (1990) 'Housing conditions, problems and policies' in S. Macgregor and B. Pimlott (eds), *Tackling the Inner Cities* (Oxford: Clarendon Press).

Rein, M. and Erie, S. (1988) 'Women and the welfare state' in C.M. Mueller (ed.), *The Politics of the Gender Gap*, vol. 2 (London: Sage).

Rex, J. and Moore, R. (1967) *Race, Community and Conflict* (London: Oxford University Press/Institute of Race Relations).

Rhodes, G. (1965) *Public Sector Pensions* (London: Allen and Unwin).

Rimmer, L. (1981) *Families in Focus: Marriage, divorce and family patterns* (London: Study Commission on the Family).

Rimmer, L. (1983) 'The economics of work and caring' in J. Finch and D. Groves (eds), *A Labour of Love: Women, work and caring* (London: Routledge).

Ritchie, J. (1990) *Thirty Families: Their living standards in unemployment* (London: HMSO).

Robbins, D. (ed.) (1989) *The Family and the Local Community*, Working Paper no. 38 (Bath: University of Bath Centre for Analysis of Social Policy, Evaluation Section).

Roberts, C. (1981) *Women's Unemployment*, Paper presented at SSRC/Department of Employment Workshop on Employment and Unemployment, London.

Roberts, E. (1984) *A Woman's Place* (Oxford: Blackwell).

Roberts, R. (1973) *The Classic Slum* (Harmondsworth: Penguin).

Robinson, J. (1975) *The Life and Times of Francie Nichol of South Shields* (London: Allen and Unwin).

Robinson, O. and Wallace, J. (1984a) 'Growth and utilization of part-time labour in Great Britain', *Employment Gazette* vol. 92, no. 9, pp. 391–7.

Robinson, O. and Wallace, J. (1984b) *Part-Time Employment and Sex Discrimination Legislation in Britain*, Research Paper no. 43 (London: Department of Employment).

Rodgers, G. and Rodgers, J. (1989) *Precarious Jobs in Labour Market Regulation* (Brussels: International Institute for Labour Studies).

Roll, J. (1988a) *Family Fortunes: Parents' incomes in the 1980s* (London: Family Policy Studies Centre).

Roll, J. (1988b) 'Measuring family income: a recent controversy in the use of official statistics', *Social Policy and Administration* vol. 22, no. 2, pp. 134–60.

Roll, J. (1989) *Lone-Parent Families in the European Community* (Brussels: European Commission).

Room, G. (1990) *New Poverty in the European Community* (London: Macmillan).

Ross, E. (1982) 'Fierce questions and taunts: married life in working-class London, 1870–1914', *Feminist Studies* vol. 8, Autumn, pp. 575–602.

Routh, G. (1980) *Occupation and Pay in Great Britain 1906–79*, 2nd edn (London: Macmillan).

Rowntree, B.S. (1902) *Poverty: A study of town life*, 2nd edn (London: Macmillan).

Rowntree, B.S. (1941) *Poverty and Progress: A second social survey of York* (London: Longman).

Rowntree, B.S. and Stuart, F.D. (1921) *The Responsibility of Women Workers for Dependants* (Oxford: Clarendon Press).

Rubery, J. and Tarling, R. (1988) *Women and Recession* (London: Routledge).

Sadiq, A. (1991) 'Asian women and the benefit system', *FSU Quarterly* vol. 46, pp. 42–7.

Scarman, Lord C. (1981) *The Brixton Disorders: A report of an enquiry* (London: HMSO).

Schuller, T. and Walker, A. (1990) *The Time of Our Life* (London: IPPR).

Scott, H. (1984) *Working Your Way to the Bottom: The feminisation of poverty* (London: Pandora Press).

Sinfield, A. (1978) 'Analyses in the social division of welfare', *Journal of Social Policy* vol. 7, no. 2, pp. 129–56.

Smail, R. (1988) 'Non-wage benefits from employment' in R. Walker and G. Parker (eds), *Money Matters: Income, wealth and financial welfare* (London: Sage).

Smith, D.J. (1981) *Unemployment and Racial Minorities* (London: Policy Studies Institute).

Smith, E. (1915) *Wage-Earning Women and their Dependants* (London: Fabian Women's Group).

Snell, K.D.M. and Millar, J. (1987) 'Lone-parent families and the welfare state: past and present', *Continuity and Change* vol. 2, part 3.

Social Security Advisory Committee (1985) *Fourth Report* (London: Department of Health and Social Security).

Spring-Rice, M. (1939) *Working Class Wives: Their health and conditions*, reprinted 1981 (London: Virago).

Stanley, J. (1986) 'Sex and the quiet schoolgirl', *British Journal of the Sociology of Education* vol. 7, no. 3, pp. 275–86.

Stone, K. (1983) 'Motherhood and waged work: West Indian, Asian and white mothers compared' in A. Phizacklea (ed.), *One Way Ticket: Migration and female labour* (London: Routledge).

Storey-Gibson, M.J. (1985) *Older Women Around the World* (Washington: International Federation on Ageing).

Svenson, M. and Macpherson, S. (1988) 'Real losses and unreal figures: the impact of the 1986 Social Security Act' in S. Becker and S. Macpherson (eds), *Public Issues, Private Pain: Poverty, social work and social policy* (London: Insight Books).

Szyszcack, E. (1987) 'The future of women's rights: the role of Community law' in M. Brenton and C. Ungerson (eds), *The Yearbook of Social Policy 1986/87* (London: Longman).

Tawney, R. (1964) *Equality*, 5th edn (London: Allen and Unwin).

Taylor, R. and Ford, G. (1983) 'Inequalities in old age', *Ageing and Society* vol. 3, no. 2, pp. 183–208.

Tebbut, M. (1983) *Making Ends Meet: Pawnbroking and working class credit* (Leicester: Leicester University Press/New York: St Martin's Press).

Thane, P. (1978) 'Women and the Poor Law in Victorian and Edwardian England', *History Workshop Journal* no. 6, pp. 29–51.

Thompson, P., Buckle, J. and Lavery, M. (1988) *Not the OPCS Survey* (London: Disablement Income Group).

Thompson, P., Lavery, M. and Curtice, J. (1990) *Short Changed by Disability* (London: Disablement Income Group).

Times Educational Supplement (1989) 'Those with designs on teenagers', *TES*, 13 October.

Tinder, C. (1991) 'Older women and the recession: how not to manage workforce reductions', *Economic Report* vol. 6, no. 2 (London: Employment Institute).

Titmuss, R.M. (1958) *Essays on the Welfare State* (London: Allen and Unwin).

Titmuss, R.M. (1974) *Social Policy: An introduction* (London: Allen and Unwin).

Townsend, P. (1979) *Poverty in the United Kingdom* (Harmondsworth: Penguin).

Townsend, P. (1981) 'Elderly people with disabilities' in A. Walker and P. Townsend (eds), *Disability in Britain* (Oxford: Martin Robertson).

Townsend, P. (1987) *Poverty and Labour in London* (London: Child Poverty Action Group).

Townsend, P. (1991a) *The Poor Are Poorer: A statistical report on changes in the living standards of rich and poor in the UK, 1979–1989* (Bristol: University of Bristol Statistical Monitoring Unit).

Townsend, P. (1991b) *Meaningful Statistics on Poverty, 1991* (Bristol: University of Bristol Statistical Monitoring Unit).

Townsend, P. and Wedderburn, D. (1965) *The Aged in the Welfare State* (London: Bell).

Training Agency (1990) *Labour Market Quarterly Report*, May (Sheffield: Training Agency).

Training Agency (1991) *Labour Market Quarterly Report*, May (Sheffield: Training Agency).

Unemployment Unit (1991) *Working Brief*, August/September (London: Unemployment Unit).

Ungerson, C. (1983) 'Why do women care?' in J. Finch and D. Groves (eds), *A Labour of Love: Women, work and caring* (London: Routledge).

Ungerson, C. (1990) 'The language of care: crossing the boundaries' in C. Ungerson (ed.), *Gender and Caring* (Hemel Hempstead: Harvester Wheatsheaf).

University of Surrey SRM Group (1983) *Patterns of Money Allocation in Marriage*, Paper given at Resources Within Households Research Workshop, Institute of Education, London, May.

Victor, C. (1991) 'Continuity or change?: inequalities in health in later life', *Ageing and Society* vol. 11, no. 1, pp. 23–40.

Vogler, C. (1989) *Labour Market Change and Patterns of Financial Allocation Within Households*, Working Paper no. 12 (Oxford: ESRSC/Social Change and Economic Life Initiative).

Walker, A. (1980) 'The social creation of poverty and dependency in old age', *Journal of Social Policy* vol. 9, no. 1, pp. 49–75.

Walker, A. (1981) 'Towards a political economy of old age', *Ageing and Society* vol. 1, no. 1, pp. 73–94.

Walker, A. (1982) 'The meaning and social division of community care' in A. Walker (ed.), *Community Care: The family, the state and social policy* (Oxford: Blackwell and Martin Robertson).

Walker, A. (1985a) 'Making the elderly pay', *New Society* 18 April, pp. 76–8.

Walker, A. (1985b) 'Early retirement: release or refuge from the labour market?', *Quarterly Journal of Social Affairs* vol. 1, no. 3, pp. 211–29.

Walker, A. (1986) 'Pensions and the production of poverty in old age' in C. Phillipson and A. Walker (eds), *Ageing and Social Policy* (London: Gower).

Walker, A. (1990) 'The benefits of old age?' in E. McEwen (ed.), *Age: The unrecognised discrimination* (London: Age Concern).

Walker, A. (1992) 'The persistence of poverty under welfare states and the prospects for its abolition', *International Journal of Health Services* vol. 22, no. 1, pp. 1–17.

Walker, A. and Laczko, F. (1982) 'Early retirement and flexible retirement' in House of Commons Social Services Committee, *Age of Retirement*, HC26–II (London: HMSO).

Walker, A. and Taylor, P. (1991) 'Ageism versus productive ageing' in S. Bass, F. Caro and Y. Chen (eds), *Achieving a Productive Ageing Society* (Westport: Greenwood).

Walsh, A. and Lister, R. (1985) *Mothers' Life-Line: A survey of how women use and value child benefit* (London: Child Poverty Action Group).

Ward, S. (1990) *The Essential Guide to Pensions: A worker's handbook*, 3rd edn (London: Pluto Press).

Warrier, S. (1988) 'Marriage, maternity and female economic activity: Gujarati mothers in Britain' in S. Westwood and P. Bhachu (eds), *Enterprising Women: Ethnicity, economy and gender relations* (London: Routledge).

Watt, S. and Cook, J. (1989) 'Another expectation unfulfilled: Black women and social services departments' in C. Hallett (ed.), *Women and Social Services Departments* (Hemel Hempstead: Harvester Wheatsheaf).

Webster, W. (1990) *Not a Man to Match Her* (London: Women's Press).

Werbner, P. (1988) 'Taking and giving: working women and female bonds in a Pakistani immigrant neighbourhood' in S. Westwood and P. Bhachu (eds), *Enterprising Women: Ethnicity, economy and gender relations* (London: Routledge).

Westwood, S. (1984) *All Day Everyday: Factory and family life in the making of women's lives* (London: Pluto).

Westwood, S. and Bhachu, P. (1988a) 'Images and realities', *New Society* 6 May, pp. 20–2.

Westwood, S. and Bhachu, P. (eds) (1988b) *Enterprising Women: Ethnicity, economy and gender relations* (London: Routledge).

Which? (1991) June issue (London: Consumers' Association).

Whitting, G. (1988) *Women and Poverty in Europe: Experiences and action from the 2nd EC Programme to Combat Poverty*, Paper to the European Network of Women's Tribunals, Brussels, November.

Whitting, G. and Quinn, J. (1989) 'Women and work: preparing for an independent future', *Policy and Politics* vol. 17, no. 4, pp. 337–45.

Whitting, G. *et al.* (1991) *Skill Shortages in the European Community*, SYSDEM Papers no. 1 (Birmingham: ECOTEC Research and Consulting Ltd).

Wilce, H. (1985) 'Y.T.S. reinforces bias against girls', *Times Educational Supplement*, 16 August.

Wilkinson, F. (1981) *The Dynamics of Labour Market Segmentation* (London: Academic Press).

Wilkinson, R. (1989) 'Class mortality differentials, income distribution and trends in poverty, 1921–81', *Journal of Social Policy* vol. 18, no. 3, pp. 307–36.

Williams, F. (1989) *Social Policy: A critical introduction* (Cambridge: Polity Press).

Willmott, P. (1987) *Friendship Networks and Social Support* (London: Policy Studies Institute).

Wilson, G. (1987) 'Money: patterns of responsibility and irresponsibility in marriage' in J. Brannen and G. Wilson (eds), *Give and Take in Families: Studies in resource distribution* (London: Allen and Unwin).

Wilson, J.V. and Davies, B. (1988) *Your New Pensions Choice: An independent guide to help you understand the new and important pensions legislation*, 3rd edn (Croydon: Tolley).

WING (Women Against Immigration and Nationalisation Group) (1985) *Worlds Apart* (London: Pluto).

Women's Industrial Council (1911) *Memo on the National Insurance Bill as it Affects Women*, TS BLPES Library.

Young, H. (1989) 'One of us, but different', *The Guardian* 8 April, p. 21.

Young, M. (1977) 'Housekeeping money' in F. Williams (ed.), *Why the Poor Pay More* (London: National Consumer Council/Macmillan).

Youth Training (1984) no. 6, March (Sheffield: Manpower Services Commission).

Zabalza, A. and Tzannotos, Z. (1985) *Women and Equal Pay: The effects of legislation on female employment and wages in Britain* (Cambridge: Cambridge University Press).

Index